Invoking the Authentic Self

The life and work of Andrew Cohen's spiritual community.
A first-hand account.

Tim Mansfield

ISBN 978-1-913663-87-2

Book category: Spiritual / Teachers / Andrew Cohen

Printed in Great Britain by
Biddles Books Limited, King's Lynn, Norfolk

Contents

Acknowledgements

I want to offer my deepest gratitude to my principal editor, Dan Nicholson. His granular scrutiny and intelligent suggestions have improved this book beyond recognition. Clare van Oosterom has been both my second editor and my guardian angel; I am indebted to her for ever, for her input and support.

To Abby Trow, Arnold Cragg, Evelyn Cavalla, Janet Holmes, Jonathan Mansfield and May Thandi, I say, "Thanks a million." Their array of fascinating feedback on my early drafts was immensely valuable.

Deeply and lastingly, I am grateful for all the help I have received.

TM

Introduction

This book tells a true story. It charts the rise and fall of a modern-day, pioneering, spiritual community. Andrew Cohen was the community's central figure; it was to his transmission of enlightenment and his teachings of evolutionary enlightenment that his students were drawn. *EnlightenNext* became the established name of the community, which formed in 1986 and dissolved in 2013. It had many Centres around the world, of which the Foxhollow Estate in Lenox, Massachusetts, USA was the most important. Foxhollow was also Andrew Cohen's home, and the location of most of the events described in this book.

The community was pioneering in that Andrew envisaged his students forming an enlightened group, or enlightened forum, that might have greater powers than an enlightened individual. He sensed that this forum might receive a form of enlightenment that had new capabilities. The "Authentic Self" was the name Andrew gave to the enhanced enlightenment he and his students aimed to invoke.

The story of Andrew's community spans twenty-seven years. I was his student and a member of the community for nineteen years. I was born and raised in England, but I lived at Foxhollow before, during and after the crucial appearance of the Authentic Self in 2001. In the community's hierarchy I was an *upper-core student*, positioned perhaps twenty-five places from the top of a group of 150 people. That position has enabled me to write this book mainly from first-hand experience, with occasional use of reports by others.

I have tried my best to write an accessible and honest account of a story that, I'm aware, can be interpreted in a variety of ways. The variety is partly explained by people's differing interest in enlightenment which, I have found, affects their understanding and appreciation of the community's work. For example, some parts of the story contrast shockingly with secular sensitivities, while other parts can be awe-inspiring. Whether readers condemn or applaud these elements will depend, I think, on their appreciation of the overall enterprise. Aware that the story will inevitably be judged differently, I'd like to reiterate my intention: I have tried to write a comprehensive and fair-minded record.

Why have I spent two years of my life independently writing this book? In large part, I have written it to correct the negative narrative that flourished after *EnlightenNext* dissolved. That dissolution, in 2013, was so sudden and unexpected that it created a vacuum. The shock of the dissolution decimated the community's prized ability to interpret human experience, leaving a void. Angry ex-students were then able to move, unchallenged, into this space and establish a narrative that dismissed the community's achievements and accused Andrew of abuse. In my view, this negative narrative does not represent either the fortitude or significance of the community's work. I see Andrew and his students as well-intentioned, courageous, intelligent and committed. I question how such positive qualities could result in the negative story promulgated by some ex-students. Hence, with this book, I have attempted to lay out a full account for public review, hoping that collective scrutiny will lead to elevated judgement and the overturning of a damaging injustice.

I have had another motive. A voice has quietly but consistently prompted me to record Andrew's spiritual work with his students. These quiet prompts seem to have come from the domain of the Authentic Self, along with the clear message: *Let the world know what happened.* That is the extent of this matter. I cannot claim there is more to say, because the sender of the message has held back from further partnership. However, I want to inform readers of the presence of this voice and say that it has quietly sustained me.

Perhaps unusually for a vicar's son, I have been a builder in my working life. This book's structure might, therefore, reflect my workmanlike approach to daunting tasks. In my Prologue, which tells of my first exchanges with Andrew in 1992, I have tried to convey the strong emotions that, I think, permeate the whole story. Part 1 then gives the background information needed to understand the community's culture. Part 2 describes the life and work of the community: students' spiritual practices, their trials, and the community's incremental progress towards its goal. Part 3 communicates, I hope, the nature of the Authentic Self, while Part 4 is explained by its title, *Development and Dissolution*.

Two general points about the book: Firstly, because each chapter is dedicated to a subject, the book's overall story initially appears in a piecemeal fashion. However, later chapters fall into a chronological succession and the book becomes a linear narrative. Secondly, at times I have judged it necessary to push against strong secular values to make space for the community's contrasting objectives. This is especially true in Chapter 14, *Engaging with Ego*, and Chapter 18, *The Women*. Therefore, I'd like to advise readers that in parts of the book my tone becomes more assertive.

Introduction

I take a risk in Part 5, the book's last section, where I review the community's work from the point of view of evolution. By looking at the overall story from that elevated perspective, I attempt to shed new light on the value of Andrew's work with his students.

Notes on the Text

- People's names have been changed, except when listed in connection to their published work, or in the case of Andrew and his wife, Alka.

- *EnlightenNext* was the registered name of Andrew's organisation. I use that name occasionally but, mostly, I refer to Andrew and his students as *the community*.

- Groups of Andrew's students were located around the world. Usually the group had a building, rented or owned, that provided space for meetings, public events and administration. This building and the students living nearby were referred to as a *Centre*.

- For two reasons, the text occasionally repeats itself. This is because some chapters have to draw on the same information to make sense, and a few of the community's terms and values benefit from more than one explanation.

- When a subject is developed in other chapters it is marked like this: (Chap 20).

- Women might appear to be underrepresented in the first half of the book. This, if true, is because the community's spiritual work was largely, but not wholly, conducted in gendered groups and my account, inevitably, draws from the men's side of the story.

- Andrew founded a magazine that was published twice a year and distributed internationally. Its purpose and physical evolution are described in Chapter 6. Over its lifespan it had two titles but, in the text, I often refer to it simply as *the magazine*.

- The community's use of two words might need explanation. *Spaciousness* can be thought of as lightness of being. Technically, this arises when someone identifies more strongly with their perceptive faculty than the activity of their mind. *Evolutionary* refers to the progression of existence that started with the universe's Big Bang. The community understood this progression to be a cosmologically powerful, purposeful impulse, experienced by human beings as the thoroughly positive desire to live an authentic life.

Prologue

Bodh Gaya, India, 1992

The Indian state of Bihar is positioned in the north-eastern corner of the country, just south of its border with Nepal. Thirty years ago, the state was known for its poverty and lawlessness: the guidebooks warned of marauding bandits. In the south of Bihar is a small town, Bodh Gaya, that famously holds the site of the Buddha's enlightenment under a bodhi tree. The Stupa, a substantial shrine built to commemorate his awakening, is the focal point of Bodh Gaya's huge tourist-and-pilgrimage industry. It was into this heady mixture of poverty, tourism and sacred history that I found myself walking in January 1992.

I was there to join Andrew Cohen's retreat for 10 days. It was the holiday period of the primary school in the Himalayas where I was a visiting teacher. I had seen Andrew teach just once before, in London the previous July. During that evening he had moved naturally across a range of human expressions. He had in turn been humorous, tender, stern and animated; and with one person (unusually for a public event, as it later turned out) he had been angry. I thought he was like an accomplished pianist, someone equally at home playing any part of the human keyboard. At the time, his evident ease of being was enough to make me think he was an enlightened man.

Initially, that teaching in July didn't seem significant. Although I was aware of my need for a spiritual teacher, Andrew had not evoked the ecstasy I thought I would feel if I met such a person. Moreover, that first meeting came at a time when my attention was on changing my life. Inwardly, I had outgrown my interest in self-improvement. My committed work with an organisation that staged personal growth workshops had run its course, and the seminar trainers I was familiar with had come to look insubstantial compared to my sense of great teachers like Jesus, Buddha and Krishnamurti (Chap 7). So, I was looking to move on. Outwardly, to make space for a new life, I was extracting myself from a settled domestic situation in London. Seeking out a teaching job in India had been part of my escape plan. The day before leaving London, I heard that Andrew would be leading a retreat, co-incidentally in India and during the exact period I had as holiday. I accepted the news as spiritual guidance and decided to attend.

In Bodh Gaya I was graciously welcomed by the group, the Sangha, that had gathered around Andrew over the previous six years. Members of this group normally lived near Andrew in California. For them, the Bodh Gaya retreat was an annual event. Each evening, Andrew gave Satsang: spiritual dialogue lasting about two hours. These were intimate and visually distinct occasions. Andrew sat on a low, upholstered, armless chair. A rug, side table and flowers completed the room's centrepiece. Around this sat 120 people on rough Indian carpets, and the scene was framed by two semi-circular rows of regular seating. Andrew took questions, mostly from his students but some from newcomers like me, or people attending for just one evening. His answers varied in length and scope as he responded to questioners directly or spoke broadly to the whole room. The only topic of discussion was enlightenment, and the tone in the room was formal and attentive.

Each evening there was a long silence before Andrew arrived. Once he was seated, we sat together in further meditation before the incisive dialogue began. For me, the intensity of the forum provoked polar opposite experiences: I was often drawn into, and nourished by, the rich current of truth being shared; but, sometimes, my lifelong Achilles heel, self-consciousness, inexplicably took hold of my awareness. During these self-conscious episodes I was unable to lift my eyes from the floor. I was afraid. My fear had one source: the possibility that Andrew would call on me to speak with him. At the end of each of my first two Satsangs these emotional swings left me exhausted, and I fled from the room to a nearby group of Tibetan restaurant tents, where something resembling chocolate cake was sold. There, I gradually stabilised.

My third Satsang brought the most significant moment of my adult life. Within the flow of the evening, Andrew turned to me and asked if I had any questions. Flustered, I answered honestly that I didn't, adding that I understood everything said so far. He asked why I had come to the retreat. At that time in my life I was plagued by shyness and in the habit of making my responses as short as possible. So, I simply told him the truth: "*I was thinking of becoming your student.*"

Andrew's instantaneous, forceful response was unlike anything I had ever known. As if it came from the heart of the cosmos, he fired the question: "*Do you have any idea how tough a teacher I am?*"

I felt stunned, but my honest answer to his first question gave me just enough surety to note the point of his second, which hit upon a subject I had – in general terms - thought about. I knew I wanted what I termed a Yang teacher, a fiery teacher, rather than an undemanding Yin teacher. So, tremulously, I replied, *"I need someone like that. The fear is so great."* There was then a pause before, in conversational tone, he asked me about my life circumstances.

The following day, members of the Sangha commented on my *'strong exchange'* with Andrew. To be friendly, I agreed. But, to me, the word 'strong' didn't capture either the shocking power of Andrew's delivery or the unusual qualities of the interaction. When it happened, the force of his response left me disarmed, with only my few grains of truth to reply with. Yet, the next day, I noticed that, despite being deeply impacted, I felt unharmed, and I saw how Andrew's words had been free of injurious intent. The exchange had another curious feature: I had no sense of having compromised myself. I had been utterly discombobulated, but I seemed to have spoken the truth, and this gave me the feeling that Andrew's cosmic blast and my tremulous reply had come from different ends of the same spectrum. Both responses had been real.

Despite my sense of having been touched by a different dimension of life, the exchange did nothing to stop my emotions from swinging. Without tools to comprehend my experience, I was unable to stand back from what was happening. I felt vulnerable to an unknown source of turbulence as my feelings oscillated between extremes. At times, I experienced a state of timeless perfection, in which I recognised Andrew's role, his words and the courage of his students to be the modern-day manifestation of a perennial, spiritual scenario. But those fragile, sublime moments were soon spoilt by the powerful insecurity within me, and by various nauseating features – such as the fly-ridden market stalls - of Bodh Gaya's teeming commerce. My dual experience continued during a day trip taken by the whole community at the mid-point of the retreat.

This trip, I could see, was an exquisite event. Early one morning I helped with preparations for a splendid picnic, before boarding one of three buses hired to take the Sangha and others to the site of an early Buddhist university. People were excited to be on the road, and more so when Andrew joined some students on the roof of one bus. Surveying the scene, I saw people's joyfulness, their prospect of a carefree day, and the pleasing picture of our beaten buses trundling through the countryside. Rationally, I could count the flawless qualities of the moment, but I wince with shame when I say that, throughout the day, my mind bedevilled me with worries about the future.

That evening, back in Bodh Gaya, my experience swung once again when I met Camilla for the first time. She was a New Zealander and an experienced member of the Sangha. With her calm, soft voice she asked if I had enjoyed the trip. I told her of my experience. When Camilla quietly replied, *"Oh, I'm sorry that spoilt your day,"* it introduced me to a novel idea: the tumult in my mind could have been experienced as incidental to the main event.

After ten days on the retreat I wrote Andrew a thank-you note. I said I thought I would see him again, but I didn't know when. I made a donation and bought his new book, *Enlightenment is a Secret*. I felt enriched, pummelled and drained, and still held in the vice that had relentlessly gripped me during my time in Bodh Gaya. I knew I had met a real teacher, and I acknowledged the guidance that had led me to him. Trusting that guidance, I knew my future lay with Andrew, but the idea of it terrified me.

In the weeks following the retreat, I continued to see only one option: joining Andrew's community in California. I anticipated that life in his community would mean facing the same emotional turmoil I had experienced in Bodh Gaya; turmoil I felt unable to bear indefinitely. So, I decided to spend twelve months preparing myself. At the end of the school year, I left India and went to live by the sea in Cornwall (UK). My plan was to build spiritual strength by reconnecting with the passions of my youth: I played football for a semi-professional team, Truro City; I worked voluntarily in a garage that restored MGB sports cars; and I bought a boat and learned to sail in the glorious estuary around Falmouth.

I'm still undecided about the spiritual benefit of my year in Cornwall, but I know my choice to move there was authentic and I look back with affection on the life I lived. There is, however, one reason to think that my decision to take a sabbatical might have been spiritually relevant: by the time I returned to London in the late summer of 1993, a new Centre had been opened there by some members of the Sangha. Joining the Centre's growing group was less of a challenge than moving to Marin, so I happily started to attend their public meetings and, within five months, I became one of Andrew's 'formal' students.

Of course, I had no idea of the highs and lows that lay ahead.

PART 1

———

Background

Chapter 1

Andrew Cohen: a Brief Biography

Please note: much of the information below is taken from Andrew's book, Autobiography of an Awakening, *1992.*

Andrew was born in 1955 into a Jewish but atheist family living in New York. He was the younger of two sons. Andrew's father loved him very much, but his parents did not love each other and, as a boy, he was unhappy. Andrew's brother was jealous of the love shown to Andrew and he physically bullied him as a toddler, leading to Andrew having difficulties at school. Consequently, when he was five years old, his mother sent him to a psychologist. Andrew later said he gained nothing from ten years of psychological help.

Andrew's parents separated when he was eleven years old. His mother left the family and went to Italy, pursuing her ambition to be a novelist. When Andrew was fifteen, his father died following surgery on a brain tumour the previous year. Andrew was then sent to Europe, first to a Swiss school and then to live with his mother in Rome. He was happy there, and he and his mother had a close relationship.

Aged sixteen, for no obvious reason, Andrew had a spiritual experience that he describes as follows:

> *"The most extraordinary thing happened to me. Late one night as I was talking with my mother, for no apparent reason I began to experience a completely new and unimaginable condition. My consciousness began to expand in all directions simultaneously and I experienced what could only be called revelation. Tears profusely poured out of my eyes and my throat repeatedly opened and closed for no reason. I was feeling completely overwhelmed and intoxicated by Love and was struck by a sense of awe and wonder that is impossible to describe. I suddenly knew without any doubt that there was no such thing as death and that life itself had no beginning and no end. I saw that all of life was intimately connected and inseparable. It became clear that there was no such thing as individuality separate from that one Self that was all of life. The*

3

*glory and majesty of the cosmic unity that was revealing itself to me
was completely overwhelming. I could hardly speak."*

Andrew didn't know what to make of this experience and, for the next six years, he pursued his ambition to become a drummer, but without success. Aged twenty-two, never having forgotten his earlier experience, he dedicated himself *"to rediscovering THAT which had revealed itself to me."* Contrary to most people's doubts about their chances of becoming enlightened, Andrew felt confident he would be successful.

Moving back to New York, he dedicated himself to his search, seeing many teachers and questioning them fearlessly. He had formal relationships with two teachers but, when these did not deliver what he was looking for, he resumed his pursuit. In May 1986, some months after arriving in India, and somewhat exhausted by his fruitless efforts, he accepted a friend's recommendation and went to see a little-known teacher, H L Poonja, living in Lucknow, Uttar Pradesh.

Poonjaji (to use his respectful title) had been a disciple of the renowned Indian sage, Ramana Maharshi (1879-1950), possibly the most revered Indian spiritual figure of the last century. Dialogues between Poonjaji and Andrew started with Andrew's declaration that he had *"no expectations."* Poonjaji's response, *"I am happy to hear that,"* surprised Andrew and triggered a series of pivotal insights. Over the next ten days, guided by Poonjaji's further encouragement, Andrew had what might be called a classic and complete awakening. He wrote in his journal:

> *"So here I am attempting to begin again in this journal of evolution, of rebirth and rediscovery of The Reality. Freedom itself and absolutely NOTHING AT ALL. So, so, so, so much every single day! Every moment is yet another moment of learning and self-discovery. How can I keep a record of something that never ceases to BE? My mind is or has been BLOWN completely out of this world. It is in shreds! Nothing solid left. Nothing to hold onto and no concepts left. Only open space and absolutely nowhere to stand. NOWHERE AT ALL."*

Poonjaji soon instructed Andrew to *"go and start a revolution among the young."* Becoming a teacher had never been Andrew's intention, but he trusted Poonjaji and, moreover, Andrew's friends were already being drawn to his radiant transmission of enlightenment. In June 1986, in the small town of Rishikesh (by the river Ganges in Uttar Pradesh), Andrew's teaching career began with informal dialogue among the eight friends and followers who had gathered around him.

He was next invited to teach in Totnes, a market town in Devon, England, where it was suggested he might be well-received. As news of his transmission spread, more people came to hear him; they squeezed into the small living-room where he taught. It was his presence as well as his words that had life-changing impact, as people - drawn into his field of consciousness - discovered spiritual freedom for themselves. It was in Totnes that Andrew and Alka, his long-standing Indian girlfriend, were married in 1987.

Andrew then taught in various European cities before travelling to America to stay for a longer period in Amherst, near Boston. Here, the gathering of newly-impassioned individuals continued, and the first signs of a community formed as committed students began to live in shared houses.

In 1989, Andrew sent some students to California, where it was suggested that people might be more receptive to his teachings than they were in Amherst. Once that idea was verified, Andrew and his students (by this time about 150 people) made the journey to the sunny hills of Marin County, just north of San Francisco. Marin's golden geography, rich economy and permanent sunshine made it a paradise well-suited to both a group of people needing to earn money and an organisation requiring offices and meeting-rooms.

During the community's years in Marin, Andrew's first books, *The Source Demands Surrender* and *Enlightenment is a Secret*, were written and published. Also, under Andrew's direction, his students were organised into groups of equal commitment. These groups started to have weekly formal meetings, the forerunners of men's and women's meetings that became powerful forums in later years.

By 1995, it was clear that spiritual interest in Marin was less than anticipated. Also, with Andrew's popularity growing in Europe, the time difference and geographic distance between California and Europe became problematic. More important still, Andrew foresaw the advantages of living with his students on one property, owned by his organisation. He longed to find a suitable ashram for his community, so scouts were again despatched, this time to search America's east coast. One year later, Foxhollow - a country estate in western Massachusetts - was found and purchased. Preparations for the cross-country move then began.

The story continues in Chapter 8.

Chapter 2

What Is Enlightenment?

Andrew was a teacher of enlightenment. He initially taught traditional enlightenment for individual benefit but, after a few years, as we will see in Chapter 4 and beyond, his work developed and he became known for his original teaching of *Evolutionary Enlightenment* and the associated group work he did with his students.

I want to help readers understand the substance of this book by offering a description of enlightenment for reference. But I should say that enlightenment is not easy to define. The title of Andrew's first book is *Enlightenment is a Secret* (1992) and, for seventeen years until 2009, the title of his twice-yearly magazine was *What is Enlightenment?* These titles suggest he saw enlightenment as something not commonly understood, even if the word itself is familiar.

Despite it being difficult to define, I should - after knowing Andrew for more than twenty-five years - be able to give a useful description of enlightenment. Here is my best effort.

The subject of spiritual enlightenment can perplex and often annoy intelligent people, who are, understandably, accustomed to regarding their intelligence as an all-terrain vehicle, capable of mastering most fields of human interest. The reason enlightenment is often experienced as perplexing is because it emerges from a part of oneself that is seldom considered. Enlightenment does not correlate with knowledge, or intellectual agility, or any steady-state experience such as compassion or bliss. What enlightenment does correlate with is the dissolving of self-importance. In other words, enlightenment is not something that one accumulates through academic learning or one's passage through life; rather, it is a pre-existing condition of natural curiosity that emerges as self-importance dissolves.

This understanding - that enlightenment is an unusual line of development - can be supported by two observations. The first is that universities, even though they contain intelligent people and advanced knowledge, have not, over time, become recognised fountainheads of spiritual enlightenment; indeed, they are at times hot-beds of self-interest and in-fighting. The second observation concerns an obvious contrast between, on the one hand, the current popularity of spiritual outlooks that focus upon well-being, and, on the other hand, the rarity of interest in teachings that emphasise – each in their own way – selflessness or the dissolving of self-importance.

In the context of enlightenment, self-importance has a distinct and, some might say, sophisticated meaning. In secular society, self-importance is generally seen as a behaviour: as pomposity, bragging, or narcissism. But enlightenment is not about behaviour, it is about the liberation of curiosity. What hinders the liberation of curiosity is a profound gravitational pull that draws an individual's attention towards the activity of their mind and, in particular, to the thoughts and feelings that arise therein. In an enlightened context this gravitational pull - the contraction of attention around thought and feeling - is seen to have a particular function: it strengthens an individual's sense of 'me', or 'I'. When attention is focused upon thoughts and feelings, a solid sense of individuality is created. In the spacious context of enlightenment, it is this contracted, solid sense of 'me' that is named "self-importance".

In this view, self-importance is not seen as the product of a deliberate activity. Instead, even while it is seen as a major hinderance to the flowering of curiosity, self-importance is seen as a response to a profound *need*: the need within our species to create a pocket of security within a largely unknowable universe.

The need within our species; this description points to our human requirement for a manageable microcosm. Highlighting the inherent, species-wide nature of this need helps to dispel the assumption that the need is either individual or blameworthy. Moreover, recognising that this need is embedded within all human beings paves the way for a particular realisation: moving beyond the need for a manageable microcosm is an enormous challenge. Once the challenge of transcending this need - this form of self-importance - is appreciated, the rarity of enlightened attainment starts to be explained.

The desire to transcend self-importance is a niche interest, attractive to only a minority of people. In this respect, I think the desire for enlightenment is akin to a love of mathematics. The two disciplines have further similarities: both enlightenment and mathematics are independent fields of study, as well as the essential currencies of other disciplines; both require affinity and aptitude; both quickly become incomprehensible to lay people; and both unfold for ever. There is yet another parallel: some people give their lives to these fields of inquiry, while others have no attraction to them at all.

The pursuit of enlightenment can be emotionally crushing. In seeking to free one's attention from what can feel like its atomic cohesion with thought and feeling, one is confronting the power of the human mind. I think the power of the mind becomes clear when we see – for example - both its capacity to observe the activity of sub-atomic particles, and its ability to generate unbearable experiences that drive people, sadly, to desperation, self-harm, or suicide. Passages in this book illustrate what has been described as the greatest challenge a human being can engage with: the challenge of transcending a particular need within one's own mind; the need for self-importance.

If risk relates to reward, the courage it takes to engage with one's mind should sometimes deliver outstanding results. I will come to these results shortly, but first I need to note that the interests of enlightened people fall into two basic categories.

In Andrew's teachings, he draws a distinction between the Being and Becoming dimensions of existence. I describe his distinction below, and elsewhere in this book, but I can introduce it by offering the following similar pairings:

- the unmanifest and the manifest;
- disengagement from the world and engagement with it;
- God at rest and God in action.

It might also help to point out that a comparison between the world's most famous religious images portrays this distinction. Buddha's peaceful repose, when compared to Jesus's crucifixion, points to the fact that, as self-importance dissolves and enlightenment flowers, some people move towards the Being dimension of existence, while others engage in the Becoming dimension.

Andrew always spoke about Being before Becoming. He said that Being, or formlessness, was the undivided, eternal background from which form briefly appears. This is also the time-honoured view of eastern spiritual traditions, in which meditation is the practice of letting attachment to all experience fall away. By letting go of all experience, one is freed from the need to be positioned at the centre of a limited space, and one's attention is liberated. In this profoundly relaxed state, having let go of everything, one is at one with the unborn nature of existence. Rare, significant people have permanently dwelt in this dissolved condition, often looked after by others, and they are luminaries, living beacons of cosmological beauty, who exhibit to others *"the peace that passeth all understanding"* and the immortality of an indivisible presence.

In contrast, enlightened engagement with the Becoming dimension of existence leads to a perfect partnership between mankind and God, or a beautiful, symbiotic exchange of self-knowledge between heaven and earth. In the Becoming dimension, an individual becomes a willing, equipped agent of divinity. The mind, once transcended - or *"seen through"*, in Andrew's words – loses much of its gravitational pull towards smallness, safety and security. It can then be shouldered and carried forward as one pursues an authentic vocation. Just as one can fall, infinitely, into the depth of Being, so one can be drawn into ever-increasing singularity of purpose, as one casts aside compromising distractions to become, in one's own unique way, a hand-in-glove expression of Becoming, or God in action.

As the aforementioned titles of Andrew's publications suggest, enlightenment is a subject that warrants repeated review. As his students, we heard him describe enlightenment in myriad ways. This book represents that feature of our lives; it will refer, time and again, by many and varied means, to the nature of enlightenment.

Chapter 3

What Is Ego?

Ego was a big subject in the life and work of Andrew's spiritual community. He and his students discovered what a powerful obstacle to enlightenment ego can be, and the strength of intention needed to overcome it. Understanding ego is very different from engaging with it, so I have elected to write two chapters. This chapter describes the community's particular view of ego. My forthcoming account of the community's engagement with ego lies in the middle of this book, reflecting how that engagement peaked in the central years of the community's history.

I suggest that the phenomenon of ego, and the community's response to it, will be one of the most contentious subjects in this book. I offer this forewarning in friendship because, without doubt, Andrew and his community were surprised by what they discovered. The story of that discovery is told in Chapter 15.

If enlightenment comes from the expansion of awareness and the softening of personal identity, ego is the force working in the opposite direction. It is the ego within each of us that seeks security in an insecure universe. If the cosmos is used as a metaphor, *Light* radiating outwards represents enlightenment, whereas *Gravity* contracting inwards represents ego. Some contraction of awareness is healthy and necessary: our individuality depends upon it. But too much contraction creates the experience of painful separation. In a tightly-contracted, egoic state, one feels separate from oneself, separate from others and separate from the great scope of existence.

Understanding ego this way – as gravity – helps to explain how we generally see ego in others. We can observe how ego is drawn towards a central point that often takes the form of a noticeable distortion in someone's character. Different elements of personal experience can act as this central point. A perceived *problem*, especially with oneself, performs this role superbly. Attention can also circle around one's *health*, or *emotions*. *Knowledge* and *intellect* are other favourites, along with *goodness* and *self-pity*. There are plenty of possibilities! Each of these elements can act as a catalyst for ego, with the result that an individual remains self-centred and reassured within their limited world.

During the first phase of Andrew's teaching career, he saw his students experiencing resistance from their egos - and plenty of it – as they sought to let their awareness expand. But, at that time, ego resistance was only an obstacle to their individual enlightenment. Ego became a greater problem when the community moved to Foxhollow in 1996, and its joint venture became its central focus. Students' egos then became an impediment to something more important than their own enlightenment.

As the community's focus changed, the nature of ego was re-evaluated. Ego was previously regarded as a parcelled, individual issue but, as the community's understanding evolved, ego also came to be seen as a single, unified force. How human beings think of *goodness* illustrates this dual understanding: it is both a quality present in humanity as a whole, and a characteristic of particular individuals. Andrew's students, therefore, spoke about ego existing in two dimensions: in one dimension it took the form of an individual's actions; in another dimension it was an independent force.

These developments, in the focus of the community's work and its understanding of ego, meant that, at Foxhollow, ego was seen as a powerful force standing between the community and its goal. As this situation came into view, so began the confrontation described in Chapter 15.

Ego is clearly a problem in secular society. Some might say it is *the* problem. But - while people express ego in many ways, for example by being difficult, boastful, unpredictable, unhappy, etc. – I would say that ego is mostly navigated around and not addressed. In Andrew's community we didn't avoid ego, and we discovered that most people react defensively when their ego is exposed and confronted.

Students would exhibit recognisable behaviours when the ego inside them was challenged. These behaviours became familiar to the community. Certain facial expressions – pursed lips, or a particular, sly form of smile - indicated ego resistance. A general demeanour of hopelessness, helplessness and defeat was another sign. An absolute lack of interest in feedback – advice about egoic behaviour - was further evidence that someone was occupied by ego. Over time, it became easy to identify students' defensiveness and refusal to change. Indeed, the features of that defensiveness became so well-known that, firstly, they could be predicted and, secondly, resistant students appeared to have been occupied by a familiar, independent phenomenon. This, I contend, is why intelligent people can be forgiven for thinking of ego as an esoteric entity, because people in a state of ego-resistance genuinely look as if they have been taken over by a recognisable, external force. When the exact same demeanour appears time and time again, in very many people, ego comes to be seen, and thought of, as an independent phenomenon.

What Is Ego?

The community's relationship to ego matured over time. Engaging with his students, Andrew gained insight into the nature of ego, and he included these insights in his teaching work. The magazine team studied the different views of ego held by a range of spiritual traditions and modern-day schools of psychology. Issue 17 of the magazine is titled *What is Ego?* and it records the team's findings. In the community, we discussed the subject of ego in our formal dialogues with Andrew and in our smaller group meetings. Each student also had to face their own ego. Over time, a lot was learnt.

In particular, our expectations were modified by our experience. The idea of ridding oneself of ego, or expecting someone else to do the same, was eventually seen as unrealistic. Instead, 'caging' the ego was our aim. (I appreciate that some readers might find this term disconcerting but, in the community, it served our purpose). Caging the ego meant, firstly, seeing it clearly. It meant being familiar with the movement of ego in ourselves, knowing our egoic habits, and recognising the onset of egoic reaction. Secondly, it meant bearing the wide range of experiences ego could generate. Broadly speaking, ego destroys curiosity while inflating self-importance. By recognising these traits we were able, over time, to simply let the activity of ego exist within us.

In short, we were taught that the right response to ego is to see it clearly but remain disengaged. *"Let it be as it is,"* was Andrew's instruction. He added, *"That's all we can do and all we need to do."* His teaching, however, applies to an ideal world in which someone is interested in seeing their ego. This is by no means always the case. Ego dislikes exposure. It detests criticism. But both of those responses are dwarfed by the ego's reaction to being caged. It took Andrew and the community five years to master the deadening force of ego. Much of this book is about the achievement of that mastery.

Chapter 4

Our Spiritual Work

At points in this book I have felt it necessary to stress the difference between prevailing secular ideas and the aspirations we had in Andrew's community. For example, in Chapter 19, *The Women*, I emphasise the distinction between empowerment and enlightenment, in an attempt to hold back the prevailing idea that spiritual freedom and empowerment are one and the same. At other points I have had to lean against the widely-held assumption that spiritual teachers should, first and foremost, express unconditional love. In this chapter, I want to root out the established notion of the spiritual journey as an individual quest and replace it with an understanding of our group venture.

In the very beginning of his teaching career, Andrew was intrigued by the personal stories of people who came to him. But, after three years, something else attracted his curiosity. He began to notice the quality of communication developing between his students. He later described how his attention was drawn to their communion:

> *"Soon after I began to teach, I made an intriguing observation: the spiritual experiences that those who had gathered around me were **sharing together** seemed to be of greater significance than any experience of higher consciousness that they had had individually …. No matter how powerful it may have been.*
>
> *It took me a few years to understand what was happening and to be able to put it into context. But it soon became obvious that a mutation was occurring. I was bearing witness to the fact that the mind of enlightenment seemed to be taking a leap beyond the individual."*

Unknowingly, I might have witnessed some early signs of this mutation in Bodh Gaya, when I saw the unusually focused communication occurring between members of the Sangha. I noticed their composed and upright posture, their consistent eye-contact, and their closer than normal face-to-face distance. I was familiar with a more casual group environment, so speaking with a member of the Sangha was quite demanding. I felt an unusually concentrated gaze coming my way that made me feel 'seen', and that a heightened sense of importance was attributed to what was said.

Andrew coined the term 'impersonal enlightenment' to describe the shared quality of attentiveness he was observing. He predicted it could grow to become a '*forest fire*' compared to the '*burning match*' of personal enlightenment. Through the years 1991-1995, the emphasis of his teachings gradually changed, as he – and, to some extent, his students - experienced a growing, intuitive sense of what this shared enlightened phenomenon could become.

As far as Andrew knew, we – he and his students - were not heading towards something that already existed. Our work was not the same as searching for an isotope or the structure of DNA. Instead, we were attempting to make something new, to forge a new metaphysical connection. I believe Helen Keller's story, told below, has the qualities of this quest. She was reaching into the dark for something unknown to her. Similarly, Andrew, largely on his own, was peering into metaphysical mist. He intuited that something - possibly a new expression of enlightened consciousness - could come from the communion he was witnessing between his students. He was uncertain what he would find, yet willing to commit all his resources to pursuing it.

During this pursuit, Andrew's students lagged well behind him. There is a reason for this. From experience, I know how the awareness of spiritual students is, ironically, occupied by self-concern. A student, genuinely aspiring to graduate from a self-centred state of mind, finds that his or her ego resists this graduation, leading the mind to contract around the question "*How am I doing?*" I have learnt that this contracted state of mind is not a deficiency, it's part of the process of spiritual seeking but, in our case, the result was that students' ability to contribute to Andrew's vision was limited.

Unquestionably, the community's mission was driven and guided by Andrew. He had the best sense of what we might find, and of its possible significance. It's true to say that both he and his students were feeling their way forward, but it should be noted that, within that joint endeavour, Andrew's students were often preoccupied with their struggle to keep up.

In later chapters I describe the physical form of our spiritual work: our spiritual practices and formal group meetings. But here, I want to tell a story that conveys the non-physical character of what we were doing. It is the true story of Helen Keller's childhood. My account is drawn from the 1962 film, *The Miracle Worker*.

> *Born in Alabama (USA) in 1880, Helen was obviously an*
> *exceptionally intelligent baby. She began to speak aged six months*

and, at one year old, she could walk. She had an older brother and her parents owned a cotton plantation. Then, aged 19 months, an illness, either scarlet fever or meningitis (it's not known which), left Helen deaf and blind.

Helen's mother was devoted to her and deeply believed her daughter could learn to communicate. Helen's father, a well-meaning patriarch, had less faith and less patience. Nevertheless, a tutor, Anne Sullivan, from the Perkins School for the Blind, was employed in an attempt to help Helen find a way out of her obvious frustration.

Helen, aged six at this point, was completely wild and unruly. She threw food, vases and crockery. She bit and scratched and rebelled against discipline. She fought Anne Sullivan tooth-and-nail: the film shows full-scale fisticuff fights as Anne struggles to gain authority over Helen and win her trust and respect. Nothing works. Relatives advise Helen's parents to put her in an institution, her father's faith all but vanishes and her mother is downhearted. But, in a memorable exchange, Helen's defeated father says, "Maybe God doesn't intend her to speak," and Anne Sullivan, with a voice of steel, replies, "Maybe God doesn't, but I do."

A last-ditch, final agreement is made between Anne Sullivan and Helen's parents. Helen will be taken on a circuitous ride in a buggy and she will be dropped at the family's summerhouse. While still within the grounds of the garden, Helen will feel she is in an unknown location. She will be solely dependent on Anne Sullivan for everything, for 10 days.

This arrangement slightly softens Helen's previously ferocious rejection of her tutor, but there is still no progress with her ability to make the connection between an object and Anne Sullivan's fingerspelling into the palm of Helen's hand. The ten days eventually expire and Helen is returned to the main house.

Everyone is exhausted, even Anne Sullivan. Helen defaults to being uncontrollable. At the dinner table, she impetuously defies the hard-won rule that she must keep her napkin on her lap. It *looks as if the situation has regressed back to the arrival day of Anne Sullivan... who... suddenly... snaps, grabbing Helen by her wrist and dragging her out to the water pump in the front garden. Maddened and enraged, she pumps water onto Helen's hand, desperately making the finger-spelling sign in her palm, over and over again. Helen, overpowered, gets the connection: the sign relates to the water; **meaning** exists between the two different entities: the object and the sign. Helen has discovered language.*

Helen's intelligence runs riot. She learns 30 words by nightfall and, in later years, she becomes a scholar and world-renowned, inspirational figure. Anne Sullivan remains her companion for the next 49 years.

The story illustrates many of the qualities needed to achieve a breakthrough. It shows the value of intention, and that friction might be inherent in the process. Helen's time spent in darkness communicates the pain of ignorance, and her emergence into light points to the existence of realms beyond our current knowledge. I find her story moving for two reasons. I love her raw wilfulness; it speaks to me of the passion I feel churning at the heart of Life. And her transcendent moment is glorious, as her profound frustration turns to impassioned comprehension.

In particular, I want to single out the quantum leap she takes from no language to language; from something not existing to something existing. This matches the nature of our work with Andrew. It explains why, in the early days, we had little idea of what we were reaching for. We had little idea because it was something that didn't currently exist. Andrew intuited what might appear, and we later discovered that French spiritual reformer Sri Aurobindo (1872-1950) had made a solid description of what he called *Supermind*, but his anticipated faculty had never been made real.

This was our task, to bring a new spiritual faculty into being. We were the boots on the ground. Philosophers had imagined its nature, Andrew intuited its existence, and his students - a mixed bunch of people, in a mixed state of repair, with mixed levels of intention – trusted him. However, no one knew exactly what we were going to find, or what it would take to first invoke and then sustain this new emergence.

Chapter 5

The Community

This chapter describes the character of the community, its demographics, and its hierarchical arrangement. Other features of the community are captured in future chapters.

I have had contact with a few spiritual communities in my life, and I think it will set a colourful context for this chapter if I note their differences.

My father was briefly the chaplain at an enclosed Benedictine abbey in Kent, UK and, in the years after he died, my mother used to take me and my sisters to visit the abbess and nuns. The abbey buildings were contained within an extensive, idyllic, walled garden that had an energetic stream winding through its centre. The stream felt like the embodiment of the nuns' fresh-faced, Christian devotion. The abbess was small, but formidable. She gave stern advice to her shy teenage visitors, such as *"Money is the God of today."* This stirred rebellion rather than reverence in our ill-prepared minds. The abbey had other qualities. Even while I disliked its dislocation from materialism, I loved its beauty, singularity of purpose, and the spiritual heights to which the nuns and their forbears clearly aspired.

Brockwood Park, in Hampshire, UK, was one of Jiddu Krishnamurti's schools. He was, possibly, the most refined spiritual teacher of recent times, and my mother used to attend his gatherings and listen to his talks. For four years, my younger sister was a pupil at Brockwood, and later I taught in one of Krishnamurti's Indian schools. From these associations, I formed an impression of the culture surrounding Krishnamurti. His followers did not form a tight-knit community, far from it, but they did form a unique genre. They were serious thinkers, focused upon the origin of ignorance. This origin was identified by Krishnamurti as the *'movement of memory'*, or, more often: *Thought*. As well as being serious thinkers his followers were, in general, well-educated and wealthy. I respected them for their dedicated introspection, but I wondered about the ultimate outcome of their study.

Among Andrew's students there were perhaps fifteen former sannyasins who had belonged to the community of Bhagwan Sri Rajneesh, the community that attempted to realise Bhagwan's Utopian vision in Oregon, USA, in the 1980s. These students - my peers - were robustly engaged, unpolished characters, strong on largesse but weak on refinement. They were friendly and easy to love, but sometimes crude with their language and personal habits. My friendships with these former sannyasins made me especially interested in two recent documentaries: *Bhagwan, his Secretary & his Bodyguard*; and *Wild Wild Country*. These documentaries, and my conversations with former sannyasins, paint an exuberant picture of happiness, indulgence and visionary zeal. Bhagwan's community – it seems – was without boundaries: no limits were placed on the community's actions as it pursued its dream of Utopia. Neither, it also seems, were any limits placed upon Bhagwan's personal indulgence and unscrupulous sequestration of his students' wealth.

The Benedictine nuns, Krishnamurti's followers and Bhagwan's sannyasins were all deeply committed to their paths. So were Andrew's students. But how did Andrew's community differ from the others I have mentioned? Below is a description of the shape of Andrew's community, along with my attempt to imagine how you might have experienced a visit to Foxhollow.

Character and Demographics

Ethnically, the community was mostly white, although it had a significant number of Asian students. Diversity came in the form of different nationalities. There were some students from outlying countries such as India, Israel, Malaysia, Japan and Chile; but more came from central European countries – France, Germany, Holland, Denmark and Sweden – and from the UK and USA. The biggest contingent – marginally - was American, with students coming from many different States.

Andrew had approximately 300 close students, with whom he had a formal, student-teacher relationship. The number of men and women was close to equal. Andrew's wider reach included people who saw him at evening teachings, usually in a city, and those who participated in a variety of longer retreats around the world. The people within Andrew's wider reach lived independent lives and used his teachings on a daily basis; numbering approximately 2000, they were recognised by Andrew and he knew many of their names. At its peak, *What is Enlightenment?* magazine sold 20,000 copies per issue, and the readership was projected to be 40,000. The magazine's readers and subscribers would have known of Andrew's work as a spiritual teacher. Sales of his books broadened this global audience. If I imagine the figures listed above – of students, audiences and readerships - accumulating over the twenty-seven years of Andrew's teaching career, and I add word-of-mouth referrals, I estimate that nearly one million people currently know something of his teaching work.

An important feature of the community was students' relative freedom from common distractions and commitments. This freedom had two origins.

Firstly, students were quite young – the average age was around 40 years – and, consequently, they were not distracted by chronic ill-health or dependent, aging parents. Secondly, only a few students had children to support; I will expand on this below. Free from commitments, students could live very focused lives. This, in turn, accelerated the work of the community and the development of Andrew's teachings.

Because raising a family is often a feature of human life, it might be surprising to read that it was not within the community's frame of reference. Within the core student community, only one baby was ever born. We were focused on our spiritual work; we didn't think of having children. Very occasionally, Andrew would say there were enough people in the world and that adoption would be a responsible choice if someone really wanted to nurture a child. But the question of having a baby was only ever seriously raised by one woman, as far as I know. In this respect, our community was like a traditional monastery. It would not have attracted people who wanted to have a family.

The minority of students who brought children into the community achieved different positions in the hierarchy. In the early years, many of Andrew's top students were parents. It looked as if their experience as parents made them more responsible people than the non-parents; they seemed more mature and able to cope with the heavy demands made upon their time. But, throughout the community's history, other parents clearly found it difficult to combine two lives – home and community - where both called for their full attention. Despite Andrew encouraging all the parents to be interested in, rather than burdened by, their challenge, I think it's fair to say that the parents found it hard to combine their parenting with our committed spiritual work.

I barely know the children – now adults – who were brought into the community. I have been told they are partly grateful for their spiritually-informed upbringing, while also feeling they suffered from their parents' divided attention. I do know that some children had to frequently move house and, understandably, found that to be disruptive.

Andrew attracted intelligent people. They found his teachings intellectually satisfying and, in him, they found an astute person who matched their acuity. This might sound suspiciously subjective but, to support my assertion, I can point to the spiritual depth in Andrew's books, the acknowledged quality of his magazine, and the calibre of his friendships and associations. I also knew the people around Andrew, for a long time. I don't think of myself as especially intelligent, but I can see others who are. Among a generally bright group of students, some were true polymaths or proven prodigies. Others were talented in a variety of creative and academic fields. I'm aware that my claim - about the intelligence of Andrew's students - is bold, but I consider it to be true.

Food was a matter of great interest, and the community had many accomplished cooks. Over its lifespan, the community's diet moved from vegetarian towards vegan and then raw. People's commitment to this progression varied, but it was led by Andrew's desire to eat consciously, be healthy and live a long life. Eventually the community's diet, especially at Foxhollow, was an element of its identity: it was one expression of the community's evolving awareness. This line of development was driven by the collaboration between Andrew and the dedicated cooks and chefs.

Andrew - by no means alone in this - disliked like the word *community*. The word was too soft-edged to describe what he had in mind for his students' collective character. He wanted us to be impressive people who represented - in appearance, manner and deed - the credibility of his teachings and our joint venture. We had an obligation to look good, dress well and speak clearly. Our standard of personal presentation was, consequently, quite high.

In the community's daily life men and women worked alongside one another, just as they do in much of western society. But the community's spiritual work was done in gender-divided groups. The reason for this was simple: Andrew thought gender-specific groups would facilitate our work. He thought students would be less distracted in same-sex configurations, and more able to focus upon specific issues, such as self-referencing, for women, or pride, for men. Because our spiritual work was our first reference, the gender divide strongly influenced our lives; we felt we belonged to an essential subset within the community, and we were aware of our tendencies, whether male or female. The importance of our gender-specific work becomes evident later in this book.

How might you have experienced Foxhollow and the community? On arrival, it's likely you would have been inspired by the grounds, buildings and interior design (Chap 8). After receiving a warm welcome and enjoying some good conversation over a nicely-presented meal, you would possibly have described the community as friendly and inquiring. However, within twenty-four hours you would probably have seen how focused students were on their spiritual activities, and perhaps you would think they had little attention available for subjects outside their field of special interest. Forty-eight hours into your visit, while still impressed by the quality of life at Foxhollow, you might well have felt like an onlooker, someone viewing an all-consuming endeavour. Possibly, you would then revise your description of the community and say it was engrossed and single-minded.

Hierarchy

Hierarchy was a big feature of Andrew's community and an important subject in his teachings of Evolutionary Enlightenment.

In Andrew's teachings, hierarchy is seen as inherent within evolving systems. One example of an evolving system is the basic progression from atoms to molecules, from molecules to cells, and then cells to organisms. Andrew also saw hierarchy as the organising principle of a cosmological progression, starting with *matter* and moving through *life* and *mind*, to *soul*. Seeing hierarchy as integral to evolution, Andrew could easily see that his students were at different levels of development, and that these differences were something to work with, rather than ignore.

The community's hierarchy developed over time. In the early days, the late 1980s, there was a simple division between those who lived with Andrew and those who didn't. Later, in 1992, when I met Andrew in Bodh Gaya, there were three tiers: the Sangha, the aspiring Lay-Sangha, and others. By the time the community moved to Foxhollow in 1996, more permutations and titles had come and gone, and yet further name changes and refinements were to follow.

Hence, I have a problem choosing titles for the community's different levels of hierarchy. I have solved this problem by creating an improvised, generic hierarchy to describe a student's position in the community at any point in its history. Not every title in my improvised hierarchy is used in this book, but the following list gives an idea of how many divisions existed, and their functions.

Senior Students led the worldwide Centres; they gave public teachings, were responsible for younger students in their city or country and were in touch with Andrew on a daily, sometimes hourly, basis. There were about ten senior students at any one time, located around the world.

Mentoring Students were also responsible for managing Centres. They led internal teaching events and held positions respected by less-experienced students.

Upper-core students had been committed to the teachings for upwards of fifteen years and lived in one of the worldwide communities. They had proved themselves capable of bearing substantial pressure and were expected to represent reliably the teachings in any situation.

Core students were similar to upper-core students, but with maybe five years' less experience. Slightly less was expected of core students.

Devoted students had their heart in the right place. They might have had a close relationship with Andrew in previous years (or not) but, for individual reasons, they did not, or could not, meet expectations placed upon the higher groups. Some devoted students lived in a city community, others did not.

Lay students had independent lives and didn't live in a community. Their involvement in the teachings supplemented their other interests and commitments. Lay students could be newcomers who were learning about the teachings - often excitedly - or they could be people who had known Andrew for a long time but had not stepped into his world.

I imagine the idea of a strong hierarchy will be off-putting to some people, because of its associations with misuse of power and the limitation of personal choice. Those associations might well be valid in a society that prioritises individual freedom but, in Andrew's community, we were committed to a group enterprise, and in that particular context our strong hierarchy freed us from two time-consuming distractions.

Firstly, the question of who had authority in a particular situation was answered. Everything to do with the community's spiritual development was in the hands of Andrew and the senior and mentoring students. Meanwhile, most practical matters fell into the jurisdiction of a department; for example, the timetabling of a weekend retreat would be decided by the events department. In this way, the existence of the hierarchy meant that students were not burdened by the often-lengthy process of reaching a consensus.

Secondly, we were, by and large, undistracted by ambition. A student's position in the hierarchy was determined by self-evident maturity, not personal desire or cronyism. Someone would move up the hierarchy when it became clear to Andrew, and usually to everyone, that they could bear greater responsibility. The signs of readiness could be seen in someone's manner, the independence in their voice, and the consistency of their participation in meetings (Chap 13). Since rising up the hierarchy was a matter of maturity, it didn't make sense for students to immaturely covet higher status. In fact, we tended to hold back from it, because the prospect of higher status came with expectations of possibly crushing responsibilities. The community's hierarchy was, therefore, more of a self-evolving structure than a competitive ladder. It was something we could trust, which meant that, again, our attention - freed from preoccupations about status – could be given to our work.

Chapter 6

The Magazine

Andrew founded *What is Enlightenment?* magazine. It played a very important role in his community and was highly respected in the wider world, so it deserves its own short chapter. Published for nineteen years, the magazine received widespread recognition, including awards for its editorial and design content (Chap 22).

The magazine was first printed in January 1992 as a fourteen-page, black-and-white, stapled publication. The first issue contained in-house material. Some articles were based on Andrew's ongoing inquiries, while others - written by leading students – were about their own challenges. By January 1995 the magazine was a twice-yearly, fifty-page colour publication containing interviews with renowned teachers. Over the next sixteen years, it more than doubled in size to become a 120-page, highly-respected, investigative periodical. Each issue, dedicated to a selected subject, stimulated dialogue and debate in spiritual circles. In 2008 the magazine's name was changed to *EnlightenNext Magazine.*

The magazine raised Andrew's profile as a teacher. It brought his name into prominence and, through its editorial and design quality, it advertised the calibre of his teaching work. The magazine occupied a central place in Andrew's working schedule (Chap 10) and it fulfilled many roles: his teaching work was informed by the editorial team's investigations; his interviews led to working friendships with many significant figures in many walks of life; and the work of producing the magazine with his students served to integrate his community.

Many students, and some external staff, were employed to produce the magazine, making it an important occupation within the community. An undercurrent of activity, focused on the magazine, ran through Foxhollow on working days, especially near to print deadlines. Our lives were further enriched by regular launch parties and, of course, the content of each issue. There was a graphics department at Foxhollow, with dedicated graphic artists, who produced inspired front covers and internal layouts. Each edition was beautiful to look at. The magazine was the community's flagship product, of which we were proud.

Here is a small selection of subjects investigated by the magazine's editors. *Is there Life after Death? Women, a Cultural and Philosophical Investigation. Ecology, Politics and Consciousness. Searching for Utopia. What does it mean to be in the World but not of it?* A full list of subjects and contributors is given in this book's Appendix. Each edition of the magazine can be downloaded for free from andrewcohen.com, and the visually-impacting front covers can be scrolled through at https://www.slideshare.net/pitneyj/the-evolution-of-en-lightennext-magazine.

Production of the magazine had to cease in 2011; the reasons for this are explained, in context, in Chapter 22.

Chapter 7

The Author

I think a short autobiography, including a description of my history as Andrew's student, will help readers understand this book.

Born in 1958, I was raised in the home counties of England. My father, Edward, was an Anglican priest. He was a very conscientious man, humorous and with high ideals. His parishioners loved him for his pastoral care and for the strong, Christian values which gave weight to his pulpit oratory. Common to his class and generation, he was socially minded and politically left-leaning. My father's background was upper-class English, not wealthy, but well-spoken, well-educated and well-mannered. He died in 1964, aged 46, from leukaemia, leaving my mother with three small children.

Dorothy was very much the youngest child of a Cornish, working-class family. She left that background behind when she passed the entrance exam of her nearby grammar school. She independently attended her local church, where my father was the priest, and where they met and later married in 1952. My mother was spiritually courageous. My father's death brought an end to thirteen years of playing the part of a young, dutiful, vicar's wife. Liberated from that role, she switched Churches and, for ten years, our family attended Quaker meetings. My mother then made another spiritual move, this time engaging with the inward-looking work of the Gurjieff and Ouspensky groups that were forming in London in the mid '70s. Her discovery and interest in the teachings of Jiddu Krishnamurti came a little later and led her, through great effort, to send my younger sister to Brockwood Park (Chap 5). Vocationally, my mother was a primary school teacher and, later in life, she taught the Alexander Technique. She died thirteen years after my father, but at the same age as him, and also from a rare blood disease.

Meanwhile, I had been a happy schoolboy. I was successful enough academically and passionate about football, girlfriends and motorbikes. I passed a respectable number of exams and graduated with a mediocre degree in Geography. My greater achievement at university was captaining the football team. College was a formative time for me, but I wasn't a high achiever. In my twenties I was self-employed, doing what I carefully termed *Fine Interior Woodwork* for well-to-do clients in London. This was lonely work, but I learnt about the building trade and, during those years, my vivacious girlfriend and

I had a dream apartment in Maida Vale and a black, soft-top, MGB sports car with chrome wire wheels. That car, as you can tell, was a prized possession. My life from this point onward is described in the Prologue.

As one of Andrew's students, I was generally middle-of-the-road in terms of performance, with my best qualities breaking through only occasionally. This was typical of students at my level in the hierarchy. I could perhaps stretch to claim association with the phrase '*When the going gets tough, the tough get going,*' as my brightest moments came during the crunch period around the year 2000 (Chap 20). But for years I was quite a sluggish student, moving along with the crowd, a resistant character from an enlightened point of view, and often frustrating to others.

I should also say – to raise my profile - that simply remaining Andrew's student was an achievement. Student turnover stabilised over time but, in the mid-1990s, students were still regularly leaving the community. This attrition continued until, simply by surviving, I was eventually one of Andrew's top twenty-five most experienced students, albeit with noticeably less weight than those above me. Rated on my improvised hierarchy, I was an upper-core student, edging, in later years, towards being a mentoring student.

Practically, I gave a lot, and had opportunities to show my capabilities. My experience in the building trade was needed at Foxhollow and I was flattered to be told - during the arrival months in 1996 - that I raised the community's level of professionalism. In 1998, EnlightenNext built a brand-new, 2000sq ft Centre in Boston - an architectural gem. I managed the construction work on that project. The biggest and most taxing job I have ever undertaken – which was EnlightenNext's largest-ever financial project - was the renovation and extension of a five-storey building in Islington, London, in 2003. I joined the venture when it was floundering, caught between the architect's grand vision and a modest budget, and – truth-be-told - I had to take overall control to straighten out the chaos and get the project back on track. Once finished, the building became EnlightenNext's London Centre.

From 2002 onward, I lived in the London student community. In 2003 I married my dear wife, Khin, who was also one of Andrew's students. She is originally from Malaysia, with Chinese ancestry. Although the London community had its own focus and character, Foxhollow – being the community's headquarters - was always a primary reference. We often travelled there for retreats, sometimes just for a weekend, and were in almost daily contact via the new – at that time - facility of conference calls.

In 2009 my younger sister died, shockingly, five weeks after her diagnosis of secondary cancer. She lived in London, near to me, and, during her last weeks,

I abandoned everything to give myself to her care. I was happy to do this; I wasn't torn; I was in the doldrums as a student and, through caring for my sister, I rediscovered my heart. I loved her very much; we were similar in many respects. Sensitive to the same matters, we shared some core values, including a sense of humour. Her illness and death broke my loyalty to the EnlightenNext community. Despite dutiful feelings, my commitment had been fractured. A future in the community held nothing that I wanted, and eventually, through a withering process that was horrible for everyone, I decided to leave in the summer of 2010. I write a little more about my experience of this in Chapter 23.

The period between 2010 and now, 2020, has been the most extraordinary of my life. Through a process that was awful to begin with, then astounding and, more recently, consistently demanding, I have been granted a rare perspective. That journey is not generally relevant to this book's narrative but, in large part, it will be the substance of my next book, *Graduation*, which will record the step-by-step process by which I graduated from my teacher's authority. Unintentionally, this book will set the context for that journey.

Eighteen months after the dissolution of Andrew's community (Chap 23), I went to visit him in India. I was concerned for his welfare and I felt the world could not afford to lose his experience. In possibly the most astonishing turn of events in my life, Andrew and I became close friends for over three years, until I started to write this book. I believe he – quite reasonably - was wary of this book. I had no track record as a writer, I think he found my writing style too informal, and I suspect he anticipated that I would make detailed disclosures that might bring him negative publicity. Feeling his ambivalence, I decided it would be best if my account were written with unquestionable independence. So, I broke our friendship and, for the last three years, there has been no contact between us.

My position in Andrew's community can be judged from two vantage points. If I adopt an in-house view and compare myself to other students, I see someone who worked hard, occasionally shone, but didn't step forward to accept responsibility for the community's teaching work. However, if I take a heightened perspective, I see myself as part of a group that genuinely aspired for the ultimate union: a group that sought to become a conduit for Spirit. In that view, individuals are barely differentiated from one another, because it is everyone's willingness to participate that stands proud and is applauded. Judged from that elevated place, each of us can proudly say, *"I was there."*

N.B. For reference, here are the locations where I lived as Andrew's student:

1993 – 1995	2yrs	London, Belsize Park.
1995 – 1996	1.5yrs	San Francisco, Marin County.
1996 – 2002	6yrs	Massachusetts, Foxhollow.
2002 – 2010	8yrs	London, Islington.

Chapter 8

Foxhollow

Personally, I like seeing where people live. I think a family's home speaks for its values. Perhaps this is why I loved Foxhollow. I knew every inch of the grounds and buildings, and I felt that the property's beauty matched the quality of our community's work. My love for Foxhollow has made this chapter, at times, quite detailed.

Foxhollow lies between the local towns of Lee and Lenox, in the Berkshire Hills of western Massachusetts, USA. The Berkshires, as the area is referred to, is an elevated, rural region, famous for its Arts institutions and scenic autumn foliage. Historically, it was the country retreat destination for super-rich New York industrialists.

The weather there is extreme by European standards. Winter, stretching from November through to April, features storms, bitter winds and deep snow. The summers are hot enough to make indoor air-conditioning essential and, although they can be unpleasantly humid, they are, on the whole, delightful. Both spring and autumn are sublime. Spring is short, but always very welcome after the long winter, and autumn is a magical time as the leaves change colour. The manor house at Foxhollow had wonderful views; Laurel Lake lay to the east and, beyond that, stretched October Mountain State Forest. That vista and the changing seasons provided a magnificent backdrop to our life at Foxhollow.

The contrast between the two towns of Lenox and Lee amused me. Lenox is a preservationist's dream. Everything is 'just so'; white fences, traditional shop signs and smooth lawns. There are no traffic-lights, potholes or problematic residents. Many local conservation societies make sure it stays untouched by municipal regulations. It is famous for Tanglewood, a music venue that stages a famous international music festival of the same name. The popularity of the annual festival raises vacation rental prices and increases the volume of vehicle traffic in the summer months. We would go to Lenox for its coffee shop, or to buy gifts.

Lee is the same distance from Foxhollow as Lenox. It is known for *Joe's Diner*, made famous by Norman Rockwell's painting, *Runaway*, of a policeman and small boy sitting on bar stools. In the late 1990s it looked as if the café was still making use of those stools. Lee has a defunct paper-mill stretching along the banks of the Housatonic River, which runs inconspicuously through the town. Main Street has the aura of a classic Western film set; the straight run of ordinary shops looks as if there might be nothing behind the facades. The roads do have potholes and there are no manicured lawns. We would go to Lee for its choice of hardware shops.

The Foxhollow estate covered 90 hectares (220 acres) and was shaped like a big quarter-circle, or baseball pitch. The straight boundaries were two roads, Summer Street and Route 7. The radius edge reached down to Laurel Lake and then swung northwards to merge with the neighbouring forest. The inner section of this quadrant was higher than its outskirts, so the land descended from a flat upper area down to the lake. The higher land comprised a grand, winding driveway with bordering pine trees, some forest, acres of lawn, a disused dressage arena and a horse paddock. The buildings of *The Ponds at Foxhollow*, a small resort with rental apartments, were also located on this flat upper area. On the lower slopes, towards the lake and partly hidden by trees, was *Lakeside Condominiums*, an extensive development of expensive, second-home apartments.

Our community, therefore, shared the Foxhollow estate with two other landowners. Before purchase, this was a cause for concern, but the joint management of what really amounted to only shared lawns and driveways, proved to be harmonious. The condominiums were hardly used. Only occasionally did we see, in the distance, wealthy, late-middle-aged couples disembarking from their Cadillacs, Pontiacs or Buicks; or those same cars obediently keeping to the slow speed limit on the sweeping driveways. The buildings of *The Ponds at Foxhollow* nestled within our parcel of land, and customers tended to be families driving their more contemporary SUVs. Again, they kept to the speed limit.

The community owned the manor house, the grandest building on the estate, positioned to overlook the lake. We also owned three blocks of rental apartments, each with twelve units, and five other residential buildings. A low-but-broad concrete building named 'the bunker' - in effect a huge garage - belonged to us; and *The Playhouse*, a unique, finely-constructed, barn-style building, became our meditation and teaching-hall.

The three million dollars needed to buy Foxhollow was donated separately by two American women students. One million dollars came from a loyal and loving New Yorker, who had been Andrew's student since the days of Totnes. Two million dollars came from a vivacious student, in her mid-thirties, of Irish descent. As I believe is the case with most charitable organisations, the sources of large donations were not common knowledge in our community. This was true of the donations made to buy Foxhollow. Nor were the donations matters of contention, until the dissolution of EnlightenNext seventeen years later. But, after the dissolution, a student from the pre-Foxhollow years compiled a list of grievances. He and his list are described in Chapter 15. An entry on his list claims that one woman was pressured into making her donation. I do not know the events of this story, or the changes of sentiment that might have occurred in later years. However, I can say that, throughout my time in the community, I did not hear of any doubts raised over the willingness with which either donation was given.

The estate had an interesting history. George Westinghouse, a pioneer in the fields of electricity and air-braking systems, and his wife, Marguerite Erskine Westinghouse, constructed the first house, Erskine Park, between 1880 and 1890. The house was built in the grand Victorian style of the era, in common with other tycoons' houses in The Berkshires. It was decorated with turrets, and the grounds were adorned with lagoons, marble bridges and crushed marble roads. Their son sold the property in 1917 to Mrs Alfred Gwynne Vanderbilt, stipulating that the house must be torn down. Mrs Vanderbilt hired New York architects Delano and Aldrich to design her a new Colonial Revival house, the building that we later called the manor house.

In 1939 this 'new' house and its land were sold to Mrs Aileen Farrell, who moved her boarding school for girls, called *Foxhollow School*, from Rhinebeck, New York. During the school's thirty-seven-year history, the estate became known as Foxhollow. In 1976 a New York developer bought the property and, soon after, constructed *Lakeside Condominiums* and *The Ponds*. In 1990 the now-reduced parcel of land was sold to Kripalu, a non-profit Yoga and Health organisation, from which EnlightenNext bought the property in 1996.

I vividly remember arriving at Foxhollow in October of that year. My friend Lenny and I were two of the first students to make the journey from California. Driving cross-country, we had become used to our life on the road, with its unpredictable doses of adventure and monotony. In California, at a party to celebrate the property's purchase, we had been shown a video that included a ride along Foxhollow's long driveway, so there was a sense of déjà vu as we drove the last half mile of our three-week road trip. The late afternoon chill and parched brown landscape added eeriness to our sense of the half-familiar. We then entered what we thought was the empty manor house.

When Lenny and I climbed the broad staircase to the first floor, we discovered we were not alone. Whooping cries of happiness issued from along the hallway, and into sight came Andrew and Alka, full of jubilation. Unfettered exuberance was one of Andrew's traits, and finding a home for his community had been his dream for some years, so this was truly a moment for him to celebrate. What's more, we were all physically affected by the surrounding volume of space. The landscape stretched away to a far horizon and the facilities of the manor house were too numerous to take in. We felt we had landed in another world.

Arriving was an overwhelming experience, but it was only the beginning of a new phase of community life. We were now the curators of an historic estate and our small advance party, soon numbering twenty people, was faced with various demands. We needed to find our personal bearings and create a new organizational structure, while being dazzled by the landscape, surprised by practical emergencies and disoriented by the size of our new home. On top of these demands, we were living with Andrew. This, for me, meant an unforgettable two-week period in his close company.

For three years I had held Andrew at arm's length; I had felt panicked in his presence and was inwardly petrified of what he represented. I wasn't alone in having these feelings, but my distance was obvious and noted. Now, suddenly, at Foxhollow, I was one of a group of spiritual frontiersmen, sharing meals with Andrew, doing the washing-up side-by-side, surveying the property, working together in planning meetings, and exploring the local area. What's more, I was in my element. The business in hand was property remodelling: my expertise.

I remember an early morning trip to the bagel shop in Lenox. It was cold, dry and sunny. Andrew said the bagels met New York standards. This information was good to know, but of incidental value to me because I was experiencing such unusual peace of mind. A life-long worry, so familiar that I was hardly aware of it, had gone. My nagging sense of a problem, existing both within me and in the general ambience of life, had withdrawn. In its place, matching the splendour of the morning, was my recognition of the perfection of here and now. Relaxed, attentive, responsive and in good company; it was a golden moment.

Day by day, we came to know the buildings: the locations of fuse boxes and air-handling units, the routes taken by heating circuits, and which windowsills were rotten. Practically, we were pulled from pillar to post by an unregulated stream of urgent repair work, domestic duties, spiritual practice and big-picture planning meetings. Each member of our advance party had creative ideas, and strong feelings about those ideas. There was, as yet, no hierarchy to organise even a daily schedule, and we didn't have agreed names for our many rooms. We lacked even the basic tools of property management. Moreover, Foxhollow's scope and beauty added to the sense of being thrown around in a cosmic drum, of revolving in a vortex of chaotic newness.

Returning to my account of the property, I want to describe the manor house and record two matters: the improvements we made to Foxhollow's buildings; and our style and standard of interior design.

Viewed from the air, the manor house was T-shaped. The original house formed the top of the T. The ground floor had four large reception rooms arranged in a line, with the building's main entrance hall dividing them into two pairs. On the first floor, twelve offices were grouped centrally, while at the tip of each wing – east and west – a large room with an exterior deck claimed the best views. The leg of the T was more recently built. It comprised an atrium, commercial kitchen, mirrored dance studio, indoor pool, various vestibules, and - in the basement - a selection of spa treatment rooms. These spa rooms included sauna and steam-room suites, one for men, one for women.

Renovations and improvements were not limited by money. In the construction department we did not feel financially constrained. Rather, we had the experience of steady progression from project to project, regulated by the availability of in-house labour and the community's tolerance of mess and disruption. There was enough space to do without one big room or hall at any one time and so, over the years, we were able to upgrade fully the meditation hall, the 120-person dining room, and all six of the biggest rooms in the manor house which measured, on average, 80 square metres, or 800 square feet.

These upgrades were not just decorating jobs. One of Andrew's upper-core students, Frank, was an architect, hitherto somewhat unfulfilled in his profession. He saw each major room in the manor house as a canvas for his talent. While some reining-in of his extravagance was required, we were, by and large, grateful to have a professional designer on board. The transformation of the blue room exemplified his work.

This room was judged to be tired and well past its best. It was on the first floor of the manor house, looking west. Two sets of French windows opened onto a deep balcony, with views of the lawns beyond. Sash windows ran along the north- and south-facing walls. Originally, it had a low ceiling. Frank's design removed this ceiling; it dispensed with the roof ties and made use of the attic space above. He designed a steeply-pitched, apparently free-hanging, new structure that could be seen as either an inverted V-shaped ceiling or a floating lining for the pitched roof. The lowest edges of this structure, running almost the full length of the room, were sharply defined. We installed various fixtures for concealed lighting. New baseboard heating covers were made from slatted maple, the doors and windows were dismantled, restored and reinstalled and, finally, everything was painted bright white, before a deep-pile, cornflower-blue carpet was laid. The job took four months and gave us a fresh-looking, spacious and stylish meeting room, conducive to inspired dialogue.

Elements of the blue room were present in all the work we did to upgrade Foxhollow to our satisfaction. Sharply-defined white walls, richly coloured carpets, and hardwood cabinetry comprised our house style, that included carefully chosen furniture and rugs. Other choices of surface, such as ceramic floor tiles, added to a theme that was clean, bright, colourful and comfortable, without being overly opulent.

Steady progress with construction work, and continued commitment to the buildings as an expression of our organisation, meant that few corners of the property were untouched. Over time, the residential and other buildings were improved, the indoor pool was boarded over to create a big construction workshop, and the outdoor pool was rescued from algae and later used for swimming laps. Our gardens were also cared for. There was a kitchen garden near to the manor house, a flower garden in the pool enclosure and a bigger vegetable garden further afield.

Andrew had a suite of rooms in the manor house, designed to suit his office needs. Later, his bigger office was built (by outside contractors) on top of the bunker, near to the apartment he shared with Alka. In the manor house there was a long conservatory close to the kitchen that became Andrew's dining room. This was next to the main dining room.

Andrew renamed our residential buildings: Freedom, Integrity, Fullness, Humility and Emptiness; and one of the driveways became Paradise Way. Our three rental apartment blocks were given the names Clarity, Purity and Truth, providing their tenants with an effortless spiritual upgrade which they may or may not have registered.

Lastly, flowers and flower arrangements were a big feature of our interior spaces. Giving flowers was customary for many reasons, and they arrived in abundance. Visitors bought flowers and the overseas Centres phoned-through their flower orders on celebration days. Students sent flowers to Andrew in gratitude, or in apology. Groups of students bought flowers, again, either to express gratitude or apology. And, for public retreat weekends or community celebration days, flowers were bought to decorate the manor house. The local flower shop, Marskandiser, in Lee, did a roaring trade and its delivery truck must have been on an almost constant loop to and from Foxhollow. We even had a dedicated flower room with racks of vases and two fridges. The students who arranged the flowers - aided by their wealth of opportunity - became increasingly expert, adventurous and inspiring with their designs.

Foxhollow's grounds and its magnificent setting imparted a sense of perfection. At times this could be hard to accept, but it often drew one's attention to the overarching, all-embracing nature of creation. Two further features of the property represented the character of the community's work. Firstly, because Foxhollow was raised above its surroundings, it had open vistas and was battered by the weather. This situation mirrored our willingness to hold an elevated perspective while bearing considerable emotional turmoil. Secondly, Foxhollow was poised between different worlds: its position on the city line between bourgeois Lenox and gritty Lee, together with the community's property partnership with two commercial enterprises, mirrored our desire *to be in the material world but not of it.*

Chapter 9

A Short Story

After an Indian meal at a restaurant, one is often given a mint or hot towel. In my experience, either is welcome. Here, at the end of Part 1 of this book, in place of mint or towel I want to offer a different gratuity: my account of a roadside adventure. This occurred as my friend Lenny and I drove across America, from west to east. The incident is relevant to this book for two reasons: it speaks of the togetherness shared by Andrew's students, and it marks the community's transition from a relatively loose-knit life in California to a more demanding one in Massachusetts.

Lenny was Canadian. He was tall, rugged and handsome, and had a distinct, lumbering gait. These traits made him a noticeable figure within our men's group of upper-core students. He could be stubborn and morose, but we also witnessed his passion for the life we were living. Sometimes he expressed this through his construction work, but his more obvious - and intriguing - strength was his oratory. He spoke with flamboyance, verve and volume, but the accuracy of his vocabulary was inconsistent. These mixed qualities made him a doubly captivating speaker: his charisma attracted half of his listeners' attention, while their remaining brainpower was occupied correcting his adjectives. Lenny's status in our group, along with his charming, hit-and-miss dialogue, meant that I was happy to be travelling with him. His presence raised my expectations for our journey.

Lenny and I shared some common ground: we were both self-employed carpenters and we had a similar physical build. But, on one matter, there was a significant difference. Lenny had a Ford pickup truck, a '92 Ranger; only four years old, it looked respectable. I had an eyebrow-raising, early 1970s Volvo 145 station wagon. Now, looking back at that car, I am troubled by two embarrassing memories: one, of driving it around affluent Marin as a mobile car mechanic and, two, of some customers who were unhappy with my work. But a year before the time of this story, when I had purchased the car, I was in a different phase of my life. I had recently arrived in the Sunshine State and was enjoying the American 'can do' ethos. In that spirit I had bought the faded-red vehicle, which had covered over three hundred thousand miles, from a church community group. I had then removed the engine, sent the cylinders to be re-bored and had the valves reground, thereby giving my 'classic gem' a heart transplant. Lenny quizzed me about its reliability but, despite a few minor faults, such as the dead heater, missing instrument lights and wandering steering system, I had faith in my 'wheels'. So, I assured Lenny I was good to go.

It was an unforgettable trip. I didn't want it to end and I will forever value the journey for showing me features of America that I might otherwise have never seen. At times I was dismayed by the unabashed American appetite for chain stores and strip malls, and I was surprised by the uniformity of the 'towns' we passed through. But, as we settled into our life and cruised along iconic highways such as Route 50 - America's loneliest - I came to value the continent's geographic richness and awe-inspiring size.

We made good progress, we drank gas station coffee, we stayed in motels and we watched the scenery pass by. After a few days, I noticed that the nearside rear wheel of Lenny's truck was wobbling, not alarmingly, but detectably. Lenny wanted to see the situation for himself, so we switched vehicles.

Driving his truck was a shocking experience. It was so warm, quiet and comfortable; the instrument lights made the cabin feel like the cockpit of an aircraft and, on Lenny's music system, as I listened to *Hotel California*, I could hear not only the plucking of every guitar string but also the musicians' fingers sliding along their fretboards. In contrast to this luxury and refinement, the sight now in my rear-view mirror was dismal. Listing heavily to one side, and with its front chrome-work crooked from years of bumps and scrapes, I saw my Volvo from Lenny's perspective; the image gave me a potent and alarming sense of how others must have seen me for quite some time.

Lenny, however, had more than self-image to deal with. Watching his wobbling wheel had made him sullen, and my attempts to raise his spirits – which he probably found hard to respect after driving my car – were futile. With a strange mixture of despondency and assertiveness, he declared that, to fix his wheel, we needed to find a garage in nearby Salt Lake City.

Lenny's declaration marked a change in the day. A similar disruption – when normal life becomes surreal - is captured in Spielberg's film, *Duel*, when the routine of a travelling salesman is intruded upon by an apparently driverless, but menacing, heavy truck. The film shows the salesman's neat life morphing into a deadly duel. In the story I'm telling now, the disturbance of my comfortable expectations started with Lenny's decision to make this detour.

All I knew about Salt Lake City was that it was Mormon territory and home to The Osmonds. Fancifully, I imagined the city to be a seat of religious power and I pictured us - as we made slow progress along the straight and flat approach road - as infidels bumbling naively towards a foreign fortress. More practically, it was early afternoon, and I judged the chances of an immediate car repair to be unlikely. My doubts were well-founded; Lenny's truck was diagnosed as having a bent half-shaft and, because the Ford dealer was out of stock, there was no chance of fitting a replacement. Shrugging, and probably keen to be rid of us, our uninterested mechanic suggested we might find a second-hand shaft at a recommended scrapyard.

The day had started so well, with a stack of pancakes. Yet now I felt caught in a downward spiral. The mechanic's bad news had simultaneously sent Lenny into deeper despair and tightened his resolve. He made a unilateral decision: we would – without a map – comb the outskirts of this hitherto inhospitable city in search of the breaker's yard. Inwardly I thought that, even if we found the facility, we would be seeking a rare spare part. These thoughts only strengthened my feeling of circling downward.

A snack at a roadside restaurant was the day's lowest point, and its absolute nadir was ten silent minutes eating veggie-burgers. From then on, our fortunes improved. I believe Americans use code to communicate their street directions. An example might be: *take i-90 to 7 south. At Roosevelt take a left onto Rodeo; it'll be there, back of Don's Drugs.* I guess that Lenny must have received such instructions from our mechanic because, somehow, we found ourselves at the breaker's yard, which thronged with life. In the crowded reception office, the man behind the counter was clearly the boss. He was working two telephones and three walkie-talkies. To receive incoming calls, he held a receiver in each hand and, keeping the earpieces clamped to his ears, he exchanged mouthpieces to speak to different customers. Meanwhile, through the walkie-talkies lying on a table in front of him, he told his yard staff where to look for requested parts, drawing only – it seemed - on his memory of the yard's dismantled vehicles.

We waited our turn. Then the call went out for a '92 Ford Ranger nearside rear half-shaft. We waited. The phone kept ringing with incoming calls. We waited a bit more. Then, like the much-doubted arrival of a train at a remote railway station, we heard distant sounds coming through one walkie-talkie. The boss listened, turned to us, and nodded. They had one! This was my point of surrender, the moment seen in films such as *Duel*, when someone abandons their original expectations of a day and engages with their real circumstances. Suddenly, I felt energised.

Out in the yard, we surveyed an extraordinary scene. Scrap cars lay head-to-tail and piled five high in an extensive grid pattern, bisected by roads of deep mud. Mechanics, to give them their most flattering title, growled along these dark channels in beat-up cars, using them as motorised toolboxes. Into sight came a forklift truck. Dangling from its raised forks were the remains – the very last remains – of a Ford Explorer. Against the odds, this limp skeleton, closely resembling the bones of a cartoon fish, still had the half-shaft we needed.

Once the remains were lowered, a mechanic let the axle oil drain into the mud before deftly extracting the critical component.

The shaft's physical presence - its weight and gleaming, machined surfaces - had restorative, almost magical properties. So, despite fading light, we decided to push forward with the repair. I had my mechanic's tools in the Volvo and, because I had changed the half-shafts in my MGB some years before, I knew how to do the job. We parked on some disused land beside railway tracks and jacked up Lenny's truck. It then took forty-five minutes to replace the bent shaft with our prized purchase.

We did not high-five our success, or chink beer bottles later that evening. Our carpenters' dignity spurned such amateurish frivolity. The job was done, and the day was over. Even so, it was one to remember.

PART 2

The Life and Work

Chapter 10

Andrew

People respond very differently when they think of the relationship between a spiritual teacher and his or her students. Some people understand why students see the relationship as sacred, while others doubt its integrity. The content of this chapter goes deeply into the nature and substance of exchanges between Andrew and his students. Before heading into that territory, I want to try my hand at bridging the gap between these sacred and doubting perspectives. To do this succinctly, I have selected for scrutiny two student tendencies that appear to divide opinion. One is students' propensity to see their teacher as perfect. Another is students' willingness to submit to their teacher's authority.

First, a simple observation: the desire for enlightenment changes people's outlook. That desire reorganises people's values and, with reorganised values, they make different judgements and are willing to take different risks. The presence or absence of the desire for enlightenment might, then, start to explain why intelligent people respond differently to the student-teacher relationship. In short, some people want what a spiritual teacher is offering, while others – freely – do not.

In a transcendent spiritual context, students' propensity to see their teacher as perfect can be explained: it facilitates their learning. A teacher acts as an intermediary, a physical representation of the formless creative force that students seek to know. That formless force is too shapeless, too intangible and too omnipotent for students to relate to directly. So, the teacher acts as a learning tool, a stepping-stone between the student and his or her destination. In this sense, the student-teacher relationship can be seen as a specific educational arrangement, that has appeared throughout history; one that originates not from human choice but from the nature of the subject being studied. Andrew said that, within this arrangement, students learn partly by osmosis; they absorb their teacher's attainment. The chemistry of this osmosis is optimised if students have no doubt about their teacher's attainment. Students are therefore drawn – by the educational process they're engaged in - towards seeing their teacher as perfect. That view expedites their learning.

Many people, I suggest, don't like being told what to do. They find the idea of being at the behest of a higher authority – especially a higher human authority – unappealing. Perhaps this recoil explains why people are sceptical about students' submission to their teacher's authority: that submission looks abnormal. Moreover, students do not just tolerate their teacher's authority, they willingly accept it, which makes their submission even harder to understand. The well-known description of the spiritual journey, *'From my way to Thy way'*, points to an explanation: changing between one authority and another is the primary business of the spiritual journey. I suggest there is a good reason why students actively seek the instruction of a higher authority: they want their life to be informed by an overarching creator. Thus, students' willing acceptance of their teacher's authority is explained: it is a means to an end.

I hope I have provided at least a rope bridge between the sacred and doubtful perspectives mentioned above. The student-teacher relationship has features that are hard to accept but, once those features are placed in context, I think they make more sense. This chapter might still provoke strong responses; if so, I can assure readers that we, Andrew's students, freely chose to be with him and were grateful for his instruction.

Andrew the Man

This is my attempt to single out the elements of Andrew's life and personality that could be called personal. In reality there were no marked divisions in his life, and certainly no timetabled distinctions between 'on' as teacher and 'off'.

The characteristic confidence of New York's citizens featured in Andrew's personality. He loved Manhattan, its charisma and its reputation as the coolest place on earth. We didn't argue with this. Even if students secretly felt that London or Paris had greater style, or perhaps depth of history, we knew New York's 24/7 upbeat vibrancy was unparalleled. Had there been an argument about which world city topped the bill, Andrew's joyfully brazen New Yorker spontaneity would quickly have overpowered more muted European reasoning.

New York set Andrew's choice of clothes and general taste. He dressed beautifully, in a modern style, which combined blacks with strong colours. He also cared about the visual character of his office. On arrival at Foxhollow it had been decorated for him using bland, brown, suburban furniture, which he didn't like, so the scheme was changed to suit his preferred look: square-edged sofas, surrounded by rugs and cushions of boldly contrasting colours.

Andrew and his wife, Alka, lived in their first-floor apartment in the house named - on our arrival at Foxhollow – Freedom. This was located furthest from the manor house: about an eight-minute walk. Visiting senior students would stay in the connected ground-floor apartment. Andrew and Alka's home originally had four bedrooms, but one was turned into a good-sized yoga studio, another into a store room/drum practice room, and a third into a walk-in wardrobe. Their apartment thereby became a comfortable, one-bedroom home, with all needs to hand.

In Marin, a student gave Andrew her Honda Accord. He didn't drive, so students drove for him. When we moved to Foxhollow, his worldwide students grouped together to buy him a new, black, top-of-the-range Volvo 850R. Andrew accepted the car, but made it clear he hadn't asked for it. In truth the car seemed to mean very little to him, apart from its safety features, which he approved of, and high-quality sound system, which he enjoyed. It was equally used by Alka for local journeys. When the Volvo was ten years old, a different student gave Andrew her five-year-old Audi A8. The roads around Foxhollow were often icy, so this car - with its all-wheel drive - was thought to be safer for Andrew.

Andrew loved his two dogs. Kensho, his Yorkshire terrier, was adored and for many years he travelled the world with Andrew and Alka, often carried in Alka's shoulder-bag. Andrew loved Kensho's feisty spirit, notably active when Andrew's second dog, Eros, arrived. Eros was a trained guard-dog, bought when Andrew's life was threatened (Chap 16). He was a sleek German Shepherd, black, remarkably quiet, but trained to defend on command. Kensho, Andrew told us, did not welcome Eros but, despite his size disadvantage, Kensho made a good show of defending his patch. Andrew was deeply upset when Kensho died of natural causes in 2012.

Andrew's humour was one of his obvious qualities. He was alert to irony, and he laughed easily. When small groups gathered informally around him, laughter was commonly heard, and humour was an occasional but valued element in his teaching style. He was an excellent mimic, known for accurately portraying national characteristics. He was also generous with his humour; he would enjoy listening to, and laughing at, other people's stories, as much as telling them himself.

Yoga was a big part of Andrew's daily life. He was an accomplished yogi and, together with three students who were, one by one, his yoga partners over the years, he and they would push the limits of their practice. He once led a yoga session for his less accomplished male English students in London. Never liking yoga, I recall it as a life-memorable experience of relentless osteopathic trauma. Andrew carried some spine and knee injuries as a result of his yoga practice.

He had personal friendships with some students based on common interests - mainly music - but these friendships existed without him compromising his teaching role. As a community, we knew these personal friendships were of minimal importance compared to our collective work, and that Andrew would drop a personal connection if a student weren't pulling his or her weight in terms of *'living the teachings.'*

Music was Andrew's greatest cultural passion. He loved jazz, and his heroes were Miles Davis, John Coltrane and Jimmy Hendrix. He was also interested in a broader range of music; Bjork, Joss Stone and Norah Jones, among others. In the year 2000, Andrew and three of his musically-gifted students started a band called Unfulfilled Desires. The name came from their unfulfilled ambitions to be musicians. The band's genre was *'jazz fusion, infused with groove, soul, and spirit.'* Andrew played the drums and other band members played the saxophone, ewi, flute, trumpet, bass, keyboard and guitar. Unfulfilled Desires played internationally, at small venues in the major cities where Andrew was teaching. Four CDs of their music were produced. When EnlightenNext dissolved in 2013, so did the band. (There is a Facebook page with music clips and further information about Unfulfilled Desires).

Andrew the Teacher

As well as working with his students, Andrew's life as a teacher included his worldwide travel, public teachings and retreats, correspondence with his global audience, radio interviews, and relationships with other teachers, pundits and authors. I heard he would spend three hours every day, responding to letters and emails from people either interested in, or committed to, his work.

The Working Environment We Shared with Andrew

EnlightenNext had ten Centres around the world; three in America, five in Europe and one each in Australia, Israel and India. Over the years some of the smaller Centres closed, for example in Israel, Sweden and Australia. Foxhollow was always seen as EnlightenNext's World Centre; it had the largest number of students and they were acknowledged to be the most mature in terms of student experience. For eight months of the year, when Andrew wasn't travelling, Foxhollow was his home.

We were not entangled in each other's working lives at Foxhollow. We worked independently, sharing an environment similar to that of a university. People were trusted to start work on time, organise their day, meet deadlines and efficiently accommodate their own business. During the working day we were individuals, strongly influenced - in my mind – by American individualism. For example, I felt it would be mildly immoral to interrupt someone's organisation of their time. In contrast, the smaller European Centres were more like families, in which relationships were understandably closer, often more personal, and occasionally fraught. At Foxhollow, the combination of personal independence and an effective chain of command meant we were not thwarted by the need for consensus at every turn; we were able to get on with our work efficiently.

Andrew embodied this independence - he was the source of it - and his daily life at Foxhollow was his to organise. We didn't expect to know what he was doing each day, just as we didn't have that expectation of each other. Hence, I am only able to share my observations of what a normal day was like for Andrew. Typically, he would start his yoga practice at the same time as our morning meditation: 7 o' clock. We would see Paul, his yoga partner, heading towards Andrew's house with a rolled yoga mat. It looked like their session would last two and a half or three hours, because Andrew would next be seen around 11 o' clock or noon, walking with Kensho up the gently winding path that was visible from the manor house.

Andrew's day would involve a great deal of communication with students and people interested in his work, plus various planning meetings to organise his travel and teaching schedule. He might also work with his co-editor on his latest book. Squeezed between these activities would be requests for decisions and approvals needed by the different offices at Foxhollow, such as the marketing, graphics or audio-visual departments.

Often Andrew would work in his first-floor office, which looked east towards Laurel Lake but, in the summer, he - and whoever was working with him - might be seen on the deck outside that office, or in the shaded area of the pool enclosure, or elsewhere in the gardens around the manor house. One could also bump into him in the kitchen. This was a favourite spot for us all because, like most kitchens, it was the focal point for making coffee and it acted as an artery for news and knowledge of people's whereabouts.

Producing *What is Enlightenment?* magazine was a big undertaking for an organization of our size. It involved more than 20 people, most of whom lived at Foxhollow. The others were dispersed around the world. Observing Andrew's schedule, his work on the magazine was clearly his most time-consuming activity. He was both Editor-in-Chief and an equal member of the six- to eight-person editorial team that researched the subject of each issue. On a day-to-day basis, this meant that Andrew and the team worked late into the night, making use of various imaginative working locations including the downstairs sauna (in swimsuits). Aside from Andrew's primary work as a modern-day western spiritual teacher and the teacher of our community, his collaborative work with the magazine team is my most abiding memory of his life at Foxhollow.

In 2011 it was decided, as a matter of financial necessity, to stop producing the magazine. The per-issue cost of $250K was no longer bearable. While this was bitterly disappointing for Andrew and the magazine team, it meant that he had more time to work with members of Unfulfilled Desires, practising, performing and developing the band's repertoire. Andrew's day would then often end in the music studio built within the thick concrete walls of the bunker, an ideal place to muffle late-night noise from a jazz-fusion band.

Communicating with Andrew

Most of our communication with Andrew was via messages. Before email these would be faxed messages, or, at Foxhollow, we would leave written messages in 'the book', managed by the student who manned the front office. In those earlier years we had pagers, which communicated a number to call, so a page from the recognisable front-office number – 435 637 6000 – could relate to something practical, or it could mean a reply or new message had arrived from Andrew. If so, his message would be read back to us, verbatim and without comment or emphasis, by the front-office student.

Some exchanges with Andrew were quite predictable. One might write, *"Dear Andrew, I'm thinking to travel down to New York to be at the teachings this weekend; I wanted to let you know."* As long as one had been living responsibly and maintaining our common standards, his reply would most likely come back: *"Great!"* Although it was possible for any exchange to be commandeered by Andrew and used as an instructional teaching tool, it was generally the case that practical requests, questions, messages of gratitude, or longer accounts of insights into the teachings, would elicit a neutral or affirmative reply.

However, this line of communication was potentially challenging. One always had a feeling of insecurity, of teetering on the edge of the fathomless unknown, when receiving a page from 637-6000. One could often tell, from a fellow student's expression, if he or she had received a page from the front office. A spectrum of possibilities would arise in the mind of the recipient. Like seeing a police car in the rear-view mirror, all one's faults and misdemeanours would stand in a suspects' parade, possible subjects of the awaiting message.

This experience lost some of its insecurity and became more conversational if one was engaged in a quick-fire exchange of messages with Andrew. As an example, I can use the back-and-forth I had with him over my desire to revisit the Copenhagen Centre. I had been there for a magical two-week period in the summer of 1999, helping a new group of students remodel a rented building to serve as their first Centre. Andrew had warned me that my ego would be fuelled by the admiration of these new students, and Ambrose, Andrew's most senior student at the time, had strengthened that warning by describing the two leading Danish women as *"very attractive."* Both warnings were warranted. I relished the admiration and was smitten by the women and so, after returning to Foxhollow, I dreamt of returning *"to further assist the Copenhagen group,"* as I wrote in my request to Andrew. His reply was, *"Do you want to go out of love or ambition?"* Driven by a boiling desire to resume an exalted role, I tried to muddle through with a minimal admission of ego, by gambling with my answer: *"Both"*. My tactic failed; his immediate response was *"Which is it?"* and, pushed to choose, I had to admit to myself that my hunger could not be labelled *'love'*, so I capitulated and replied *"ambition"*, which brought the matter to a close.

The arrival of email saved a lot of fax paper and removed the need to find a fax machine, which was often difficult when travelling. For a few years, Andrew's personal assistant – a new role from 2001 - still acted as an intermediary, but eventually Andrew decided to receive and reply to emails himself. This brought the sending and receiving of messages into even sharper definition.

Students' relationships with Andrew, their spiritual teacher, made them sensitive to every detail of his messages. To us, it seemed that he used every comma, exclamation mark, salutation and signature to maximum effect. Whether he wrote them spontaneously or by careful design we didn't know, but we took his emails to be precise expressions of his approval, disapproval, encouragement, correction, exasperation, condemnation, support, etc. He could apply great pressure by, for example, responding with *"What do you mean?"* to a long, carefully-crafted email from oneself about an insight thought to be important. His short question would force one to completely review the insight, maybe leading to a deeper understanding or a simplified description.

Interacting with Andrew

In the first years of Andrew's teaching career, when he was interested in people's personal history and circumstances, he would take long walks with individuals, or people might speak to him on the phone or go out with him for coffee. Ten years later, these kinds of one-on-one personal conversations no longer happened. We would not knock on Andrew's door 'just for a chat', or invite him to the coffee shop in Lenox. This distance from him was not maintained by rules, it was our accepted habit; it wouldn't have crossed our minds to think of approaching him with such familiarity. A level of formality existed at Foxhollow which meant that casual, chatty, conversation with Andrew was uncommon.

My day-to-day feelings towards Andrew would vary, depending on whether I was concerned about myself or passionately engaged in the life we were living. Self-concern, as we all know, comes in myriad forms, leading to the contraction of awareness and the extinguishing of curiosity and generosity. Conversely, attention placed on a wide-angled picture of existence - which, at Foxhollow, meant the deep-time scope of evolution – led to a sense of being an integral part of that formative process.

To me, Andrew seemed naturally sensitive to the state of mind of his students. I have no memories of him being badly out of tune with my fundamental motives. Over time, my awareness of his perceptive powers made me feel that he always knew *'where I was at,'* or, in other words, which part of myself I was choosing to validate. Therefore, my experience of moving around Foxhollow, which included the possibility of crossing paths with Andrew, could be freedom and happiness if I had nothing to hide, or anxiety and guilt if I knew I was hand-in-glove with self-concern.

Whether I actually crossed paths with Andrew was, in a way, immaterial, because the sense of being seen was constant. His omniscience, as I experienced it, followed me wherever I went. It didn't matter whether I was living at Foxhollow, setting up a retreat in India, or driving to Pittsfield (the local town) to visit the dentist: I was always accompanied by my sense of his sense, of my relationship to my experience.

However, if I did cross paths with Andrew there were a few possible outcomes. Surprisingly, given my propensity for doubt at such moments, the path-crossing might go quite well and take the form of naturally exchanged, warm greetings. But if I were inwardly engaged in negative activity while outwardly exhibiting some sort of ego-masking behaviour - such as exaggerated nonchalance or cheeriness - Andrew might walk by without remark. Occasionally there would be a question to ask or news to share but, over the years, we learnt that chance encounters were not the time to raise either important or unimportant matters. As with anyone, it would have been unfair to bombard him with information and, in our context, impromptu advice-seeking would have undermined the formal, respectful relationship we had with him.

You might ask whether Andrew wasn't sometimes grumpy or out of sorts with himself and, therefore, inconsiderate. It might be hard to believe, but I don't think so. His responses could be skewed by wrong information or lack of information – occasionally this happened in formal meetings – but his spontaneous responses were – as I experienced them – natural, balanced and on-point.

Despite the high level of formality, Andrew was not aloof or distant when the going was good. The community enjoyed a range of informal activities. Yes, there were plenty of periods - months, sometimes years - of tension and stress between Andrew and different groups of his students, which prohibited informal socialising. But, especially in the early years at Foxhollow, we would have welcome-home parties, men's saunas, film nights, music nights, five-star dinners, and launch parties for his books and each new issue of the magazine. Andrew's birthday celebrations were special occasions. His students with acting and musical talent would often perform, or we'd have a visiting band, or our resident professional magician (a student) would put on a show. These informal occasions would include free-ranging conversations about world events and trends, news from the world of music, the noting of students' career successes, cultural observations, etc. If and when a satisfying degree of spiritual progress was being made, we had great parties.

Our relationship with Andrew was a long way from being '*fellow travellers muddling along together.*' He held absolute authority and wouldn't compromise his responses to students' innumerable, varied attempts to place their egoic desires centre-stage. These attempts came in the form of tantrums, casualness, self-pity, inertia and more. Chapter 15, *Engaging with Ego*, gives a full description of our interactions with Andrew on this subject, but here I can offer an aperitif by imagining what might have happened in my exchange of messages with Andrew about Copenhagen.

The exchange could have gone badly wrong. If my desire for further exaltation had been stronger than my interest in what was true, I could have seized on my feeling that Andrew's use of the word *ambition* wasn't quite correct, and used that criticism as the catalyst for a storm of resentment and mistrust. This would be an example of an adult tantrum, one that might have resulted in me leaving the community. My disintegration might have proceeded like this: further to-and-fro messages with Andrew, of increasing intensity, plus correctional meetings with my peer group and one-on-one meetings with more senior students. Had I resisted all attempts to help me - or make me - see sense, I would have destroyed my relationship with Andrew. Without question, Andrew would never have said, "*Oh well, I can see you really want to go; it's not ideal, but I don't want to lose you as a student so I guess I have to agree to you having your way.*" This apparently minor incident could have become – as many did - a do-or-die situation, but Andrew would never compromise either himself or our work to mollify his students' egos. Stories in future chapters confirm this.

Meetings with Andrew

Meetings were central to our lives. Each week we had men's and women's meetings, and smaller 'holon' meetings (Chap 13). Gender specific groups also existed for the men and women in relationships, for the celibate students, and for our different physical practices such as yoga, weightlifting and running. Working departments also had their mixed-gender meetings. Our meetings with Andrew were the most momentous, and they happened every two to three weeks.

Meetings with Andrew lasted about three hours. Usually, we would wait in silence for twenty minutes before he arrived. Students would sit on cushions on the floor facing Andrew, and he would sit in a chair. If the men and women met with Andrew together, we would divide right and left respectively. Sometimes core and senior students around the world would join via a conference call. Andrew always had an innate sense of who was missing – I was impressed by this; he seemed to sense absences, and would often start by confirming who was missing and why. (For reasons of sickness or travel, most often). The business of these meetings was, in a way, always the same: to review and advance our progress as a community. But they would start in different ways. For example, Andrew might have some observations to make, or he might raise a particular issue, or he might want to hear our experience of the community's collective progress.

Formal meetings with Andrew had their own status and expectations. They were given high status because we were meeting with our teacher, in a purpose-built room, confident of surveying our work from a sophisticated perspective. Expectations were also high. We knew how these meetings could be pivotal events and, therefore, that both Andrew and our peers were expecting everyone to listen attentively and speak precisely.

Meetings with Andrew had their own ambience. In his presence, our familiar sense of belonging to a peer group – in my case, a men's peer group - diminished in strength. It was superseded by the potency of our individual relationships with Andrew. As our attention moved to him, our awareness of each other lessened. In this way, we were drawn into Andrew's enlightened field and the meetings were reliably spacious and focused.

The subject of a meeting might simultaneously have been a recent theme in Andrew's public teachings, the title of an issue of the magazine, and the ongoing subject of discussion in our men's and women's meetings. An example might be '*authentic individuation*'. (A process in which an individual becomes autonomous while still integrated within a community). Quite possibly this subject could also have been the general topic of inquiry within the community for the previous six months. In this case, the content of the meeting would be a mixture of students' questions and observations on the matter of authentic individuation, Andrew's responses, then students' responses to Andrew's responses, followed by more questions arising from this dialogue. This is what we called an enlightened inquiry: following a thread of interest into uncharted but defined territory.

One couldn't go to these meetings 'armed'. It wouldn't work to anticipate a subject, study it, and memorise material to produce at an opportune moment. Had one tried this, the memorised quality of one's contribution would have landed badly, disclosing one's intention to avoid the common requirement to step into the unknown. So, preparing *knowledge* was useless, and something we didn't do. But, perhaps confusingly, it was possible to prepare *oneself* for these meetings.

Being prepared meant being curious. Ideally this would be cultivated by ongoing, engaged inquiry. *Ideally.* This was the great upheaval that Andrew was pushing for; the birth of independent interest. This might not sound like much to ask for, but the request is thrown into sharp relief once one understands that a powerful and pernicious part of oneself is committed to maintaining self-centeredness (Chap 15).

I'd like to describe Andrew's nature in these, our highest-calibre forums. The meetings were in-house, with his most experienced students, inquiring into a loved subject, using tailored language and a refined form of communication. In short, conditions were perfect for Andrew to fire on all cylinders. I think anyone appreciating the context would have been impressed by his composure, and the speed and precision of his responses as he led the discussion. Witnessing him at work in his milieu was like watching an archer hitting bull's-eyes, one after another. He would, for example, straighten-out confusion. Sometimes a student would struggle with a description; there might be a slight pause, then Andrew would give a concise, simple version of what the person was attempting to say. His abundant interest was also evident. One could be quietly feeling replete and thinking the meeting had surely run its course, but Andrew would be as alert and responsive as he was at the start. The inexhaustible quality of his interest had an important effect: it set our meetings with him within a vast context.

Worldwide Community Exchanges with Andrew

Meetings to organise celebrations did not involve Andrew, but they played an important role in creating the culture that supported his teaching work. A happy by-product of our ego-challenging spiritual endeavour was that preparing for such celebrations was easy. Resistances and obstacles often present in event management were low hurdles compared to the rigours of our spiritual practices. Students fell happily into line, grateful for the opportunity to contribute to what were often full-scale extravaganzas. For events like weekend retreats, Andrew's homecomings, or annual celebration days, the organised machinery of a willing community whirred smoothly into action.

Andrew, not deeply involved in these preparations, might be asked to approve a proposed idea or itinerary but, often, our celebratory events were organised in secret. In these cases, our relationship with him became cat-and-mouse, as he tried to wheedle clues from unguarded students. In general, events were organised to meet unspoken standards of creative excellence and to properly position the significance of an event within the context of the life we were living. Through failure, we developed sensitivity to this all-important matter of making the tone of an event fit with the community's uneven progress. For example, if a group of experienced students had underperformed on the annual European retreat, a happy welcome-home party was inappropriate. There was another refinement we had to learn. While it was an achievement to have the logistics run smoothly, we had to find the right balance between the sacred and the celebratory. So, community meetings at Foxhollow, often involving the lay students, were frequently spent discussing the perfect combination of location, food, decorations, messages, readings, music, etc.

The worldwide core student community was eventually able to 'meet' together with Andrew when improvements to conference-call technology made it possible. On occasions we could have 250 people online, grouped together in different countries. These calls worked best when Andrew gave an introduction and then heard back from students, one city at a time. Speaking in these meetings could be an unfamiliar, hair-raising experience as one looked at a telephone keypad while feeling as if one were talking into outer space. The sense of exposure was strong: 250 pairs of sensitive ears could detect circumspection, and there was the danger of letting down the forum by waffling. The requirement to meet people's expectations of someone at your level in the hierarchy was a further pressure.

Although these calls weren't as powerful as being physically together, they had three new qualities. Firstly, it was exhilarating to use new technology for our pioneering work, as we felt we were riding a new wave. Secondly, the conference-call facility enabled us to be together as a complete, worldwide body, which had not been possible before. And finally, the fact that we could communicate across different time zones, not seeing but sensing each other, while referring to Andrew as the centre of our invisible union, seemed to represent nicely our wider sense of existing between the material world and the spiritual realm.

Andrew the Guru

Throughout this book I have used a small 't' when referring to Andrew as a teacher, thinking this would make my narrative more accessible to a public audience. In the community, we used capitals for *Teacher* and *Teachings* and, in our most devotional messages, we referred to Andrew as our Guru.

I appreciate that the idea of deifying someone might alarm many westerners. However, in Andrew's community, we understood it to be an inherent and necessary part of engaging with a formless, higher power. We wholeheartedly accepted Andrew's role as a conduit of divinity. We saw, and related to, him as a guru. We also studied the guru's role, and came to understand both its traditional and modern forms. Unabashedly, we revered our teacher while knowing such reverence was culturally incongruous. Consciously, we both surrendered to Andrew and maintained a meta-level western perspective on what we were doing.

Andrew's response to our reverence – which I will come to - was interesting, but first I'd like to take a retrospective look at how the student-guru relationship can be seen as a symbiotic process, more beneficial to the student than the guru and, ultimately, serving a greater awakening.

As a student, I didn't see the relationship as a two-way flow; I thought I was only a recipient of Andrew's guidance. But, in retrospect, I can see how students, through the process of deification, partly create their teacher. Through expressions of love and devotion, they lift their teacher high above themselves, enabling him or her to report back from an elevated place. How does this happen? Quite simply through the flow of attention. A teacher receives a large amount of focused attention - or spiritual energy - from his or her students. This energy further enlightens and energises the teacher, helping him or her perform the function of a trusted intermediary, *needed* by the students. From a certain point of view, the students' devotion can be seen as self-serving, as an investment in someone from whom they want a return. However, standing even further back, the whole exchange between student and teacher can be seen as an activity – a circular flow – that produces people useful to an evolving universe.

I suggest, therefore, that our deification of Andrew was more our doing than his. As our teacher, he wanted proper respect, and he would respond very strongly if that was not given. But the desire to write devoted messages, prepare his table, give him gifts, etc., came from within us. We were not ordered to show devotion, and we didn't do so out of fear. We delighted in praising him. We created the figure we needed.

Andrew certainly took his role, and the identity that came with it, seriously. He recently said that he saw himself as a *Jivanmukta*, a Sanskrit term for someone who is fully liberated and completely free of ego. People might judge his sense of himself to be deluded and the product of self-aggrandisement, but he had many of the qualities of a big, spiritual figure. His students' perception of him as a guru was based upon abilities which, in my understanding, cannot be contrived. The following paragraphs describe his curiosity and positivity, the sense he had of his role, and my experience of being in his presence.

As I have already mentioned, his curiosity was boundless. For example, on the last day of our big summer retreats in Tuscany, he would stand in the hotel's garden and speak to participants one-on-one. A long line of people would wait to talk with him. Andrew would spend three hours, attentive to each person or couple. Afterwards, he was quite capable of going with his senior students to Florence, for dinner, and diving into a detailed discussion of a matter that was of concern or interest to him. All this would occur at the end of a ten-day retreat in which he had spontaneously taught, or engaged in dialogue with, a group of 250-300 people, twice a day, for three hours at a time. This level of focus and energy is, I believe, something not normally found in human beings.

Alka once observed that Andrew was never cynical. He would never relapse, collapse or drop out of his function as the provider of an intelligent and positive relationship to life. It wasn't in his nature as a guru to do that. Similarly, while he could be relaxed and quiet, he was never sloppy in his comments, or languid in his posture. Nor would he abandon his composure. When someone in his travelling party had made a mistake in Paris and the group had arrived at the wrong railway station, Andrew didn't get caught up in the panic to cross the city. He'd rather have missed the train than lose the spacious beauty of the day.

Although something not discussed at the time, I felt that Andrew worked with a strong sense of the boundaries of his role. My experience in the building industry, with its distinct trades, might account for my awareness of the boundaries he maintained. It's quite easy to see why these boundaries are important. Students are prone to making the false assumption that their teacher is an expert in all matters, or that he or she wants authority over every aspect of their life. They can also easily act on misplaced deference by, for example, expecting their teacher to be an oracle of wisdom on health issues, finances, family relationships, etc. I felt that Andrew was keenly aware of the limits of his role as a spiritual teacher, and therefore good at fielding his students' misguided expectations.

Andrew's presence, his guru's weight, was most keenly felt at the blurred boundary between form and formlessness, where even his competence with spiritual mechanics melted away into stillness and nothingness. It was in this largely dissolved condition that the contrast between him and an ordinary person was most obvious. Even in a regular conversation in the corridor of the manor house one could feel this 'there-but-not-there' quality, as if the solid core of a normal person, made up of their preferences and resistances, didn't exist in him. In those conversations, one had the experience of not hitting an expected target; one's words would travel into his consciousness but, instead of bouncing back from a hard surface, they would apparently drift away. His response, centred on the same subject of discussion, would come as if formed from different material, yet to the point and entirely original.

If one were feeling at all insecure – quite likely in his company - a disabling sense of mismatch could become overwhelming. His stillness and detachment could nudge one's emotional gyroscopes off-kilter. One's sense of balance, the control of one's limbs, and one's sensitivity to appropriate personal distance, could all waver, leaving one feeling incapacitated. In recent years I have come to understand this experience a little better, from an unproblematic place. It's similar to how two boxers of different weights might feel standing next to each other. Each would sense the difference in hierarchy and know the origin of that feeling. Between student and guru, the difference is between their degrees of attainment: their independence from the movement of their own mind. Andrew, as guru, stood like a rock face. One's conversation as a student could just bounce off him and drop to ground, and this, his detachment from the need to respond reassuringly, could be very unnerving.

Over the twenty-seven years of Andrew's teaching career, his students' relationship to him as a guru changed markedly. His emerging teachings placed evolution centre-stage, and this move away from traditional ideas of enlightenment broadened the attention of Andrew's students. As I now describe, the intensity of their focus upon Andrew softened, and their acts of devotion changed.

Andrew's second book, *Letters of Love*, contains letters written to him by students in the community's early years. The letters convey the exhilaration, inspiration and willing submission that could overcome people in his presence. In those years the community would celebrate Guru Purnima Day, a Hindu and Buddhist festival dedicated to spiritual and academic teachers. Our celebration of this traditional day would often take the form of a picnic in a beautiful location, such as one of Marin County's Pacific beaches. Andrew would sit under a canopy, with rugs, cushions, etc., and he would ceremoniously be presented with a mala (a garland, or string of flowers) in recognition of his status. Preparations for the event would take many days, a message of gratitude – beginning 'Beloved Master' - would be written and refined by many people and, in addition to the traditional gift of fruit, Andrew would be given – for example – a fine, leather jacket.

At Foxhollow, from 2002 onward, we no longer celebrated Guru Purnima Day but, instead, marked four important dates in our own history (Chap 22). Events to celebrate these dates were simple affairs compared to previous Guru Purnima Day arrangements, and they had a more commemorative tone. Andrew was gratefully acknowledged as our foundational inspiration, but it was no longer his role or nature that was being celebrated. Instead, we were taking time to respect the crossing of important thresholds in the community's evolution.

The new 'holy-days' were indicative of a general, but not complete, movement of attention away from traditional Buddhist references and Sanskrit terms. They were also signs of our emerging, new, spiritual genre. Original Eastern influences were increasingly either supplemented or replaced by the substance of Andrew's teachings, by discoveries made in our work as a community, by Ken Wilber's work on Integral Theory and by the investigations of the magazine team.

Our devotional acts upholding Andrew as our guru also evolved. Our choices of gifts, flowers and messages were refined through experience. They became increasingly creative and, viewed over a broad time spectrum, these devotional acts could even be seen as a specific art form. For example, we laid out an intricate, circular mandala (like a tapestry made from different-coloured pebbles), twenty-five feet in diameter, on the driveway in front of Andrew's house. It was lit by sixty candles in jars every evening. We also set up light shows, with projections onto buildings, and rivers of flower petals to welcome him home from his longer teaching trips. Planning and executing these expressions of love and respect used to unify the student group. In my experience, it was when we were working together - artists of different materials - on these multifaceted presentations, that we felt most like a family.

A Closing Anecdote

As a student, I witnessed the different demands made of Andrew. These were composed of students' neediness, their changes of heart, untrustworthy declarations of intent and semi-conscious attempts to corner his attention. In public teachings, he often said he wouldn't wish the job of spiritual teacher upon anyone, saying it was like being married to 300 people. Even so, it always felt as if his description of his experience had little impact upon a powerfully-held, mainstream idea. That idea is that exalted spiritual figures ride magic carpets, and are immune to stress, doubt or self-concern. It's an idea that appears to be so strongly held, by so many people, that little can be done to correct it.

With that idea in mind, perhaps this tender anecdote is useful. I remember a London teaching in which a woman questioned Andrew about his experience. She asked, *"How does a free person, not identified with their experience, reply to the social greeting, 'How are you?'?"* Andrew answered, *"Well, basically, you say you're fine."* She pressed him further; *"But what is your experience?"* and Andrew said, *"Well, most of the time, I'm pretty rattled."*

Chapter 11

Andrew's Evolutionary Teachings

I believe Andrew's teachings are best read in his own words, so I would like to refer readers to his latest book, *Evolutionary Enlightenment*. Here, in this chapter, I want to convey the substance and value of Andrew's teachings in terms of their effect on my relationship to life. By doing this, I will be drawing readers' attention forward to 2020, briefly disturbing this book's timeframe. Focussing upon my personal experience will also be a departure from the book's main narrative, which concentrates on the community's group work. This departure is deliberate; I see it as an opportunity to illustrate how Andrew's teachings can benefit an individual.

I will first give a brief overview of his teachings, then a short description of myself as an incoming student in 1993, before writing about how I have benefited from the transformative power of Andrew's work.

Within today's wide spectrum of spiritual paths, Andrew's teachings are transcendent teachings: they aim to unite an individual with a higher form of Self. They are not about the pursuit of bliss or well-being, or about becoming a good person. Rather, they are instructions for someone who wants to rise above the activity of their mind and engage in the primary activity of existence: awakening. To help someone rise above the activity of their mind, Andrew has five tenets. These are listed in the Appendix. Andrew's five tenets lead an individual to enlightenment, or clear-sightedness. The journey to enlightenment is acknowledged to be a tough one, but someone who is successful transcends the often intimidating or seductive power of thought and feeling. Delightedly, they then discover spaciousness. Andrew calls this spacious dimension of existence the *Being* dimension. To some people this *Being* dimension is their preferred destination but, in Andrew's teachings, it is seen as an origin: the place from which self-nature appears. In his teachings, the purpose of self-nature, which is as varied as the people it arises within, is to contribute to the physical form of universal awakening, or evolution. Contributing authentically to evolution is thrilling; someone who does so feels at one with the primary, thunderously positive, driving force of existence. Andrew calls this driving force the *Becoming* dimension of existence and his six principles of evolutionary enlightenment - also found in the Appendix – highlight some of its emergent features.

Andrew's teachings do not include the practice of worship, but other spiritual practices are seen as very beneficial, and often necessary. Even so, no single practice is prescribed. What Andrew does stipulate is the need for clear intention and great effort. In addition, his conception of a higher form of Self – *'the force of love and evolution'* – is not a deity with parental qualities. So, appeals or offerings to a greater entity are not part of his teachings. Instead, his teachings insist upon a high level of personal responsibility and take the form of precise instructions, set within the context of evolution, concerning the management of one's mind. His teachings also contain detailed considerations of particularly challenging subjects like ego, sexuality and gender. The work of the magazine team provides further insights into questions about – for example - self-mastery, ecology, life after death and many others.

I first saw Andrew teach in July 1991. I became his student in 1993. At that time, I wasn't very different from the inwardly split, outwardly withdrawn, person described in my Prologue. I loved the scope of Andrew's teachings, yet I was terrified of the destiny they pointed to. Andrew was someone I held back from. The leaders of the London Centre, while friendly enough, told me I was *"full of fixed ideas"* and *"chronically quiet"*. Their words remain in my memory! Some years later, Andrew mimicked my upright, wooden style of walking, and the tremulous way I spoke with him. More seriously, he said I was *"charming, and very skilled at it [being charming],"* an observation I found both flattering and worrying. As a citizen of the world I was a regular fellow; reliable, paying my way, hard-working and well-mannered. Being English, I had a mildly smutty sense of humour (soon ironed out in the community) and I liked drink. But I wasn't notably aggressive, gross-minded or selfish. Looking back, it was my inner relationship to life – my wavering ability to accept the positivity of existence - that was the source of both my own problems and other people's frustrations with me. My passion for Andrew's teaching work was strong and could be sensed by many people, but very little of that passion saw the light of day. I had self-respect and substance, but I didn't give of myself. Scared of the enormity of life, I was, at first, barely able to engage mentally with my teacher's teachings.

In the UK, we have a television programme called *Homes Under the Hammer*. It features unloved properties, bought at auction and then improved. Once the improvement work is finished, the programme has a method of comparing *before* with *after*. For example, an image of the old fireplace will be shown, and then – *swoosh* – the screen will swipe across to reveal an image of the new fireplace. Frame by frame, swoosh by swoosh, old is compared with new. What is not shown is any of the building work done in between. Similarly, when comparing my relationship to life in 1993 with my relationship to life now, I feel I should say that it is not only the ideas contained in Andrew's teachings that have made the difference. I also lived in his auspices for over two decades and benefited from his community's disciplined culture. In addition, as with anyone, my life's circumstances have played into my development.

What has helped me immeasurably is to see my life in the context of evolution. I find it profoundly useful to know that life is on the move. Of essential value is the knowledge that *my mind* is on the move, and always will be. This knowledge destroys a destructive idea: the idea that a state of permanent equanimity, happiness, contentment, or any unchanging experience, is achievable. I no longer live with that idea. I do not refer to *'how my experience ought to be.'* A powerful habit has died: the habit of comparing my experience with an ideal. That habit dogged me deeply throughout my adult life, forever generating the conviction that there was something wrong with me: that I had a problem. I now know that my experience will always drift, swing, pitch, toss and change like the weather. Knowing this, I can let my mind be. I'm not fighting myself as I used to, nor am I dragged down by bad days, or seduced by the belief that good days will last forever. Crucially, I now understand that, as long as I can bear my arising experience, I am free to be interested in it, not controlled by it.

Free to be interested. I will be forever grateful to Andrew for this. In his teachings, consciousness is the primary field of existence, and its derivatives – awareness, attention, curiosity and interest – are the elements of divinity alive in human consciousness. *I am not my experience; I am the interest that perceives my experience.* This shift of identity defines spiritual liberation. It is an unexpected homecoming, as – with surprise – one realises that, to be free, nothing more than perception is needed. The bonanza following this shift of identity is proportionate to its profundity. Free to inquire, one can gaze into the nature of existence and the mechanics of evolution, just as an unchained hound might race off to sniff around its neighbourhood. With similar alacrity, there are two horizons I love to explore.

Firstly, I like to see the backstories to – for example - political issues and the ideologies of today. Marxism can be seen to arise from an evolutionary drive towards Utopia that has been corralled into a political context and then harnessed by the arrogance of men. Patriarchy can be seen to have developed from thousands of years of necessary provision and protection, now experienced by women as oppression. Seeing the lengthy, intricate, unavoidable chain of events trailing behind today's big issues, and understanding the primary character and strength of the forces driving them, is, I find, fascinating.

Secondly, I love to conceive of existence not as an *It* but as a *Who*. I love this conception for its abrupt departure from convention, and for the shocking, explosive rush of passion that comes back at me for merely considering that the universe has Self-nature and is working to know itself. I find that by imagining existence to be purposeful, adaptive and possibly self-aware, my curiosity is awakened. I then think to myself, *"If curiosity is, in large part, the nature of Self, then the awakening of more curiosity means I am moving in the right direction."* Conceiving of a self-aware universe, and observing how that conception affects my curiosity, leaves me feeling lightness of being. This feels wholesome, because the movement away from stultifying rigidity and the need to think in static, mechanical terms is, I feel, consistent with the desire to be free. Being able to think freely and inquire on a vast scale is another product of Andrew's teachings that I greatly value.

Along with this capacity for untethered exploration, I am free to see my individuality. As well as enjoying the challenge of asking big questions, I can see my position on important spectra. I'd like to give three examples of how my knowledge of these positions guides my choices. Firstly, I want to look at the spectrum of worldliness versus mysticism. 'In the world but not of it,' was the phrase used by the community to describe our desired involvement in society. We knew our first reference was to love and evolution, but we also wanted to have an effect on culture. Similarly, I love spiritual philosophy and I also love the nuts and bolts of the material world. On this spectrum, I have no desire to be more mystical – more removed, or melted away - than I am. Secondly, I see that spiritual teachings have different degrees of complexity. Some use models, quadrants, pyramids, planes and all sorts of grades and shades of categorisation as aids to self-knowledge. I appreciate that many people like these sophisticated tools, but they don't attract me. I've learnt how happy I am with my unorthodox, pared-down, dust-and-sweat, Christian love (see Appendix). Feeling connected to the passion emanating from the Christian story and being informed by the perspective gained from Andrew's teachings, I find myself equipped to live an authentic life. Lastly, I know what I care about. Two obvious facts - that nobody can be all things to all people, and no one can respond to all the world's needs – stand in my awareness, as if they were two of Henry Moore's monumental sculptures in my back garden. Their presence drives a plethora of unwanted possibilities from my mind, leaving the timeless message, *Give yourself to the world*, prominent in my awareness. The singularity of that message reveals the gifts I have to give and fuels my desire to give them. I care about people's spiritual and mental welfare and about using enlightened intelligence to disentangle cultural knots (Chap 24). I am also excited by the spiritual potential of my nation. This ability, to discern the direction of my vocation, is, I feel, a precious product of my time with Andrew.

Andrew's teachings have freed me from dependency upon my mind, especially my feelings. They achieved this by draining religious sentiment from the spiritual endeavour and, instead, making it a practical matter. Some people might wonder what the goal is, if acquiring feelings of spaciousness, joy, bliss, peace, or compassion is not the aim. I can offer the following answer. Anyone who has a professional relationship to their work will be familiar with an enlightened relationship to experience. A professional person will prioritise the task in hand. To do this they will place their personal feelings aside and keep an open mind about what a job might entail. Knowledge and intuition remain valued and available, but transitory feelings of irritation or excitement are treated as incidental. The benefit of being a professional person is that one contributes to society; one is not just an observer, or consumer, one is a valued participant. Andrew's teachings have a similar but loftier objective. They teach people to become participants in evolution. This has been their great gift to me. The activity of my mind no longer constantly undermines my relationship to life. I know my gifts and I want to give them. The enormity of life is now more fascinating than overwhelming. After twenty years as Andrew's student, and ten subsequent years of independent inquiry, I now consider myself a capable contributor to evolution: someone who has won enough independence from conditioned impulses to pursue his true vocation.

Chapter 12

Spiritual Practice 1 – Traditional Practices

London, February 2019.

I lay awake one morning with my wife, Khin, beside me. I had been downstairs to fetch tea, which we'd finished, and I'd slid down beneath the covers until I was half propped-up by pillows. My left arm was outstretched and my hand lay open on the duvet. With my eyes closed, ruminating on life and the writing of this book, I said to Khin, *"I'm dreading writing the chapter on practice; it was never my strong suit."* Her response was two light pats on my outstretched hand.

Maybe her *'there, there, dear'* touches were genuinely sympathetic, but I experienced them as patronising. Bristling, I felt a rush of self-assertion. This jolted me from a dozy state to a condition of resolve, and I was reminded of the context in which Andrew's community did spiritual practice: unless conducted while fully awake and with conscious intention, practice was seen as ineffective.

Lying there, I went on to imagine a diving-board, somewhere high in the cosmos, busy with spiritual aspirants who'd declared their intention to jump into the unknown and live a life of free-fall. Some clung to the railings in terror. Others smoothly reassured their friends about the bliss of detachment. A few were biding their time, chatting over coffee, while another group diligently – and with visible superiority - worked their way through a list of prescribed preparations.

The question *Who will jump?* re-evaluates the scene and reveals the purpose of the metaphor. Decades of dedicated practice can be eclipsed in an instant by a newcomer who walks directly to the edge and leaps. Or someone clinging limpet-like to the rail can suddenly detach, dash, and dive. There's no telling who is actually going to let go, or when. Earnest preparation might, or might not, be fruitful.

Andrew's teacher, Poonjaji, did not recommend spiritual practice. He was a proponent of *'radical immediacy'*. I'm guessing Poonjaji used those words to help his students destroy a truth-denying idea: that finding spiritual freedom is a time-dependent process. In Poonjaji's view, practice was either unnecessary or the dangerous source of a new spiritual identity. Andrew also started teaching this way. At first, as he said himself, he did not understand the need for supporting structures, such as the Buddha's community, or for supporting practices like regular meditation. But, over time, he saw how his students needed their intention to be strengthened and, eventually - surveying Andrew's whole teaching career - he employed many traditional Eastern practices. These are listed shortly.

As Andrew's students, we did a lot of spiritual practice, knowing it was only to support our intention and not itself a path of incremental improvement. *Clarity of Intention,* in Andrew's teachings, is the name given to the first of his five foundational tenets (see Appendix) and, in his eyes, *Intention* – the focusing of one's desire to be free - is essential for spiritual success. He says there is no substitute for intention and, while practice can help cultivate intention, practice does not act like a savings scheme in which one builds credit and later receives a spiritual pay-out.

Practice was taken seriously in our community. Students were not cajoled to do it, nor was it done under the watchful eye of superiors. We had great respect for the importance of practice; its value was widely upheld. Andrew periodically stressed the importance of doing practice both beautifully and with dignity – do it with *'positive pride,'* he said – while also warning against vanity.

At Foxhollow, a typical day's practice started at 6am with 600 prostrations (see below). An hour's meditation followed, from 7.30 to 8.30am, and then many people would do their physical practice – yoga, running, weight-lifting, etc. – before having breakfast and starting their working day at the official time: 10am. Students who worked off the property had to adapt their timetables. Evenings were unscheduled, while Sundays were usually given wholly to different practices, including the men's and women's meetings described in the next chapter.

The following list of practices starts with the least significant – in terms of its status in our community - and proceeds to meditation which, I suggest, was the most influential of our traditional practices.

For a year or two we did a mala every day. This Buddhist practice involved memorising a prescribed passage from Andrew's book, *Enlightenment is a Secret,* and repeating it, either aloud or in one's head, while keeping track of the number of repetitions by feeding a string of beads through one's fingers. The challenge was to stay with the meaning of the words during each repetition. Mechanically repeating the passage was fairly easy, but staying focused was difficult. One could do this practice sitting in a chair or, if living at Foxhollow, walking in the grounds: a pleasant option. It would take about 45 minutes to complete the mala practice.

Some students were given the traditional practice of Mauna: being silent. This involved withholding from unnecessary communication for an open period of time and thereby living a contemplative life. People with this practice would use a notebook for necessary communication, and not resort to using gesticulations or facial expressions. Andrew probably had different reasons for giving students this practice; one appeared to be for its calming effect, another to rescue students – if need be - from emotional tailspins. The practice was more common in the community's early years and, like the mala practice, it was not used after the year 2000.

Andrew gave some students spiritual names. These were substitute names given for an open-ended period of time to deepen a student's awareness of an ingrained characteristic. Some men's names were: Sincere, Shadow, HG (for His Greatness), Nar (for narcissist) and Cas (for casual). Some women's names were: Vacance, Dizzy, and Tamasa (for tamasic/lethargic). Of sixty core students at Foxhollow, there were between six and eight people with spiritual names at any one time during the seven years 1996-2003. After 2003, this practice was not used. I didn't have a substitute name but, observing my fellow students, I could see it was impactful to receive a name, and a triumph to transcend it. Some students would hold their names for years and we'd almost forget their original names. We didn't view these names as punishing or shameful, nor did we see them as signifying higher status; they were respected and seen as one of Andrew's tools for responding to his students' egos.

Physical practice was a daily commitment and we did yoga, weight-lifting or running. The purpose of the practice was not only to be healthy and fit, but to push through limits, so this practice was done with planned programmes and stated goals. I didn't do yoga but, judging from the discipline of those who did, and their well-kept studio, they did it to a high standard. The men doing weight-lifting were easier to spot by their buffed upper torsos - sometimes highlighted by tight T-shirts - and their presence at the snack bar, where they'd mix protein shakes. I was one of the runners, grateful for the lovely country lanes around the property and the varied weather. We ran some marathons, notably our first along the coast of Rhode Island and another that we organised near to Foxhollow. We once ran a torturous, one-mile sprint which split body from mind: the body begging for mercy, but the mind set on reaching the finish line. (The winner's time was five minutes twenty-five seconds, interestingly noted to be forty-five seconds *slower* than a top marathon runner runs every one of his or her twenty-six miles).

We also wanted to look good, and physical practice was done with this in mind. An hour's work-out every day meant that most people were in admirable shape and, with many years on a vegetarian diet and drinking little alcohol, students tended to look younger than they were. Physical practice was managed and monitored by students. We had to accommodate it whenever we could. Andrew was interested in our targets and breakthrough moments, and he applauded the general level of rigour. I was happy when he congratulated me for winning our in-house marathon, (my time was 3hrs 25mins). He seemed as impressed and surprised as I was. Living on a campus made physical practice easy, especially once we had built the gym in the basement of the manor house, as everything was to hand. The women students did 600 prostrations a day (see below), which was a physical challenge in itself. Many women also did their own physical workouts, of different kinds, but these were done on a solo basis, whereas the men tended to do their physical practice in groups.

Celibacy was a challenging and greatly respected practice. I was not celibate and, therefore, I'm not best placed to comment on this revered commitment. However, I can, with respect, give an outsider's view. The practice involves disengagement from sexual desire. If, as a community, we were watching a film which included a sexual scene, the celibates would avert their eyes. This action was once described to me as a celibate's overall relationship to the arising of sexual interest: the turning away of attention. Andrew would say, *"Celibacy can take someone all the way,"* meaning all the way to freedom, because the power of arising sexual interest is close in strength to the overall power of the mind. If one can successfully turn away from sexual interest at all times, in all places, then one is well-placed to transcend the activity of the mind in its entirety. Hence the respect due to the practice of celibacy.

Having a shaved head was part of the celibacy practice and every month, at the traditional time of the full moon, the celibates would come together to shave their heads and celebrate their refreshed state. This was a dramatic and humbling event to witness. The bareness of their heads exaggerated their facial features, an effect that made them a striking-looking group. At these monthly events, they looked obviously happy and unified by their commitment, which made the overall spectacle an inspiring reminder of the extreme life we were living.

Between ten and twelve students were celibate at Foxhollow, fewer than in the earlier years. The ratio of men to women fluctuated around one-to-one. We understood that a shaved head was a greater renunciation for a woman. In everyday life, the celibates wore caps and scarves - to suit the weather and their working situations - which meant they looked quite similar to everyone else.

The practice of celibacy added greatly to our sense of ourselves as a community. By their example, the celibate students raised our overall willingness to renounce and sacrifice personal concerns, and the practice was an important feature of our spiritual culture. In our own minds, the serious practice of celibacy put us in the company of credible lineages and historic monastic traditions.

The celibate students seemed to revere and love the practice. For some, one could see it became part of their identity, especially if they were celibate for many years. Clearly, it was a major event when someone came to the end of their celibacy practice, because we all felt as if that person was moving from one world back into another.

Being in a sexual relationship was also a practice. A sexual relationship was seen to be a place of conscious engagement, not one of refuge or indulgence. In 1994, Andrew, staying in New York en route from Europe, famously sent a message to the Marin community, *"I'm not coming back until some relationships are formed."* There had been such avoidance of sexual interest among his students that Andrew felt forced to do this. He judged a sexual relationship to be a natural part of life – providing companionship and sex - and he wanted his teaching work to embrace this sustaining aspect of human nature, through committed relationships.

There were about sixty couples among Andrew's worldwide body of close students, both married and unmarried. About half of these relationships started after the community arrived at Foxhollow. Students in relationships had formal meetings, the men separate from the women, to share and inquire, with dignity, into their experience.

Generally speaking, Andrew's teachings help an individual to see his or her life in an evolutionary perspective; one could say his teachings help someone see life from a different point of view. In this different view, the importance of some secular values is reduced. In particular, Andrew wanted his students to reduce the importance of a sexual relationship. Instead of looking to a sexual relationship as a source of fulfilment and emotional succour, he wanted his students to refer, first and foremost, to the spiritual context of their lives. Within that context, he wanted them to be most at home in their same-sex peer group. He said that if students used their peer group to resolve personal issues, they could be together with their sexual partner in a way that was unburdened, or free. Hence, the practice of being in a sexual relationship was a form of renunciation. It involved conscious disengagement from the type of intimacy that is emotionally dependent. Andrew said, *"Keep things cool,"* meaning not heated, and it was this suggested state of coolness that became the benchmark for couples in a sexual relationship.

Broadly speaking, serious problems did not arise in sexual relationships and, therefore, only a few relationships broke up while students were in the community. There are a few simple reasons for this. Students were largely free from common challenges such as raising children, money worries, demanding careers, or the temptations of infidelity. Students also lived in a disciplined environment that kept immaturity in check. Finally, and perhaps most importantly, the everyday challenges and rewards of living a spiritual life did lower – as Andrew's teachings instructed – the expectations placed upon sexual relationships, which helped to diffuse tensions that did arise. On the whole, couples in sexual relationships in the community tended to stay together.

Sex itself was, of course, a significant activity. Chapter 18 is dedicated to the subject.

Chanting became a significant practice over time. We did not chant to music or to any intonation or rhythm; our chanting was always in the form of reading aloud, in unison. Mostly we chanted prescribed texts from Andrew's teachings, either as a prelude to meditation, or as an allotted section of longer practices such as the Absolute Practice mentioned below.

In the years 2004-6, concerted effort was made to raise the quality of our chanting. It was felt that a transformative resonance could be achieved if both the action of chanting, and of listening to the chant, were made more conscious. On a ten-day retreat in India, a group of thirty people was given the task of finding a higher level of vocal synthesis. Through effort, they experienced chanting in a new way. The chant acquired a momentum of its own, nourishing the chanters who, in turn, engaged more fully with the chant, and so a symbiotic exchange came into play. I equated this with the sublime synchronicity – or 'the zone' - that athletes speak of. It was a peak experience, one that showed what was possible and informed our chanting thereafter.

Our most impressive chanting practice continued around the clock, every day, for the four years 2006-10. Co-ordinated between America and Europe, it was arranged that someone would always be chanting one of two texts centred on the core principles of Andrew's teachings. Each participating Centre had a room dedicated to this community-wide practice and, on the hour, at the switchover moment, the incoming person would telephone the outgoing person to confirm continuity.

Chanting, although perhaps not a natural fit with our self-image as a leading-edge community, was a significant practice.

Doing prostrations was another important and respected practice that was an integral part of our community's history. Students in Marin often completed the Herculean challenge of one hundred thousand prostrations. The practice was special to Andrew's core women students, who did at least 600 every day. At one time or another, all of Andrew's core students experienced what it was like to do this humbling, traditional sadhana (discipline).

Quite possibly, just the idea of prostrating oneself raises alien feelings in a westerner's mind. To be prostrate is, I suggest, not a generally desired state. If true, this is for a good reason, because it feels submissive to be prostrate and there's a part of oneself that doesn't like to submit. Repeatedly facing this part of oneself is what makes doing prostrations a powerful practice.

The action is to bend from a standing position and then slide forward with outstretched arms until one is lying fully extended on the floor. Retracing those actions back to a standing position completes one prostration. Once one has assumed a rhythm, 500 prostrations take about an hour. Some equipment is needed, most importantly a smooth floor and two sliding mats. We did prostrations with an accompanying three-part chant: on the first descent we would say, "*To be free is to have nothing;*" on the second, "*To be free is to know nothing;*" and, lastly, "*To be free is to be no one.*" These chanted statements steered one's attention away from the thoughts and feelings circulating in one's mind, and towards the greater scope of existence.

As with all practice, prostrations could be done mechanically or contemplatively. A mechanical state of mind made prostrations little more than an athletic and counting exercise, whereas even attempting to maintain concentration and hold a spiritual context would yield humility and self-respect. Ultimately, this practice was about consciously and repeatedly subordinating oneself to a higher presence.

Prostrations combined physical exertion with emotional submission. After doing prostrations for many hours, students looked both washed-out and dignified, and they evoked the same admiration one feels for exhausted Olympic athletes. Instinctively, one would not want to bother anyone immediately after their prostration practice. Over time, this natural inclination to honour sincere effort could be seen accumulating in a student's attitude towards himself or herself; even from a distance, one could see how prostrations built spiritual strength. That strength could be seen in people's posture, heard in their voice, and observed in their choices.

Meditation was almost synonymous with practice. For most of us, most of the time, it was our main form of practice, and meditating together as a community brought us together on a daily basis. We meditated on our big public retreats, on silent retreats, before and after our other practices and, if we were travelling, it was the practice that we somehow made time to do.

We did not use any mind-quietening techniques. Andrew taught direct meditation: be still, relax and pay attention; have no relationship to time, thought or feeling. This meant not engaging with the content of consciousness. He often used the metaphor of seeing a street beggar in India: one has a choice whether to engage or not. The same is true of the thoughts and feelings that arise in meditation.

Our main meditation practice was called the Absolute Practice. It had longer and shorter versions. Students would come to Foxhollow for three months to do the longer, eight-hour version, which involved doing practice in the morning and practical work in the afternoon. The whole community did the shorter, three-hour version every Sunday morning. The Absolute Practice was about having an absolute relationship to Time, Thought and Feeling. There were dedicated chant sheets for each subject, containing Andrew's precise description of what an absolute relationship to these three basic components of our experience actually means. Here is a brief description.

An absolute relationship to time is one in which we have stopped waiting for anything, inner or outer, to improve before we engage with the life we deeply want to live. An absolute relationship to time destroys excuses, brings one's attention into this moment, and saves one from the incapacitating promise that life will get easier in the future.

An absolute relationship to thought is one in which one sees the arising of thought as an independent process, distinct from oneself. It gives one distance from one's thought stream, so that one is neither dismayed by destructive thoughts, nor glowing with pride about clever thoughts; nor, indeed, drawing any limiting or overblown conclusions about oneself from the thought stream. 'Thought is not Self': this is the nub of this teaching.

An absolute relationship to feeling is one in which one remains emotionally stable, desiring the cool, spacious sanity of spiritual freedom more than either giddy episodes of ecstasy or grim descents into despondency. An absolute relationship to feeling eventually establishes a consistent preference for level-headedness, saving one from emotional indulgence in either direction.

As Andrew's students, meditation was central to our lives. We meditated a lot together, but the hours allotted to sitting still were only the physical representation of a practice which permeated our culture. Meditation is the practice of healthy detachment. It leads to salvation from the pitching and tossing of one's mind. This salvation is consciously pursued during dedicated practice, but it can also be subliminally absorbed. At Foxhollow, meditation was ambient; it was the ground on which we interacted with one another, enabling mature participation in all facets of our life as a community.

Chapter 13

Spiritual Practice 2 –
Men's and Women's Meetings and Retreats

Men's and Women's Meetings

The formal peer-group meetings provided the context for our most demanding spiritual practice. Andrew said that our other practices were done to prepare us for these meetings. They were always the central event of a regular week but, as the community's spiritual work took shape and gathered momentum, the men's and women's meetings gained further prominence. Increasingly, they were seen as the forums that would invoke the Authentic Self.

Because I was in the men's meetings, I cannot comment on the women's meetings. However, to complete my record of the community's work, I have commissioned a research project which, I hope, will capture the character and content of their meetings. Chapter 19 has further details of this project.

Men's Meetings: Form

Although, over time, the quality of participation in men's meetings developed enormously, the physical form of these meetings remained largely the same. A typical men's meeting would see fifteen to twenty men sitting in a circle on meditation cushions. In later years we sat in order, according to the years we had known Andrew. We would meditate for ten minutes before starting the meeting, which would last for about two hours. Often our discussion would find its own thread but, sometimes, Andrew would send a message that gave us a focus, or an event during the previous week would provide an obvious starting point. There were no appointed leaders in our peer group, but the senior students often came to broach a subject, and we would then defer to them during the inquiry that followed. In the community's early years, the purpose of the meetings was to improve our understanding of Andrew's teachings. In the middle years, it was to develop our ability to interpret our experience in the light of his teachings. And, in later years, the meetings served to advance the community's relationship with the Authentic Self. While all types of discussion were challenging, and the meetings were not perfect pictures of mature exploration, the context of the meetings – the aspiration to be a conduit for spirit – made them, I would say, admirable events.

Men's Meetings: History

By chance, I moved from London to Marin at a time of pivotal development for the men's meetings. This means I am able to convey the history of the men's meetings by weaving together three threads: I can say why I changed locations; I can describe Andrew's integration with his men students; and I can take two snapshots of men's meetings in their early stages of development.

My first experience of a men's meeting was in 1994, in London, where students had been in the teachings for about two years. The meetings were characterised by competitive scrambles for airtime and by individuals trying to make clever points, or subtle points, or points laden with profundity. At that time, making a good point was thought to be the name of the game, active inquiry was minimal, and the primary concern of each man was - in essence, and especially compared to later years - personal performance.

During a formal meeting between Andrew and his students in London in 1995, he suggested it would be good if one or two students went to live in Marin. To perhaps everyone's surprise, including my own, I raised my hand to volunteer. I heard later that Andrew and the senior students were flabbergasted. They had been hoping for stronger voices to come forward but, instead, they received only my spontaneous response, with its noticeable conviction. Looking back on that moment, I am amazed that it happened. So much of my life has hinged on that raising of my hand (as will gradually become evident in this book), and it was generally recognised as a bold action. Yet, at the time, I was acting only from a faint sense that the Marin community would be more spacious than the London group.

Some months later I moved to Marin, where I joined a bigger group of men who were older in age and who had seven years' experience of men's meetings. To me, their meetings were scary affairs. The men had great erudition and confidence, like speakers at a G7 geo-political conference. This compared to the London meetings, in which the men were akin to jostling, town-council wannabees. *'Out of my depth'* only begins to capture my experience of those Marin meetings. I dreaded them, I was happy to make do with one or two stammered sentences as my contribution and, afterwards, I counted down the days, with increasing terror, to the next meeting.

Those weighty Marin meetings - in late 1995 and early 1996 - existed at a remarkable time in the community's history. Before my arrival there, Andrew had decided to draw his men students closer to him. His decision meant more formal meetings with him and more social outings to San Francisco. I arrived just as a new degree of intimacy was developing between Andrew and his men. As part of this development, Andrew called us to an unprecedented meeting in his home. At this time, he and Alka lived with six senior students in a big, rented house on Spring Grove, San Anselmo.

Please forgive me if the following description sounds star-struck. I accept that it might, but I judge the risk to be worth taking in my attempt to capture the transcendent qualities of this particular meeting. The Spring Grove house was high on a hill, with fabulous views. When I and the other men drove up the looping approach road and saw the vista, I felt we had arrived on a higher plane. Sitting on the floor of Andrew's living room, I felt uplifted by the beautiful location and excited by my proximity to him. The ambience was – to me – scintillating, and alive with a quality of intimacy quite different from that of a crowded public teaching or Moksha Foundation's business-like meeting rooms in nearby San Rafael. (Moksha Foundation was an earlier name of EnlightenNext).

Especially delightful was Andrew's total freedom from the men's normally eloquent and impressive expressions of self-mastery. He simply ignored anyone's attempt to impose knowingness upon the purpose of the day. In the presence of his higher intention, the distinctions between us dissolved, along with our shields. His even-handed, spacious attention to each person, and to all matters arising, filled the room with what I might call shimmering sanity. This quality seemed to blend with the nature of life outside the room and stretch away beyond us all. In my experience, the air was filled with an inexhaustible and unassailable form of soft curiosity. I felt I was in touch with the ambient nature of existence.

The Spring Grove meeting happened at the beginning of an important osmosis. The nature of that osmosis was the infusion of inquisitive intelligence into the relatively rigid mass of Andrew's men students. The softening of this rigidity continued during 1996 and, when the community moved to Foxhollow, it was accelerated by a number of events. Some of the group's older, weightier men chose not to move from California, while some younger men came to Foxhollow from Boston and Europe. The process of moving cross-country was also rejuvenating: as men scheduled their own journeys, the group gradually melted in Marin and was then freshly reconfigured in Foxhollow. As well as these events, an obvious new condition affected all of Andrew's students: the community now lived on one property. Adapting to new living conditions gave people new roles, which changed the ideas they had about each other. One further evolution in the men's (and women's) circumstances was fundamental – indeed, it was the whole reason for moving to Foxhollow - Andrew could now work more closely with his students.

The men's meetings at Foxhollow therefore started with a rich recent history. Chapter 20 resumes this eventually climactic storyline.

Men's Meetings as a Spiritual Practice

How could a meeting be seen as spiritual practice?

In a men's meeting, we built individual spiritual strength through discussion. This medium provided both basic and specialised training. The basic training - as with all spiritual practice – was to set aside self-concern and give one's attention to a higher purpose. Specialised training involved listening attentively, speaking clearly and building the emotional strength necessary to participate responsibly in conditions that were sometimes chaotic.

The three instructions listed previously in connection to our prostration practice also applied to men's meetings. *'To be free is to have nothing;'* this meant going into a men's meeting empty-handed but ready to respond. *'To be free is to know nothing,'* meant suspending the secure feeling of already knowing what was likely to happen. And *'To be free is to be no one,'* meant discarding any perceived position of importance, higher or lower, in relation to anyone else in the meeting. All three instructions worked towards freeing one's intelligence and curiosity from a contracted state of awareness. We called this contracted state: Pride.

"Pride is the enemy if you want to be free," is a line from Andrew's book, *Enlightenment is a Secret.* He says Pride is the central obstacle to freedom, especially for men. In essence, we wrestled with Pride in all our men's meetings up to the year 2001. Arrogance is definitely Pride, born from the conviction that one is a terrific guy, on top and in charge. Cowardice is also Pride; it arises from the equal certainty that one is a pathetic wimp. Both conditions are contracted states of mind, formed from deep-rooted conclusions, and neither leaves much room for inquiry, exploration, discovery and development. Pride equals resistance to change, to opening up to a greater context, and it was the emotional coalface we chipped at in our men's meetings for many years.

Here is an example of a good meeting. Let's say that the subject of *autonomy* arose in our discussion. At the beginning of the meeting someone might suggest *autonomy* as the subject or, more likely, it would appear in our dialogue and be identified as the best thread to pursue. Our inquiry would gradually illuminate the difference between the ego's idea of autonomy – which is essentially *indulgence*: the power to do whatever one pleases whenever one wants to - and spiritual autonomy, which is the flowering of authentic choice, made possible by seeing the ego's idea of autonomy as a spiritual dead-end. This understanding of autonomy might be teased out over the course of an hour and a half, with the help of a variety of observations, and their refinement. The result would be a group of men sharing an elevated understanding of autonomy.

However, in any meeting, a lot could go wrong. Men had many ways of making their personal concerns more important than our joint inquiry. Imposing one's knowledge was one way to crush a fledgling theme. Interrupting a discussion to propose a new direction was another. More subtly – as, of course, often happens in secular society - someone might respond dismissively or not at all to a previous speaker, or, conversely, pretend to value the contribution of a previous speaker but actually introduce an entirely new take on the meeting's subject, thought up five minutes before and polished for presentation. Other hindrances existed: a cohort of silent men could dampen an inquiry; or a self-conscious man could add an abstract point, dressed up to appear relevant, but which actually only obstructed the natural progression of an exploration. The position of self-appointed grand master was popular: a fellow who would offer a meta-level analysis of the meeting so far, ostensibly to hone the discussion but, in fact, serving only to take everyone's attention away from the common thread. In summary, any meeting could be a tumbling mixture of genuine insight, spontaneous description, inertia, cowardice, bluster and various familiar pretences.

Inwardly, a meeting could be a heavenly, or significantly less-than-heavenly, experience. From a personal point of view, risking everything was the route to having a good meeting. This meant consciously adopting the attitude of wanting nothing from the meeting for oneself. It meant genuinely employing the instructions to have nothing, know nothing and be no one, and being willing to accept whatever came from simply being alert, interested and ready to respond. Anyone following these instructions might turn out to be a key player or a keen listener. This vulnerable approach meant one had to participate in the meeting without any reassurance of a particular outcome for oneself.

For myself, I would often be consumed by self-concern. This meant worrying about speaking enough. Worrying about speaking could consume 95% of my attention. It was often a burning anxiety that would gather momentum through the meeting, leaving me with very little attention available for what was happening. The result was insubstantial participation, an inability to care about the success of the meeting, and a lack of awareness of other people. It was a pitiful and painful state to be in. All of Andrew's students had a chequered history, coloured by their strengths and weaknesses; for me, this patchy progression meant that, for many years, I was one of the weaker participants in men's meetings.

But I was not alone in my struggles, or lack thereof, and my participation was not the whole story. Meetings could be peak experiences. Our inquiry could catch fire, and the consequent updraft would draw us together into one unit. 'My curiosity got the better of me;' this phrase describes what could happen. When the balance tipped, our interest overwhelmed our reservations and our years of training would come to life. We'd enter our own zone and become an astute unit, finding our way through entangled assumptions, refining one another's insights, course-correcting if we hit a dead end, and allowing ourselves to trust the path that unfolded before us. These were the best of times, when we were 'on song', enjoying the fruits of our spiritual practice and the beautiful experience of inquiring together.

The challenge of men's meetings was to leave everything behind. Through our struggles to do this we came to know each other extremely well, and to identify the common shades and shadows of male pride: we became taxonomists of our own egoic natures. The weekly men's meeting was the creative core of our spiritual life, where we were stretched, scrutinised and, with tough-love, supported by one another. Our sensitivity to each other's progress, compromise, courage, habits, strengths and weaknesses became intuitive. The men's (and women's) meetings were our highest order of spiritual practice.

Retreats

Each year the community held two big retreats. One in the summer in Europe, the other in the winter in India. They lasted for either ten or fourteen days, and each consisted of different combinations of meditation, dialogue with Andrew, teaching by Andrew, group discussions and silence. These events were open to the public and attendances varied between 250 and 350 people, of whom about a third would be new to Andrew's teachings. For his students, the retreats were periods of intense spiritual practice.

Travelling to a retreat was enjoyable. It provided a break from one's familiar routine and, most often, the retreat's distant location was alluring. The winter retreat in Rishikesh, on the banks of the river Ganges, was set in the context of India's majestic spiritual heritage and the raw, overcrowded, richly chaotic nature of that country's culture. The summer retreat in either the south of France or in Tuscany, Italy, was an opportunity to enjoy a snatched moment of European high life. In later years, the location of the winter retreat switched from India to America - either Colorado or Arizona – a reflection of how Andrew's teachings moved away from their eastern origins.

The physical beauty of our retreat locations in southern Europe deserves special mention. In France we would land in Nice and, once free from the complex road network surrounding the airport, we would find our way to Tourrettes-sur-Loup. From that small town, situated on a typically rocky Provencal promontory, we ascended a long, steep drive up to Les Cormettes. The property's large main building was built of stone. Its varied history – as a family home, sanatorium and wartime HQ – made it architecturally curious.

It had the decorative arches, stone paved terraces and grand staircases of a chateau, but its overall shape was low and sprawling. While the house was something of an oddity, there was no doubt about Les Cormettes' stunning setting: the property and its surrounding fields looked out over the Côte d'Azur. This view was spectacular, and especially pleasing at night, when the dense network of lights shining from surrounding towns made the coast and its inland areas look like a mirror image of the starry sky above.

Tuscany's landscape - rivalling the South of France – has its signature lines of cypress trees, rocky grandeur and plentiful connections to medieval history. Florence – Tuscany's capital city - has an added attraction: it holds the riches of the Renaissance. In that historic context, the community's students felt very much at home; for better or worse, either with justification or blind self-glorification, we saw ourselves living in similarly significant times, at the crux of a new emergence. I well remember many post-retreat, alfresco dinners in the squares and lanes of Florence, with tables of thirty animated people enjoying the riches of Tuscany's cuisine, the palpable sense of history, and the uplift that followed ten days of spiritual engagement.

The idea that a retreat is an enriched holiday appears to be widely held. Many retreats are clearly sold on this basis and, if their locations are exotic, the presumption is easy to understand. On Andrew's retreats some participants – the general public and his newest lay students - probably held this expectation, and had it fulfilled. They could, for example, be seen 'topping and tailing' their attendance with pleasurable excursions, while treating the retreat as a distinct episode of dedicated, but managed, spiritual exploration. Meanwhile, Andrew's older, and sometimes more static, lay students brought their respected loyalty, and his younger, active lay students brought their evolutionary zeal. All these retreat participants – the public and lay students - were beyond Andrew's direct authority and, therefore, able to enjoy the retreat, untroubled by the possibility that it might change their regular lives.

It was a different matter for Andrew's core students. I think it's true to say that it took more than ten years for his students to really accept that retreats were not enriched holidays but – as Andrew saw them - spiritual accelerators. In his view, a retreat was a rare opportunity for his students to build spiritual strength. It was only a retreat – a withdrawal - in the sense that we were free from distractions; otherwise, it was an opportunity for advancement, for spiritual stretch, for the application of more effort than usual.

There was, therefore, during these ten years, a mismatch in expectations: students hoping for a period of relief from a pressured life versus Andrew's idea that a retreat was an opportunity to engage in serious investigation and development. Frequently, this mismatch resulted in failure. At successive retreats, his students would arrive unprepared. Andrew would want and expect us to apply ourselves, to be interested in pushing the boundaries of our understanding and experience, to be thinking freshly about what he was teaching, and to be making use of the time available for contemplation. But our response would be sluggish and minimal; we would hide within our own ranks and inwardly wonder why Andrew was frustrated with us.

This reliably deflating situation turned full circle after 2002. We matured. Andrew's expectations and ours came into closer alignment. Momentous, hard-won victories (Chaps 20/21) enabled us to hold a broader perspective. This improved our ability to bring to retreats only the most constructive parts of our experience. Moreover, Andrew's leading students now had greater spiritual weight. This enabled him to redesign the format of his retreats. With more leaders available, participants could be optimally placed in peer groups of about twenty people and, with the progress of the groups shared each day, a potent learning environment developed.

Being 'on retreat' – as we termed it – was a unique experience. The regular daily schedule included a lot of meditation, starting early in the morning and reaching late into the evening. The teaching hall was open at all times for those who wanted to meditate during or through the night. Andrew would teach twice a day for three hours, we would have discussion groups and, at all other times, we would be in silence. We didn't read, or watch TV, or engage with the outside world. Our attention was on Andrew and what he was teaching, which created a unified field of common interest and intent. Was *everyone* unified in this field? Probably not, but it was certainly the strongest feature of these events, valued by the majority.

Among our retreat locations, Les Cormettes held a special place in my heart. Isolated high above the world, animated by the frenzied hum of insects and baked by wonderful sunshine, the grassy slopes and stunning vistas evoked the feeling of being in heaven. Typical of France - I thought - it exuded confidence in its own beauty and was easy to fall in love with. Maybe it's not surprising that the very first manifestation of what Andrew intuitively felt was possible between his students - the first sign that our collective work might bear fruit - took place during a retreat in Les Cormettes in the summer of 1999.

Ten of Andrew's core women students had been meeting in the afternoons for some days. They had met the usual difficulties of groups at that time, with various forms of self-concern suppressing the women's curiosity. The group's meetings appeared to be getting nowhere; they were discordant, frustrating, lacking in direction and fragmented by conflicting personal agendas. In a moment of despairing honesty one young woman, a Canadian from Saskatchewan, commented on how separate she felt and how disparate the group seemed to be. In reply, an Englishwoman with previous experience as a Buddhist nun– whom I knew very well, hence my knowledge of this event - said, "*But we're not separate.*" She was speaking from her direct recognition of life as one undivided whole.

These two injections of realness – the first personal, the second truthful - somehow relocated the group's centre of gravity, at least enough to move the women's attention away from their personal concerns and towards a bigger picture of life and deeper truths. Primed by days of Andrew's teachings, while held within the retreat's focused environment, and with their curiosity ignited, this group of relatively young students came alive. As if a switch had been thrown, their interest expanded beyond themselves, giving them a new point of view in which they saw their experience as the raw material from which common, yet profound, truths could be gleaned. Their passion for describing what they saw in this new perspective was contagious. Although this passion was not uniformly felt - there were differences between the women - the group as a whole was carried by those who felt it most strongly.

In a meeting with Andrew their spontaneous inquiry continued. This itself was remarkable because, normally, the temptation to clam up or play safe in meetings with him was strong (for both genders). However, infused by hitherto unseen and extraordinary curiosity, each woman was noticeably and naturally herself, and he confirmed they were experiencing and exhibiting what, for seven years, he had been hoping his students would find. The significance of the event was obvious: it supported Andrew's intuitive sense of what was possible. But it also demonstrated something that became very important in later years, when Andrew's women students were having great difficulty. This event in Les Cormettes showed that women were equally capable – (of course, at the time, it looked as if they were more capable) – of receiving the force of love and evolution that Andrew sought to invoke.

Closing Observations

Men's and women's meetings, and retreats, were particular forms of spiritual practice. Compared to the traditional, largely individual, practices described in the last chapter, these meetings and retreats were collective engagements in which, potentially, whole groups of students could advance. Therefore, Andrew and the senior students had a keen interest in the results of these events, and we were often subject to their scrutiny, advice and correction. As one might expect in these circumstances, the community's group practices sometimes yielded heartache and failure and, at other times, ecstasy and breakthrough.

Chapter 14

Tales from the Property

After spiritual practice comes the best moment of the day, breakfast! Having risen early and diligently applied himself (in my case, for example) to disassociating Self from Mind, and then maybe worked hard at his physical practice, a dedicated student can reward himself with the delightful business of choosing from the breakfast menu.

This chapter is intended to evoke that commonly enjoyed, exquisite moment: the first well-deserved cup of coffee of the day. It can be a contemplative moment, with the ascending sun promising well. Or a moment in which to savour early accomplishments. It can also be a convivial moment to engage with friends and discuss the day ahead.

Yes, purified and fortified, breakfast is a great time to review what's afoot in the neighbourhood and get a sense of the daily lives of others. For my part, I offer the following three tales, each providing a window into the life of our community.

Jason and the Sewage Pumps

Jason was a good man, an Australian, an upper-core student and the maintenance manager of the Foxhollow property. He and I were peers, working closely together for five years and, although close friendships were not a feature of our culture, we were good friends and I have lasting fondness for Jason's intelligence and good intent.

He had an interesting mixture of qualities. He was affable and, ostensibly, easygoing, like a typical Aussie, but he was also precise, controlled and meticulous. These traits coexisted within his surprisingly dishevelled personal space. His messy office was an example of this dishevelment, as was his appearance. Jason was a handsome man, yet he chose to dress from the lost-property box – literally – which unfortunately made him a walking exemplar of a very useful Australian term: *daggy*.

Jason was a great manager and, over the years, he taught me the value of people who maintain control of their workload. For him, no detail was too boring to warrant accurate record, careful consideration, and appropriate response. This penchant was a godsend when it came to managing small repairs in our community's rental apartments or residential buildings. I loathed these unrewarding jobs, and I know the other three members of our team also detested them, but to Jason they were important, and he would keep each job on the docket, week after week, until it was completed. He was also the most willing labourer imaginable, a feature of his character that a generous person might use to excuse his choice of tatty clothing. On our larger projects, he would happily take on the less glamorous broom-and-bucket work while the rest of us relished the juicier, more satisfying, big timber and nail-gun activity.

Jason first met Andrew in Bali, Indonesia, in 1993, as one of a loose group of ten westerners who eventually became Andrew's students. He had a very beautiful, intelligent and gentle girlfriend called Raya. She had the island's generic western woman's appearance: slim, tanned, elegant and delicately wreathed in translucent white chiffon.

I mention Raya to introduce Andrew's dilemma when a couple became interested in his teachings. Neither he, nor they, could tell if both partners had independent interest, or if one was clinging to the other. Every permutation arose. For example, one person could become enamoured by the teachings while the other clung to the relationship, and then these positions might reverse. Couples could split, when just one would join the community. They could both join and, later, decide to separate; or both join and stay together. And, of course, they could both buckle under the threat of anticipated separation, and disappear. In Jason's case, it first looked as if he were tagging along and Raya had the deeper interest, to the extent that Andrew quizzed him repeatedly about the independence of his interest. But, in fact, Raya eventually chose to leave the community, during the Marin period, and Jason turned out to have the stronger commitment.

In amongst Jason's mixture of qualities was his mathematical acumen. He later became a maths teacher in Lenox but, at Foxhollow, a surprising event drew forth his passion for numbers.

Lakeside Condominiums had a swimming pool, shared by the largely absentee owners and, beside the pool enclosure, some five metres away, was an inconspicuous, green metal cabinet mounted on a larger concrete base, surrounded by lawn. There was a two-door hatch lying flat within this concrete circle, giving access to a large, subterranean chamber about twenty-five feet deep and twelve feet in diameter. Into this chamber poured the sewage and rainwater from all the buildings on the Foxhollow estate, before it was pumped onward by two giant pumps that worked alternately, day-in, day-out. One morning, an alarm sounded from the metal cabinet.

So began something equivalent to a Freudian dream sequence. A day that had started in normal sunshine suddenly demanded that we peer into the active bowels of the property. We had had no idea this chamber existed. For years the pumps had faithfully done their gruesome work, dispatching whatever effluent came within reach. But the surface alarm signalled the failure of one of these loyal workhorses and, unexpectedly, we acquired a new responsibility. Opening the hatch, we looked down – a long way down – to a swirling, churning ocean of foul water, and to the brown, encrusted shapes of two whopping electric motors, each at least the size of a wheelbarrow. Under the foaming surface were the actual pumps, as big as truck tyres.

An army engineering corps would have relished the job of retrieving these pumps. They were mounted on vertical, toothed rails, enabling them to be wound to the surface using a geared handle. They could then be winched onto the back of a truck with the help of a large, overhanging tripod. Once we had the pumps in the workshop – where they lay like dormant alien pods – we were able to scrape them clean, send them for repair and later reinstall them.

Never has a man accepted a mission with more alacrity than Jason brought to this project. Here was a proper job that needed proper management, and someone willing to take on a grisly task in order to maintain Foxhollow's infrastructure. No more mincing about with broken door-handles and window-catches, or sweeping beneath lads on ladders, this was a vital utility matter on which the function of the whole property depended. Moreover, as well as its importance, the project had enticing potential. The green cabinet, now known to be the periscope of a dreadful vessel, held electronic recording devices that monitored the work of each pump. In Jason's eyes, these devices were portals to a mathematical paradise.

Each morning he made a pilgrimage to the green cabinet, where he retrieved the night's data for the two motors. He recorded the data on a chart and plotted the figures on a graph. If asked, he would sweetly inform people about the pumps' behaviour. They were – indeed - quite fascinating, operating as they did on a seemingly random basis, like two unruffled brothers sharing a joint vocation. The pumps' irregular participation meant that their use of electricity varied on a daily basis: it was this variation that made the data exciting! I suspected that Jason kept his own more sophisticated analytical figures, correlating variables of different sorts, integrating and differentiating multiples of this and that, with tangential sine and cosine equations, predictive flow charts and the like.

Foxhollow often surprised us with its secrets. Each surprise called on our talents and, in this tale of the sewage pumps, it was Jason's infectious enthusiasm for data that was added to our skill set. With the pumps working reliably, he monitored their flow charts and Foxhollow functioned as freely as before.

The Freedom Trail

Wherever Andrew lived, the students living near him developed faster than those elsewhere in the world, creating certain imbalances within the community. This second tale recalls an example of the kind of confrontation that could arise during attempts to address such differences.

In this instance the straggling group - the upper-core English men – had been my peer group three years earlier. So, when they visited Foxhollow in the spring of 1998, my loyalties were briefly divided. I was English and, therefore, a compatriot of the visitors and a former brother in arms. Yet, since leaving that group, I had lived closer to Andrew than they had, first in Marin and now at Foxhollow, and so I had a new sense of kinship with my largely American group. However, any uncertainty about where my loyalties lay was soon dispelled when the English men arrived: seeing the obvious difference between the dignity of the two groups made it easy for me to stay aligned with the Foxhollow men!

The fifteen travellers pitched up in buoyant mood. They appeared to see their visit as a transatlantic meeting of brothers, not a correctional exercise. They brought a gift that affirmed their mistaken assessment. I should first explain the significance of gifts. It was customary for visiting students to give one to Andrew. This custom was not policed; it was something we did naturally, much as people might take gifts to a social occasion. Generally speaking, students brought Andrew a gift out of love or gratitude, although sometimes we were motivated simply by our knowledge of what was appropriate. As I experienced this custom, gifts were not given to win Andrew's favour, they were given to acknowledge his leading role in our joint endeavour.

The English men did not bring Andrew a gift. Instead they presented a football to the Foxhollow men and suggested a match. This football, possibly the most incongruous object ever seen in the manor house, proclaimed the expectation of an easy, convivial weekend, and perfectly exhibited the English men's disconnection from our community's commonly-held standards and focus.

The purpose of the intended five-day visit was soon under way, with formal meetings between the London and Foxhollow men acting as spiritual fitness tests. Many of the visitors, being out of shape, were overwhelmed by the rigorous levels of scrutiny. Shocked by the news that there was a problem, and the problem was with them, they responded in a number of ways: some protested their innocence, others expressed their disbelief, and a few resorted to blame.

Such defensive responses revealed an unwillingness to accept responsibility for, or be curious about, their spiritual condition. Both behaviours were starkly at odds with the qualities we were seeking to cultivate within ourselves. The football was soon forgotten as it dawned on everyone that raising the English men's standards – of self-discipline and interest in our work - was going to take significant effort.

In this type of situation, the currency of formal meetings – spoken description - was useful for clarifying a problem. But, if there were too many meetings, they became repetitive and unproductive. People needed time to reflect on their situation and develop curiosity about their predicament. In this instance, there was another consideration: the Foxhollow men had work to do, and could not down tools entirely to support their struggling peers. Both circumstances meant that a daytime project was needed for the English men. A senior student, who had an affinity with nature, proposed they clear a path within Foxhollow's woodland. He envisaged the path becoming a Zen-like trail – *The Freedom Trail* – that might become a famous attraction. Others thought the basic idea was good, and so the English men started work.

They laboured for three days clearing a route. Heavy tasks included building a bridge to span a stream and laying stepping-stones across boggy hollows. Lighter work included clearing brushwood, digging-out roots and levelling uneven ground. It is safe to say that both the heavy and the lighter occupations were relatively easy compared to the spiritual wrestling-match active in the men's minds.

Men versus their pride; the timeless contest playing out even in these mildly challenging circumstances. In Chapter 13, on the subject of spiritual practice, I have described pride as a state of contracted awareness, frequently expressed by men through arrogance or cowardice. Pride can also be seen, in its essence, as a state of refusing to change. In the men's meetings described in that chapter, we were trusted to manage our own pride. But, in this story, the English men were under greater pressure. Others were demanding that they change, so they *had* to confront their pride. This pressure provoked a variety of reactions: despondency, helplessness, defiance; sentiments which extinguished any sparks of interest that might have led them out of their preoccupied state.

What I want to highlight in this story, is the contrast between the men's almost melodramatic responses to spiritual pressure and – if seen from Andrew's point of view - the reasonable nature of that pressure. As described above, the English men were swept up by the riot of resistance arising in their experience. But, in fact, they were simply being asked to take two reasonable steps: firstly, recognise that they had fallen behind and, secondly, make some effort to catch up. As Andrew's students, we encountered this time and again:

the drama generated by our minds when we were asked to develop spiritual maturity. Andrew would say to us, "*Be true to your original intention*" but, by fixing our attention on the strong feelings that arose in response to his command, we would feel helpless, claim helplessness and disobey him. At that point, battle lines would be drawn.

In the story of the Freedom Trail, Andrew was in the background. It was two of Foxhollow's mentoring students who oversaw the English men's visit. But their authority was backed up by his authority which, in our context, was absolute. So, when the English men turned inward and refused to change, they put themselves at odds with their teacher. Blindly, they were then challenging the cosmological force that Andrew transmitted. That challenge can only lead to failure, and this was the case for four of the English men, who, demoted, returned to London as lay students. The other eleven men showed sufficient interest and made enough effort to, eventually, see their situation dispassionately. Humbled, they kept their status. It was not a transcendent episode in the history of our community: it was more of a pruning exercise, necessary to safeguard the potential of the majority. The Freedom Trail, having perhaps fulfilled its purpose during the course of the visit, was slowly reclaimed by the forest.

The Kitchen Roof

We were lucky to inherit a well-equipped, commercial kitchen when we bought Foxhollow, but its roof was in poor shape. As I've said before, the two-storey manor house was T-shaped when viewed from above. Both the original part of the house - the top of the T - and the newer 'leg' had pitched (sloping) roofs. The kitchen roof nestled at a slightly lower level than the bottom edge of the pitched roofs, in the south-facing corner of this T shape. It was flat and it covered a 20ft x 20ft single-storey extension. For some reason the manor house did not have gutters, so rain and snow falling on its pitched roofs discharged directly onto the kitchen roof.

The kitchen roof leaked; not badly but, under certain circumstances, bowls and pans had to be positioned to collect drips. It had the potential to be a fabulous viewing-deck, as it overlooked the lake and the grounds stretching towards the condominiums, but its undulating and suspiciously soggy surface made it feel perilous underfoot. It was also home to various machines, sitting over apertures in its surface: two large intake-and-extract fans for the kitchen's ventilation, and an air-conditioning compressor. Electrical supplies and switches servicing these machines also poked through this cracked and blistered membrane.

Many people over many years had obviously seen that the roof needed repair. It was peppered with signs of attempted quick fixes - perhaps made hurriedly on Friday afternoons by tired roofing contractors en route home: "*We've done what we can, ma'am, no guarantees, that'll be $200.*" Clearly there was a bigger bullet to be bitten: the roof needed to be stripped and rebuilt. This job was given to me, and I relished its delicious complexity. It provided a challenge that, positioned nicely beyond comfort, was enticing. Jason and I agreed a start date, Tuesday, September 11th, 2001 and - edging closer to the relevance of this story - I was given two English aristocrats as labourers.

After eight years as Andrew's student, I had a lot of experience managing volunteer labour, acquired mostly during preparation for the big retreats, but also on the sites of our bigger construction projects. Spiritual seekers, as one would expect, generally make excellent volunteers, although excited newbie seekers tend to talk too much, and long-term seekers can be glum if assigned to lowly work. Different nationalities have their pros and cons. One might expect the Germans to be the best, but they spoil their usefulness by tending to know better than their manager. Israelis, although hard workers, have an annoying need: they must argue to confirm their existence. The Swedish are just a little too quiet, cool and competent for comfort, while the French are massive snobs when it comes to non-intellectual work and are nowhere to be seen. Americans are a mixed bunch, who use much of their attention to translate instructions into their own bite-sized, comprehensible shorthand. By far the best are the Dutch, who are hard-working, practical, and so thoroughly conditioned by their advanced egalitarian society that they automatically assume the position of willing collaborators, thereby slightly undermining their manager's authority, but only to a degree that feels like a fair trade for their productivity. My two English aristocrats, however, were newcomers to the world of volunteer labour. They stood on unfamiliar turf, creatures of novelty, willing, but not necessarily able, and clearly a breed apart from the average volunteer.

In terms of aristocrats, mine were the real deal. Ambrose and Linley were cousins, whose ancestry reached deep into England's medieval history with all the heraldry, land, titles and royal friendships that accompany names such as Arundel, Howard, Spencer, Boleyn and Churchill. Both had been educated at Eton College and, although they were products of the sixties and had, therefore, toned down their aristocratic traits to suit that decade, their mannerisms - to an eagle English eye - were still identifiably ruling-class.

The kitchen-roof project provides an opportunity to review the cousins' journeys under Andrew's auspices, partly because it was an unusual time when, briefly, they shared the same student status. Seen in retrospect, their stories resemble two halves of a biblical parable that ostensibly tells of cousins making different choices, but actually describes an archetypal struggle between social privilege and spiritual surrender. Both men, in my opinion, stand as representatives: Linley for well-intentioned students who lacked resilience; Ambrose for high-flying students who hit unforeseen obstacles. I regard them as significant figures within the history of Andrew's community.

Linley was a generous man. He was also intelligent, likeable and humorous, and he had a degree of courage. However, I believe it's true to say that he lacked the necessary steel to engage with the level of spiritual pressure exerted by Andrew because, eventually, Linley accepted the position of loyal lay student and we became used to seeing him in that - to us - compromised place. However, I knew Linley in the community's earlier years, the mid-nineties onward, and I want to acknowledge how strongly he felt the spiritual call because, following a few years of soul-searching, he chose to leave his wife, teenage children and Yorkshire farm, to become Andrew's student. I could easily have been a family man; I have those traditional values and, therefore, I can feel the wrench experienced by Linley and the heartache felt by his wife and children when he left home. Their story is a classic example of how Spirit can disrupt conventional life, leading one to appreciate why eastern teachings have the model of a man (as it has been) completing his duties as a householder before pursuing self-realisation. Considering Linley's family situation, I empathise with them all. I believe his children now feel they benefited from his choice, and I have heard that his wife carried her situation very well. I find their story humbling and moving.

It must also be said, to be true to the view and standards held at Foxhollow, that Linley's choice to hang back from the live action was judged negatively. There really were no excuses for removing oneself from the front line, and Andrew felt our work was undermined by people who wanted to belong to our endeavour but were unwilling to engage with their ego. We repeatedly and unequivocally declared ourselves to be a radical, spiritual outfit and, although Andrew made repeated efforts to integrate those who felt they could only tag along, he also deplored the compromise of his students who refused to be true to their intention. He had not asked them to become his students, that was their choice, and they were provided with the same assistance as everyone else. Hence there was collective frustration felt towards those who adopted a permanently peripheral position, because they were, essentially, siding with the part of human nature that the community was committed to transcending. Occasionally this frustration was expressed as full-blown disdain, but disapproval was the more consistent attitude held towards students in Linley's position, and he would continually have been aware of this.

The contrast between the two above paragraphs illustrates an important distinction. The first paragraph acknowledges Linley's bravery and empathises with his family's heartache. The second stresses the need, in the context of enlightenment, to give up personal preferences and obey common truths. This distinction shows the different values held in the top two tiers of a popular reference: Maslow's hierarchy of needs. Drawn as a pyramid, Maslow's hierarchy shows self-actualisation occupying the peak position, with psychological needs – social belonging and self-esteem – lying beneath. Linley's student history stands as an exemplar. He had strong social strengths, he was agreeable, hard-working and well-meaning; but these values are neither helpful nor unhelpful in the higher tier of self-actualisation, where self-sacrifice and obedience to independent principles are required.

Ambrose's story is iconic. Other students wrestled with common human dependencies such as arrogance, casualness, flirtatiousness, self-consciousness, or queenliness; dependencies that have been faced and transcended throughout humanity's spiritual history. But Ambrose had to face a less familiar dependency through which fewer, if any, paths had been cut. His spiritual journey led him to a confrontation with the entitlement and privilege that prevailed in history's most recent and extensive empire.

Ambrose did not obviously exhibit English imperialism. He was the youngest of six siblings and had youthful energy. He wasn't stuffy, or a pompous traditionalist, and he didn't trade on the trappings of his privilege. He was tall, and on the slim side of perfectly athletic; he was also handsome, smart, charming to women when he chose to be and, according to Linley, nicknamed 'cool-cat' at Eton due to his ability to remain attractively aloof. Before becoming Andrew's student he had trained as a therapist, but it was our common understanding that he had never needed to work for money. Born in 1952, he would have been in his forties and early fifties during the period covered by this book.

Although not a traditionalist, Ambrose had an effortless air of authority. Literally effortless. In his personal mind space, there appeared to be plenty of time and more than enough room for him to maintain an intelligent and composed outlook on life. This was not an affectation, this was his actual state of cool-headed awareness, which undoubtedly played a big part in his rise to become, at first, one of Andrew's lieutenants and, later, his closest student.

Ambrose's status developed during the period between 1993 and 1998. He was more independent than his peers. He spoke with authority, both in general and, when required, to large audiences. Compared to other respected senior students, he had some different qualities: he was more spacious, unproblematic, direct and uncompromising. Ambrose led weekend retreats and made a teaching trip to Australia. He came to be seen by other students as existing in a league of his own, and he was publicly acknowledged by Andrew to be *"the best I have."*

I happened to spend the winter of 1998 in London, building a loft conversion for my sister and her husband. One evening, at the London Centre in Belsize Park, Ambrose called the upper-core men students to a meeting. *"A rift has developed,"* he said, *"between me and Andrew."* Ambrose told us he had been asked to write some publicity copy about our community's work, which he'd failed to complete satisfactorily. Andrew, he informed us, judged that, as his foremost student, the subject should have been front-and-centre in Ambrose's mind and an easy matter for him to write about. I guessed the rift must have started some weeks before, and that it was unresolved, because the meeting itself was an unprecedented event. Normally we had no idea of the dynamics existing between Andrew and the senior students. Yet, surprisingly, we were being informed that Ambrose was not living up to Andrew's expectations.

I will repeat myself a few times in this book, when I say that Andrew scrutinised his top students more closely than those lower in the hierarchy. To us, his close scrutiny was foundational to the integrity of our community. It gave us confidence that neither favouritism by Andrew nor student ambition for status was active in our ranks. We knew life was a lot tougher at the top. So, when Ambrose failed to write a simple description of our work, Andrew sought for the reasons, and discovered that Ambrose was dependent upon his aristocratic entitlement: his inborn sense of being above other people. In other words, Andrew saw that Ambrose was not a completely free man.

Profound entitlement can, ironically, make someone appear enlightened. I observed this irony in one or two of Andrew's upper-class Indian students. Entitlement delivers confidence, from which follow calmness, spaciousness and the ability to use intelligence with economy and precision. An unruffled, intelligent person - especially someone informed by sophisticated scripture - can look noticeably unselfconscious and very impressive. However, entitled people often lack the beautiful qualities of unfettered spontaneity and perfectly weighted, authentic transmission. Compared to a truly free person, an entitled person can look measured, managed and circumspect.

English imperialism proved to be impenetrable. Ambrose struggled with his sense of entitlement, but without success, and his status gradually declined. More people became aware of him being on the wrong side of himself. He was given less important roles. He must have lost confidence, in the same way that we all did if we were at odds with Andrew. Eventually, Ambrose was not included in community events and he was, uniquely, on what could be thought of as a walkabout, or a period of permanent reflective estrangement from his teacher. This came to be called his banishment, which lasted ten years.

I do not know of Ambrose's experience, or the nature of his inquiry during his fall from grace and his years of banishment. My view from within the community was that he came and went. Hopes of him achieving a breakthrough were occasionally raised, but they invariably dissolved. Each time we saw him at Foxhollow he would be softer than before, but this was at the cost of his confidence, presence and status. Meanwhile the teachings developed, and he came to look a little like someone frozen in time. This was a common feature of students who returned after some time away; they exhibited an earlier stage of the community's development. In the middle of his banishment I met with Ambrose in a café in London, for a practical reason, but we also talked about how he was doing. I could feel his joy as he reconnected to our world and, when we touched on the subject of blue-blooded entitlement, he let out a sigh, as if thinking of a respected opponent, and said, *"It's quite a thing."* At that moment, I really felt the struggles of someone called to give up profound privilege in favour of an empty-handed life.

Before ending this chapter, I think it's worth examining some of the reasons for Ambrose's banishment. Andrew did not want his former leading students visibly struggling within his community. This would have been bad for morale, a drain on resources and a source of confusion in the hierarchy. But neither did he want to give up on people - in this case Ambrose - who had travelled the furthest into his world, given enormously to our endeavour and who were actually - even with their stumbling-blocks - his most highly-developed students. Ambrose, on his side, had deep experience of enlightenment; easily enough to know that no other life was possible for him. He had the intelligence to recognise the scale of what he was fighting within himself, and the necessary maturity, love and integrity to maintain a relationship with Andrew even while being put under immense pressure. As we will see in the next chapter, sometimes – or perhaps often – the spiritual path includes impasses that, because they exhaust human effort, put all parties in the unknown.

Work on the kitchen roof went very well, despite starting on the day of the 9/11 attacks on New York's Twin Towers. Jason and I had been for breakfast at a truck-stop in Lee. We had seen the first smoking tower on a TV screen as we left. It was only after we had torn away half the roof's rotten surface that we were informed of the nature and extent of the disaster. By then, the Foxhollow community had encamped around our large television, but - with some unease about our decision - we continued with the work because the kitchen was now vulnerable to rain.

America's timber supplies are plentiful, making it possible to buy 20ft lengths of 2"x 6" joists. Once the roof surface was stripped, we set about laying a new support structure. I marked out the notches to be cut on each joist, and then the aristocrats would cut and bolt together my original joist plus one copy. These pairs were then laid across the roof at 12" centres, each supported at either end, and by two intermediate structural beams. Over a number of days, we developed a satisfying rhythm and a congenial (and well-spoken) working partnership. Once the supports were in place, we screwed down two layers of plywood and called in the Sarnafil roof membrane sub-contractors. They paid us a great compliment, saying our work was the best they had seen.

Chapter 15

Engaging with Ego.
And Hal Blacker's 'A' List

A feature of enlightened consciousness is fearlessness. In particular, a fearless relationship to ego, the part of oneself that wants life to be known and manageable. How is this fearlessness achieved? In theory, one could simply observe the impulses of ego and choose not to respond to them, but that relationship to ego requires tremendous resolve, or attainment. Alternatively, a fearless relationship to ego can be achieved by engaging with it; by learning - hands-on - about the strength of ego and its multifarious forms. This chapter describes how the community learnt in that way, the hard way. It records a struggle that was sometimes vigorous; a quality that I have tried to represent fairly in this chapter.

I think a quick review of Chapter 3, *What is Ego?*, will be helpful. It forewarns of this chapter and says that the community's engagement with ego peaked in the middle years of its history. It describes ego as a contracting force that acts positively, because it shapes individuality, but also negatively, because it often creates the painful experience of isolation. Two further points explain how the community was forced to confront ego when it became an obstacle, and that students' aim was not to rid themselves of ego, but to cage it. The chapter also notes that undisturbed ego is experienced very differently from ego that is exposed.

This chapter has been challenging to write for two reasons. Firstly, as previously noted, the elusive nature of ego defies description. Secondly, the community's engagement with ego, a thorny subject in itself, has been made thornier by some ex-students who have successfully cultivated a new narrative. Their new narrative is that our engagement with ego was the product of wilful abuse.

Wilful abuse? Yes. The motives of these ex-students will be examined in a later chapter but, here, I want to explain how their seedling narrative was able to take root. Some of the upcoming ego-engagement stories will land badly, as they have done already, in today's liberal society. They are stories about the assertion of unbending authority that are almost guaranteed to inflame the sensitivities of people who are wary of authority in all its forms.

Such people have provided the receptive, fertile soil in which the ex-student's accusative narrative has flourished. Furthermore, the community's unusual relationship to ego, being hard to understand, has itself provided the space for misinterpretation. When aggregated, the above conditions make it easy for someone to propagate a story of abuse from the community's engagement with ego. Enter Hal Blacker and his 'A' List. He and his list are described at the end of this chapter, but I can introduce him as one of Andrew's students during the Marin period, and someone I regard – in the grand scheme of things – as a creative antagonist.

I have been advised, and tempted, simply to allude to the community's history with ego. But four powerful reasons have compelled me to give a full account.

Firstly, one purpose of this book is to overthrow a damaging injustice. The ex-students' story of abuse prevails, but I believe the community's work was well-intentioned and that it could still prove to be immensely valuable to humanity. Seeking justice, I want to create a jury to hear my case. That jury is you and other readers! I hope that, by placing the full story before a number of intelligent people, my case will receive fair judgement.

Secondly, I have been mindful of the understandable human propensity to respond to allusions and non-disclosure with suspicion. This has also steered me towards giving a full account.

Thirdly, I considered what to do about Hal Blacker's 'A' List, which sits on the internet proclaiming its narrative of abuse. Through my building work, I have learnt that a thorough job produces a durable result, so I thought hard about what a thorough response to Hal Blacker's list might be. Eventually, again mindful of the relationship between public scrutiny and fair judgement, I decided to draw his list further into the light of collective awareness, where its true character could be assessed.

But my most compelling reason for giving a full account is that this book makes a bold claim. It claims that Andrew's community developed a hugely significant, evolved spiritual faculty. I believe such a claim cannot credibly be made without showing the birthing pains involved. (For the same reason, the upcoming chapters on the women, and the men, are equally unreserved).

To further help readers understand this chapter, I'd like to offer a description of ego at rest and another of ego when exposed. To do this I will first describe my ego, then I want to use a hypothetical situation to convey how ferocious ego can be when challenged.

Thinking back to myself at Foxhollow, I imagine my ego as a cone-shaped spiral. Common human characteristics are contained within the upper/outer rings, whereas personal features exist in the lower coils. Using the community's view of ego, I will start my description with the outer rings and work inwards. I had a man's ego: I walked with importance, my ideas of myself swung between heroic and hopeless, and I was, to some extent, a rigid knower. I also had an English ego: reserved, superior and dutiful. But my personal ego, at the core of the spiral, was the most secretive part of myself. Like Tolkien's Gollum, I had two inner voices: one resentful, the other self-aggrandising. The repartee between these voices formed the core of my ungiving ego. They turned me into someone who looked to give little but receive much. This self-centred core constantly called for my attention, yet hid from the eyes of others. It was obstructive. It limited my free participation in the work of our community.

Luckily there was more to me than my ego, but it was real, and came with the common features of ego: impoverishment and the desire to stay in the shadows. To convey what happens when ego is pulled from the shadows, I want to create a scenario. If six of the world's most powerful nations were to group together and say to America, *"You must change your relationship with guns, or we will impose an embargo,"* one can imagine America's response. Many Americans would feel their national identity was under attack and they would, most likely, react defensively. It is unlikely that a majority would say, *"I see their point; everyone would be better off if this were changed; we should express gratitude for the opportunity to evolve."* If America resisted, but the six nations were resolute, the situation might escalate, as was often the case when we engaged with ego in the community.

General Observations on Ego Engagement

We knew the score. Unlike my imagined scenario above, students had chosen to participate in an ego-intolerant community. Andrew advertised his understanding. He said people often needed to spend six years in the auspices of his teachings before they could accept that they had an ego. While new students might pay lip service to having an ego, it took time for them to see, know, feel and talk about that part of themselves. For this reason, incoming students had a long period of grace before being challenged and, even then, the challenges to their ego were gentle to begin with. It was impossible for anyone to become part of our community without knowing the score, without knowing the stand taken with ego.

Engaging with ego cannot be glorified or sanitised. It was often a boring, draining, war of attrition. While nearly all adults react predictably - either defensively or aggressively - to their ego being challenged, their subsequent responses – soon described - are unpredictable and irrational. Everyone involved in ego engagement has to bear the fact that no one knows when, or if, an individual's spiritual chemistry will change for the better. Ego engagement is also undignified. It often makes people act ridiculously and then, of course, look ridiculous. In our context, students allowed themselves to become monosyllabic, miserable, wraith-like creatures; walking vessels of resistance who would say anything or do anything to assert their wilful refusal to change. Those with the job of handling a peer's egoic responses could feel they were being drawn into an alternative reality, a hazy world of loopy associations and erratic emotions. At the same time, a student in the grip of their ego would use all manner of misleading tactics to create the impression of sincere intent to change, when none actually existed. All of Andrew's significant students spent time on both sides of this wearing process, as the community came to understand this deeply resistant part of human nature.

Ego engagement was also a thankless task. Speaking about battles with his students' egos, Andrew said, *"Usually, I lose."* In all serious confrontations there was a good chance the student would quit the community. And if, instead, they *'came through'* by choosing to side with the more honest part of themselves, a student would often bask in their newly-discovered spaciousness, valuing their experience over and above the lessons of the episode. In these instances, success would often be temporary and, even if permanent change were achieved, it would only represent incremental progress. With ego engagement, job satisfaction was unreliable and minimal.

In mainstream society, the law imposes appropriately weighted punishments to correct anti-social behaviour. In people's minds, therefore, powerful associations exist between misdemeanour, correctional action and the maintenance of acceptable behaviour. It would be easy to assume that the community's engagement with ego was a similar form of policing, but there is an important difference. The reason for caging ego was not to control destructive or immoral behaviour, because students didn't engage in such behaviour. Instead, we wanted to cage ego to create space within ourselves, to make ourselves the empty vessels through which something new could emerge.

The Community's History with Ego

At the start of Andrew's teaching career, the community was in bliss and ego was an untouched subject. But, from 1988 onward, students attempted to *'take-on'* each other's egos. In retrospect, this was like the blind giving the lame a hard time for their shortcomings. Students living together had house meetings. These could be distressing events lasting into the early hours, with students of assorted attainment expecting immediate ego submission from bewildered peers. The meetings sometimes resulted in lasting bad feeling. Ego was also addressed outside these meetings, in face-to-face conversations. In tough cases, when someone was in a state of resistant lock-down, that person would find themselves avoided and alone. With little experience and minimal supervision, students' engagement with each other's egos had a rocky beginning.

Between 1996 and 2002, the confrontation with ego came to a head. This chapter's upcoming case histories, and the content of future chapters, convey the nature of that confrontation. Broadly speaking, expertise developed during this intense period. A graph, plotting *intensity of engagement* on its vertical axis against *time* on its horizontal axis, would show a typical, bell-shaped curve, with its peak coinciding with the turn of the millennium.

Over time a lot was learnt. The development of hierarchy in the community brought order, humility and structure in many forms. This included, from 2002 onwards, 'holon' meetings of five or six peers. These same-gender, more personal, weekly meetings could be used for different purposes. They could take the form of free ranging discussions, or open-hearted conversations about students' experience, or they could be used as forums for examining individual egoic habits. Holon meetings greatly improved students' handling of each other's egos until, after the community's bumpy start, students eventually engaged with ego with informed precision.

What Was Learnt?

Formality was important. Dedicated meetings, with everyone informed of the meeting's purpose, were found to work better than spontaneous moments of individual feedback.

Experience of caging the ego was also important. Since caging the ego is, in essence, a matter of encouraging someone to accept greater responsibility, it worked better if the people addressing an individual had achieved the aspired-for level of responsibility themselves. This principle meant that students did not engage with the egos of people above them in the hierarchy. In fact, there was a second reason for this protocol: less-experienced students just didn't have the weight - the combination of status, maturity, experience and respect – to impact those above them in the hierarchy. No matter how willing both parties were, the chemistry of dealing with ego worked in one direction only.

In peer-to-peer situations, it proved more effective if two or more students spoke to an individual. That configuration created useful formality, from which came mutual respect. Clearly, a two-on-one situation created a risk of bullying, which maybe occurred at times, but that risk was offset by the development of trust, as follows:

If one's ego was being addressed, trusting the motives of one's advisers made a big difference to the effectiveness of the exchange. It was important to know that they were not acting from personal impulses, but from their desire to forward our collective endeavour. This was a precise matter. If they cared too much for one's feelings, the exercise became sugar-coated, inauthentic and ineffective. If they were remote, the exchange became inhuman and, again, unproductive. But if one's advisers genuinely cared about our community's work, everyone - and the issue at hand – became part of a bigger picture. In an ideal ego correctional meeting, everyone shared not only the same picture, but also the same obligation: to care for something greater than themselves.

Our expectations of what could be achieved were refined by experience. No one can instantly drop the habits of a lifetime, but it is possible to make effort and be interested. A quiet person might be told they were not contributing enough to our important meetings. For that person, caging their ego would mean setting aside whatever form of self-concern lay behind their non-partici-pation. To expect that person to become a leading speaker in the next meeting was too much to ask. But it was satisfying to see him or her making effort in the 'right' direction, especially if that effort was maintained. Ultimately, the situation we arrived at with regard to ego was one in which everyone knew they had an ego, knew its behaviour, and was making enough effort to keep it caged so that it was not an obstacle to our work.

The community's engagement with ego – as with many other human endeavours – shows how evolving awareness makes human beings more sensitive and effective. The early, roughshod years were fruitless in comparison to the informed later years, when the community knew how to contain even the immediate, reactive defensiveness of ego. Eventually, students knew what was involved in ego engagement. From that knowledge arose a common moral standard of care: students were no longer willing to spoil the beautiful life we shared by taking themselves, their peers, or our joint enterprise into a prolonged, undignified stand-off. Through hard-won experience, we learnt that ego denies a very simple truth: *transcendence requires great effort.*

Andrew's Responses to Ego

In day-to-day interactions, Andrew sensed, but did not respond to, ego. When walking among us, or in conversation, or when he was teaching, he would notice signs of ego but ignore them. Observing him respond, one could see him weave his way through his students' different states of mind with a seemingly instinctive sense of where their allegiances lay. These allegiances could quickly change, from *freedom* to *ego* and vice versa, so it was always fascinating to witness Andrew's fluid responses when he was with us.

When Andrew was teaching – either in public or to his students – he didn't allow ego to get a foothold in dialogues. If students clammed-up in formal meetings, Andrew would not let the situation dry up; he would say *"Don't keep me waiting,"* and force a student to say something that would keep the conversation alive. If we received a message from Andrew, via his assistant, he would expect a reply within hours, not days. Students gave each other time when dealing with ego, but Andrew either instinctively avoided ego, or pounced upon it. He didn't allow it to establish momentum. His outward responses seemed to mirror his inner responses. For example, he appeared to pass over anything arising in his own mind that he identified as being unfree.

Did Andrew have an ego? This is a useful question. Many people insist that he did, but, as students, the question would not have arisen in our minds. We would have felt the motive behind the question to be greedy and cynical, and that the question itself was unconsciously sacrilegious. I have tried to explain students' unquestioning relationship to Andrew in Chapter 10. Here, I can add that we only experienced him as a forward-leaning force. We didn't experience him withholding from the call of evolution, we saw him as surrendered to it. In this respect, because he didn't exhibit self-concern, he was, in the eyes of his students, without self-concern. Others might wonder whether thoughts and feelings arising in Andrew's mind were selfless but, in Andrew's teachings, thought and feeling have only the value they are given. So, the answer to the question *Did Andrew have an ego?* depends on the value given to thought and feeling, versus the value given to action. *"You are what you do,"* Andrew used to say. Later in this book, we shall see that Andrew's concerns changed during the community's dissolution.

If ego were imagined as the criminal element in society, upper-core students would be county magistrates, the senior students would be circuit judges, and Andrew would be the supreme court. He dealt with the tough cases that couldn't be handled at lower levels. These cases might involve a group of students that had settled into a dull routine, or individual core students who were making a drama of their experience, or senior students whose sense of responsibility had relaxed. When a situation developed to the point that Andrew had to step in - usually after a lot of talking had failed - events could become colourful.

Case Histories

I'd like to reiterate; I am aware some readers will dislike this section.

A whole chapter devoted to the community's engagement with ego might create the impression that it was the main subject of our lives. At times it was but, mostly, it was just one of many activities. Leafing through a newspaper, one can see a range of headlines. Had *The Foxhollow News* existed, ego engagement would have been one of many issues reported upon. Some stories selected from the community's twenty-seven-year history would, quite rightly, have made major headlines, but lesser incidents would have been placed on the inner pages, or among Letters To the Editor. The following case histories exhibit this range.

'German student receives pork chops,' would be a lesser headline. In this story, Andrew sent a brash, muscle-bound young man a Tiffany gift-wrapped box containing two uncooked pork chops; a reflection of the student's curt and gross-minded manner. Another report would have centred on Emma, an overly sensuous English woman. In her movements and speech, she delivered an inviting message, inappropriate to our community. Andrew arranged for her female peers to decorate her bedroom as a boudoir, and for them to strip down to the minimals and pamper Emma while mimicking her seductress's ways. The result was that Emma dropped her exaggerated allure. 'Hypochondriac lies on mattress,' might also have drawn attention. This incident involved Tess, a student living in Boston. The prospect of helping with weekend practical work at Foxhollow reliably made her feel sick, so she was told to lie on a mattress in the midst of her colleagues as they tidied the attic of the manor house. I believe this event made Tess less resistant to practical chores.

As well as tailored responses, Andrew had standard methods of engaging with his students' egos. He might apply pressure by excluding a student from formal meetings, or from the manor house, or from the whole Foxhollow property. In a few cases, he sent senior students to the EnlightenNext Centre in Sydney, Australia, for months and even years. As described in the previous chapter, Ambrose was on walkabout for ten years. In a similar situation an upper-core student, Rhett, lived within range of Foxhollow, exiled but connected, for five years. These graduated responses by Andrew created positive tension within students, between their ego's resistance and their desire for spiritual freedom. This tension was an essential element in the work of our community. It benefited both individual students, who slowly matured, and the whole community, which felt the need to be alert and make effort.

Having students thrown in Laurel Lake was one of Andrew's short-and-sharp responses. I can convey the respectful attitude with which this was done. Baraz, a student, was like an Iranian prince. He was smooth-talking, hypnotic and handsome. I imagined him to be Svengali's nicer brother. Baraz was failing to meet his proven standard of responsibility. He was spiritually stuck. The trip to the lake was a formal event. Four men and Baraz drove there in silence; we took care of his shoes, expensive watch and classy wallet, gripped one limb each, and swung him into the lake on the count of three. Once he had climbed out, we wrapped him in a blanket. He thanked us, and we drove back to the manor house. Like all the following case histories, Baraz was not instantly restored to the best of himself. But the event brought him out of an isolated, slow decline and put him in contact with his teacher and his peers.

Seth was a smart guy, but he was casual, arrogant and immune to criticism. He had been like this for years. Earnest conversations over more than a decade had not impacted these traits. A 'beating' was arranged, either in consultation with Andrew or instructed by him. This involved - at an arranged time and place, and with Seth's expectation - six men wrestling him to the floor, pinning him down and subjecting him to five minutes of miniature, withheld 'rabbit' punches to safe areas of his body. We were shown how to do this so that Seth would experience being overpowered and pummelled, but without injury or pain. A number of these harmless but vigorous beatings occurred, at appointed hours until, one day, the activity was changed to pampering. Seth found our soothing strokes and gentle caresses intolerable and he asked if we could revert to "*having a scrap.*" As with Baraz, Seth did not change dramatically afterwards, but the episode placed his arrogance on an open stage, making it a matter of common knowledge and containment.

Harvey was a polymath, an effusive genius, congenial and slightly overweight. He had the bearing of a supremely self-assured man. Imagine a fellow with John Wayne's build and confidence, triple his IQ, remove his gun belt and add irony to his humour. Andrew gave him the spiritual name 'H.G.', standing for *His Greatness*. He was easy to love, but also rather loved himself. Harvey was fascinating to listen to. He was a composer of language and music and, when speaking, his talents would synthesise to become a mesmerising show of eloquence. Listeners would be drawn into his spellbinding oratory, but then, at a certain point, they would realise that he, too, had been drawn into it. In an amazing, cogs-turning exhibition of narcissism, onlookers would see Harvey's attention contract and seemingly wreathe around his own unfolding monologue. Before long, members of his audience would find themselves stranded, mere spectators of Harvey's self-absorbed stardom.

Although technically an upper-core student, Harvey lived in a rarefied world of his own. In both his mind and the minds of others, his genius put him on a par with Andrew, and they had a friendship unavailable to other students of lesser intelligence. However, Harvey also had an ego proportionate to John Wayne's, with which Andrew had to engage.

In 1998, while travelling, Harvey met a young woman with a blossoming interest in Andrew's teachings. She was a successful businesswoman, a single mother and a Mormon. Later, she was a student at Foxhollow. Harvey had an indulgent side to him and he mixed his charismatic nurturing of this woman's spiritual interest with his physical interest in her. This was a heinous crime by our standards. Our informal protocol frowned upon close, platonic friendships with newcomers, because such friendships interfered with a precious, formative process. Having sex with a fledging spiritual aspirant was an extreme breach of our ethical code but, to a man with HG's self-assurance, it was probably – in his eyes - just part of an independent lifestyle.

Andrew's response was to confine Harvey to his room for three days. His meals were taken to him but, for company, he had only an inflatable sex doll, pile of pornographic magazines, and bottle of whiskey. The aim was for Harvey to reflect on his indulgent behaviour. He noticeably mellowed afterwards.

Selina was from Texas. Andrew said that, of all his women students, she had travelled the furthest into the impersonal dimension of his teachings. This meant she had achieved the most spacious relationship to her experience. As a result, she was a powerful leader in the community between 1995 and 2001. She was invigorating to be around: direct, simple, punchy and decisive. She pushed weights in the gym with vigour, broke sweat, and had a swift and effective management style. I loved her; during her years as a leader she truly flew the flag of freedom, beyond gender, and was a great inspiration to many of us. Her demeanour was bright, eager and alert, and she freely expressed her humour.

In retrospect, I think the leading women at that time – who rose to prominence one by one - found themselves isolated. Their experience of enlightenment took them far beyond their peers, creating unseen tension between their level of attainment and that of the women around them. A small event could then catalyse the leader's return to the common centre of gravity. This would explain Selina's trajectory, and the trajectory of women who came before and after her. It would have been a small matter that grounded her but, from Andrew's point of view, her return to a contracted condition of self-concern was a disaster. He was putting great effort into developing a stable, supportive hierarchy that would contain an upward-moving developmental current, beneficial to our work. The collapse of a brilliant leader and, instead, the depressing presence of a fallen star, was exactly what he didn't want.

In response to this predicament, Andrew put pressure on Selina, pushing her to recover her trail-blazing role. This pressure - after many attempts at spiritual resuscitation - culminated in her office being moved to the basement of the manor house, where the janitorial and kitchen supplies were stored. To portray the negativity of her ego's resistance, her office was painted in devilish blacks and reds. Ultimately, as happened with many students at the time, she did not regain the relationship to her experience that had made her such an inspiring leader.

Effects on the Community's Culture

The community's engagement with ego gave it an essential edge. Awareness of ego kept everyone on their toes, awake to its movement within themselves and others. It made us realise we were not living a moderate life and gave us the idea – for better or worse – that we were an elite outfit. Knowledge of ego was also unifying. We knew everyone's mettle would be tempered by their struggle with the same negative force. Although the confrontation with ego reduced our numbers, we were proud of our engagement with what we regarded as a perennial spiritual obstacle.

Andrew's unyielding stand against ego created the circumstances for profound change. It turned the community into a pressure cooker. The need to maintain this transformative pressure meant that neither Andrew nor his students could condone someone's choice to leave the community. Had an open back door existed, students would have made use of it at potentially fruitful moments of crisis. Instead of an easy exit, there was – and I would say there had to be - a final backstop.

The form of this backstop was not material; students could physically leave Foxhollow whenever they chose. Instead, three powerful matters of integrity combined to form an emotional barrier facing students who wanted to leave. The first was their own commitment to becoming spiritually free. The second was our collective commitment to our work. The third was Andrew's dedication to his role. If a student chose to leave, they had to abandon a profound personal commitment, walk away from the community and turn their back on their teacher.

Knowledge of the ramifications of a student's choice to leave gave Andrew and his students a view on that choice, and an attitude to it. The view was that leaving the community was a drastic and possibly irrevocable action, damaging to the student and to our endeavour. The attitude was one of intolerance; it had to be, because, as stated before, leniency would have facilitated students' compromise. Hence the backstop - as I'm calling it – had two components: a predictable reaction (consternation); and an attitude (strong disapproval). Sometimes, in combination, these took the form of condemnation. At other times, Andrew might shake his head and give a one-sentence summary of the reasons why a student had chosen to leave. I must add, to round out this difficult subject, that the minority of students who later returned were welcomed, circumspectly but warmly.

Success or Failure?

Before judging the success of the community's engagement with ego, I think two matters should be borne in mind. Firstly, the context of the engagement. Secondly, the credibility of strongly-held alternative ideas.

The context, transcendent spirituality, is neither within human control nor entirely beyond it. On the one hand, Spirit stands aloof from human siege and our attempts to lean ladders against its walls do not predictably succeed. On the other hand, the law of cause and effect can be relied upon and we can confidently say that human effort improves our chances of entering a new, enlightened citadel. Egoic impulses are an inevitable feature of this context and, unsurprisingly, the same hit-and-miss success rate is found: no practices guarantee victory, yet the intention to cage ego does produce results. When judging the community's success or failure with ego, the uncontrollable nature of transcendent spirituality needs to be borne in mind.

Many people hold strong ideas about the transformative power of sympathy, empathy and unconditional love. These ideas conflict with the community's response to ego, raising the questions: *Was it necessary to confront ego so directly? Couldn't people have been coaxed and encouraged through their difficulties?* Our understanding was that sympathetic approaches would be ineffective and endless. We saw ego as an anti-transcendent force that would take any shape and accept any form of attention, as long as it could continue to do its work: keeping an individual in a contracted state of mind. We thought that sympathy, empathy and unconditional love suited ego very nicely.

To clarify, our view on this was as follows. Transcendent spirituality is a niche interest. People interested in transcendence have a rare desire - they seek what might be called a miraculous relationship to life. The desire for a miraculous relationship to life is different from the desire for a state of untroubled equanimity which, we thought, is many people's goal. Sympathy, empathy and unconditional love might be useful in the pursuit of untroubled equanimity, but our understanding was that these empathetic emotions did not contain the discipline necessary to lift someone into a miraculous relationship to life.

Success or Failure? I think expertise is hard won. I can see how, in my life, I repeatedly had to reach beyond myself to learn what I needed. Without venturing into the unknown, I would never have acquired useful capabilities. In relation to ego, Andrew and the community achieved their goal: sufficient strength to cage this well-known spiritual foe. He and his community acquired extensive experience of the subject, at great human cost. In my opinion, everyone involved is due great credit. We struggled for a decade, failing repeatedly, but the result was that the community did not cower in the face of ego; we found a way to cage it.

Hal Blacker's 'A' List

Hal Blacker's 'A' List has played an important role in discrediting Andrew Cohen's reputation, and the reputations of his teachings and teaching work. Given the purpose of this book, I feel I should comment upon it, and this chapter feels like the appropriate place to do so.

That said, I think Hal Blacker's 'A' List (henceforth simply 'the List') deserves a more comprehensive response than I have space for here. So, I have decided to write a separate book which will set context for, and respond to, every item on the List. This future book, titled *A Rebuttal of Hal Blacker's 'A' List*, will be available on or before December 1st 2021. It will be revised twice, at six-month intervals, and I hereby issue an open invitation for assistance in scrutinising the List and composing my *Rebuttal*. (I can be contacted by email: tm@invokingtheas.com)

Hal Blacker was an upper-core student of Andrew's until the community moved to Foxhollow in 1996. As a student, he was an editor of *What is Enlightenment?* magazine. He is a lawyer, registered in California, and a spiritual teacher under his banner REAL DHARMA (his capitals). The website for REAL DHARMA lists his authorisation to teach in the traditions and lineages of Advaita Vedanta and Tibetan Buddhist Nyingma Dzogchen.

The full title of the List is, *The "A" List of Andrew Cohen, a Catalog of Trauma and Abuse*. In his introduction, Hal Blacker makes clear that the list is only representative, *"not exhaustive,"* of the trauma and abuse committed - in his view - by Andrew Cohen. He also says that all acts on the list have been *"reported, verified and corroborated by first person witnesses."*

The list has fifty entries, divided into five categories. For example, Category 1 has the title *Physical Abuse*; Category 2, *Financial Exploitation*, etc. Regarding the purpose of the list, he writes:

"It is hoped that this list will aide [sic] former students in coming to terms with their history and trauma, and that it will serve as a warning and wake-up call to those who are currently engaged with Andrew Cohen." Hal Blacker proceeds to name six of Andrew Cohen's top students - those who have embarked on their own spiritual vocations - plus *"the Integral Community and others."* Thereby, he declares his hope that his List will warn people away from everything and everyone connected to Andrew Cohen.

As I believe is intended, Hal Blacker's List is shocking and persuasive. Purely a prosecutor's document, it does not attempt to present context, mitigating circumstances or counter-arguments. Reading it, I am repelled, not so much by the content of the List, but by the author's zealous intent.

The List also provides a learning experience; a window into a lawyer's mind. So much is made of so little. I can recognise the origin of all entries except four, yet, by various emphases and inferences, Hal Blacker builds a terrible picture of what was, to me, a well-meant endeavour. In his descriptions, mistakes become punishments, creative responses are given devilish intent, occasional events become prevailing practices, and retrospective anger is valued more than feelings felt at the time. Without doubt, his list is a skilful construction.

This book contains many stories that either are, or could be, taken and included on the List. The case studies in this chapter are examples, as are accounts in future chapters. Pioneering work proceeds by trial and error, and is - evidently - vulnerable to bystander criticism. To illustrate the content and character of the List, I am going to take two entries and contrast the List's description with my understanding of the same event. The first entry is by far the most extreme in the history of the community. The second is the most baseless.

John and the Prostitutes

The List's account: Under Part 3: Violation of Sexual and Reproductive Rights and Privacy, and Interference with Family and Personal Relationships

"Requiring a student to visit prostitutes repeatedly over a several week period and to provide detailed faxed reports on these visits to Cohen, despite the student strongly expressing his strong disgust and emotional trauma over having to do this and daily begging Cohen to be allowed to stop. Witnesses saw Cohen reading and listening to the reports of the prostitute visits with great interest, enjoying and laughing at them."

My understanding

John was a senior student of many years standing. He was a prominent, respected and experienced figure among Andrew's students. Andrew needed him to lead one of the community's important Centres. This meant that John was separated from his girlfriend, who stayed in the Foxhollow community. In a fit of petulance John, secretly and of his own choice, visited prostitutes.

Once this was discovered by John's peers and found to be something John was unwilling to give-up, Andrew had a dilemma: one of his highest-profile students was engaged in addictive behaviour damaging to himself, and threatening the reputation of Andrew's teaching work. Andrew decided to try and achieve a catharsis by saturating John in his chosen indulgence and, with John's agreement, a number of further prostitute visits was decided upon. The result? No change in John. So, Andrew instructed John to make a second set of visits. These were also unsuccessful and the trial came to an end. Andrew did receive faxed reports from John, he did read them with interest, and he does remember laughing at some points in the proceedings in the company of students who, at the time, were trusted.

The Ladies in the Lake

The List's account: Under Part 1: Physical Abuse

"Having women repeatedly do full-immersion prostrations in a freezing cold lake in New England in the autumn (on EnlightenNext's Foxhollow premises) as penance for perceived faults and 'women's conditioning,' some to the point of hypothermia, delirium and unconsciousness. Some women had to be rescued or helped from the lake, and some developed illnesses afterwards. Some women were berated and ordered to repeat their attempts to complete a required number of prostrations despite having become delirious or suffering hypothermia. No medical care was provided for women who passed out, suffered hypothermia or became ill, even though there was a doctor in the community and on the Foxhollow premises."

My understanding

Andrew was informed that a group of women had decided to do prostrations in the lake. This was not an unusual activity at that period in the community's history. From his point of view, it was their decision. He had not suggested the idea to the women, or issued an instruction, and he presumed that, being adults, they would look after all aspects of an event they had elected to do. The event was on the periphery of his awareness that day. No medical emergencies were reported to him afterwards, no doctors or ambulances were called, no one had to go to hospital, there were no lasting injuries. He was surprised, years later, when the incident was selected as an example of his harsh treatment. At the time it had passed without notice.

Summary

The community's engagement with ego was an unpleasant matter at the time and, today, it is a contentious issue. Former students hold a range of attitudes, from loudly critical to quietly admiring. Some feel damaged by their experience, others are deeply grateful. Meanwhile, the responses of onlookers have, so far, revealed a defining threshold. People recognise the existence of ego and see the widespread problems it causes at all levels of civilisation but, invariably, they stall at the threshold we reached in the community. That threshold appeared when every reasonable step had been taken and repeated for many years. We were then faced with a choice: either admit defeat, or take unreasonable action. We crossed that threshold. As is generally known – and evident in this chapter – unreasonable action can achieve breakthroughs or create chaos. Personally, favouring bravery over caution, I'm happy we engaged with ego in the way that we did. More importantly, we would not have invoked the Authentic Self by playing safe.

Chapter 16

Three Key People

The previous chapter describes the community's engagement with a common human obstacle: ego. In contrast, this chapter centres upon the individual challenges and progressions of three key figures. Within this more personal context, I hope to capture further features of community life and explain students' relationships with one another. The intimacy between students was distinctive. Below, I describe what that intimacy was based upon and, in Chapter 19, I write about the interactions it engendered.

Although I haven't seen the people selected for this chapter for many years, I still feel a profound bond with them. This, perhaps surprisingly, might be because that bond was not one of personal love; it was never a one-to-one connection, characterised by personal feelings and intimate knowledge. Instead, our bond was always based on our commitment to a third party. At first, it was to Andrew himself; later, it was to our shared spiritual narrative, or perspective. I believe this kind of union shows how human beings can be deeply connected, not by blood ties, shared history or day-to-day contact, but by commitment to a common purpose. A noticeable and, some might say, sacred feature of this bond is that it is not time-dependent: by sharing the same narrative, people can unite very quickly, while neither geographic distance nor periods of separation seem to weaken that union.

Andrew's students were united in a perspective. We knew of each other's relationship to our overarching, common reference but, on other normally familiar matters, we were quite ignorant of one another. For example, we often knew nothing about each other's family background, siblings, parents' occupations, or early life history. No one at Foxhollow would have known that my father was a priest who died when I was six years old. Our relationships had another unusual feature: we didn't try to explain our strengths and weaknesses. That meant we didn't examine each other's life stories. Instead, we each accepted and lived with the demand to change any behaviour detrimental to our work.

Our minimal interest in each other's personal stories might leave some readers perplexed, and certainly there is now criticism by ex-students and others about the community's lack of attention to personal psychology. But, as Andrew's students, we understood that we lived in a transcendent paradigm, not a psychological paradigm, and that our individual responsibility was to change any hindrances we brought with us. In the life we were living, we didn't have the time or the interest to root around in our interior compositions. We were expected to shoulder shortcomings, rise up and join together in the pursuit of a common goal.

My affection and admiration for the three people described below are, therefore, based on my knowledge of the journeys they made within Andrew's teaching work. My description of Alka, Andrew's wife, focusses on her life with him, whereas the passages on Stathan and Bernard are stories of change. All three people were easy to choose. They lived and worked closely with Andrew, and – to me – they were exciting people, each colourful in their own way.

Alka

Alka had sterling qualities. She had gravitas. She lived in the eye of an evolutionary storm for twenty-seven years, and she had greater commitment to Andrew's teaching work than many of his other students. She was a beautiful woman, body and soul, who made many sacrifices while fulfilling her role as Andrew's wife. With that status came greater demands, greater expectations and greater temptations than most of us had to handle. In my view, looking back on her contribution to our work, she is an unsung heroine.

As I have said, students generally knew little about each other's backgrounds. But, with Alka, we knew even less. She was, perhaps, a private person by nature. She also had to uphold the dignity of her position as Andrew's wife, which meant that aspects of her life were, quite reasonably, not matters for common discussion. Moreover, the community held the idea that Asian people – especially those from the upper-middle-class – were inscrutable. This, if true, was another reason why Alka was one step removed. My following description has, therefore, been drawn from miscellaneous sources: from fragments of information, intuitive deductions, memories of small events, and my recollections of her responses and comments.

I deduced that Alka came from a progressive family. She had two sisters, who had moved to America and married American men, and a strong mother, who lived independently in Mumbai. Alka told me that, as a young woman, she had been a triathlete. Her tough workouts in Foxhollow's gym suggested this was true. She had clearly been a youthful, independent, spiritual seeker, who chose to marry Andrew - her boyfriend before his enlightenment - in his earliest days as a spiritual teacher.

At Foxhollow, Alka loved to work in the gardens. Each year, she organised a small army of volunteers to rake pine needles from acres of grass, and with limited resources she cultivated the fruit trees and flower beds that gave the property flashes of eye-catching colour. When living at Foxhollow, Alka did spiritual practice with other students and attended important student meetings. She also cared for the home she shared with Andrew and organised most of his travel needs.

She could be authoritative, even haughty, when organising logistical matters. This was a useful characteristic at Indian train stations, where luggage had to be ferried through crowds, and perhaps that quintessential Indian scenario points to the origin of that trait in her. She also, rumour had it, enjoyed sweets and chocolate; perhaps another Indian habit? On a few occasions, I had to visit Andrew and Alka in their home for practical reasons and, in that relaxed situation, she was often carefree, boisterous, irreverent and slightly flirtatious.

Andrew and Alka looked good as a couple. Both were of slightly less than average height, so their figures matched nicely. They dressed well, in a modern style, and, because Andrew's glossy dark hair and olive skin made him look Indian (Indians assumed he was Indian), there was a pleasing harmony to their appearance. They also worked well together in an everyday, practical sense, moving at the same pace, having shared tastes, and knowing each other very well.

It cannot have been easy being Andrew's wife. Alka was essentially a student like the rest of us, chipping away at her resistance to spiritual freedom. Yet she lived with her teacher, who ceaselessly expressed and effortlessly revelled in that freedom. Being around Andrew – for any of us - was mostly a sublime, uplifting experience, but it could be very demanding and, at times, unbearable. Alka would have experienced strong doses of both extremes.

Alka usually travelled with Andrew and, over the years, she enjoyed the benefits of his varied itineraries. He was invited to speak to spiritual communities, such as Esalen, in California, and at a variety of international conferences; for example, The World Parliament of Religions (Chap 22). As founding editor of the magazine, he met and interviewed a wide range of people, from heavyweight boxer Evander Holyfield to spiritual avatar Ammachi. Andrew's teaching trips also involved worldwide travel, as he moved between EnlightenNext's Centres. Anyone travelling with Andrew experienced many contrasting cultures and the diverse responses of different nations to his public teaching events. For his students these tours were, in part, dazzling and enlivening. The freedom from routine, the stimulation of new environments, the food, people, parties, picnics and gatherings were all infused with happiness. Being on the road with Andrew could be a delightful life. A life that Alka would often have enjoyed.

On the other hand, these teaching trips could be gruelling. As well as managing endless travel logistics, adjusting to new environments and being drained by repeated flights, there was often spiritual work to do in each community. Alka, and anyone travelling with Andrew, were not just visitors to foreign Centres. The community's work was one integrated endeavour, and travelling students were expected to get involved in the transformative meetings stimulated by Andrew. These formal men's and women's meetings, described in Chapter 13 and later in this book, were often deeply taxing, especially when a result – such as closer communion, or a more profound understanding of a subject - was expected before Andrew moved on.

As the wife of a renowned teacher, Alka had to face people's expectations. Andrew had a New Yorker's outgoing personality, whereas Alka had upper-class Indian reserve; her responses were measured and considered. If people expected Alka to be a female form of Andrew, it could take time for them to reconcile the difference. Likewise, there was perhaps an expectation that Alka would have a leading voice, or *the* leading voice, among the women students and the student body as a whole. However, this expectation, over the years, was not fully realised. Instead, her spiritual strengths were traditional Indian strengths, which centred on her inner enlightened values - stillness, emptiness, detachment - and it was to this dimension of our life, the Being dimension of enlightenment, that she contributed.

Alka's spiritual strengths were shared by other students who had met Andrew in the first years of his teaching career. This generation of students had either come from western Buddhist backgrounds or they had been involved in the 1960s' burgeoning interest in eastern spirituality. They often remained – I think it's fair to say - rooted in Mother India's historic embodiment of the here and now. Alka not only brought this, her nation's spiritual depth, to our community's culture, she provided another valuable asset. As one of only two remaining members of the enraptured group that gathered around Andrew in Rishikesh in 1986, she represented the very first days of Andrew's teaching work. She was, therefore, someone whose presence, alone, reminded us of the origin and many phases of his work.

A significant event gives a little more insight into Alka. As mentioned before, Andrew scrutinised his leading students more closely than any others. This was common knowledge, and one reason why they were respected. In 1998, when the community had adjusted to living at Foxhollow, Andrew asked his leading students to take more independent responsibility. Alka's group of senior women did not respond sufficiently to his request. Raising the stakes, Andrew instructed them to live together, still on the Foxhollow property, but apart from their partners, including him.

At the time, this was felt to be a draconian change of status and living arrangements. Other students, somewhat settled into an enjoyable new life, were shocked. Alka's group of five women went from being admired, elevated students to whom one deferred, to being seen as a problem group, working in the kitchen and separated from their partners.

The change in Alka's status prompted a memorable moment of vulnerability, when she tearfully told me that she had never believed Andrew would exert this kind of pressure on her, because she was his wife. That she was in tears in front of me, a man, with whom she had no closer relationship than anyone else, points to how shocked she was. I suggest the incident shows how Alka – like the community at that time – was resting in her sense of worldly security. In her case, she was relying upon the security that came - she thought - with her status. Clearly, the event also reveals an emotional person existing behind her customary composure.

The incident is significant for two further reasons. Firstly, I think the shock felt by the community illustrates how any society is unnerved when its leaders are seen to be fallible. Secondly, the incident can – in retrospect - be seen as the first tremor of a much greater confrontation. The story of that confrontation continues in Chapter 19, *The Women*.

My lasting memory of Alka is of her quietly organising something in the manor house at Foxhollow. Most likely she would be carefully arranging something for Andrew, while carrying her black Longchamp Le Pliage bag, and manoeuvring Andrew's beloved, yet wilful Yorkshire terrier, Kensho, on his lead. In the grand scheme of things, I see that Alka sacrificed a lot of personal preferences (as we all did) to willingly and tirelessly support Andrew's teaching work. I believe she is due more recognition than she has been shown hitherto.

Stathan

Stathan was a man whose capabilities made one question whether he belonged to our species: he was multi-lingual, a martial artist, practised in various healing disciplines, ultra-fit, never ill, muscular, informed, and he had organisational skills that could have marshalled the troops of an invasion force. He had the physique of a middleweight boxer: solidly built and six feet tall. His expression, while generally serious, or even grim, could easily break into a surprisingly radiant smile.

Stathan was not universally liked. This is not a euphemism for saying he wasn't liked at all, but anyone wanting to see themselves as top dog in their field had trouble with Stathan, because they were likely to be overshadowed by his attention to detail and decisive approach to life. I saw him as something of a hero, not just for his comprehensive competence, but also because, during his twenty years as Andrew's student, he underwent a phenomenal transformation.

I first met Stathan in 1994, in Pokhara, Nepal, following Andrew's yearly retreat in Bodh Gaya. I was not yet Andrew's student, unlike Stathan, who had moved to Marin from his native Holland over a year before. In Pokhara four men – Stathan, Joe, Jack and I - made a plan. We would take a five-day recreational trek along the famous Apple Pie Trail, a journey that started high in the Annapurna Massif area of the Himalayas and descended back to Pokhara.

I had high hopes for this trek. I loved walking and, seen from Pokhara, the mountain range looked beautiful and challenging. I imagined that we, the four trekkers, would become a convivial group. But my hopes were soon dented. Stathan had spotted that I sat awkwardly in meditation, and he and the others quizzed me on the condition of my troublesome knee. *"That's a diligent question,"* I thought. But their military-style interrogation, and stern warnings that a tough attitude would be taken towards stragglers, were disturbing. Nevertheless, I assured them all would be well, and we boarded the tiny plane that took us up to base camp.

Indeed, all was well for the three of us who walked together: Joe was a little fussy about the micro-regulation of his body temperature; Jack used a supply of tall stories to support his chosen identity as a born-tough American frontiersman; while I and my well-behaved knee quietly made the most of the scenery. The trail was beautiful, we kept to our schedule, and met for dinner.

Aside from these evening meals, Stathan was hardly seen. Only when the trail gave a vista stretching three miles ahead could we catch a glimpse of his silhouette. At agreed meeting-points he made short, dismissive comments about the poor quality of this or that and, in private, he efficiently listed Joe's and Jack's character faults. Then he would punctually hit the trail once again. These daytime absences and condemning critiques continued throughout the trek, forming an oppressive cloud over our journey, which concluded without mishap or any sense of camaraderie.

When I moved to Marin a year and a half later, Stathan was a changed man: an asset to the community. He had his own acupuncture practice, used by many students, and Andrew trusted Stathan's advice on his own health. Stathan was still a self-reliant loner - for example, he was the only person to ride a motorcycle - but he was significantly more integrated in the community than when he had arrived. He had also made progress with what Andrew termed his *'latent violence'*.

Earlier in his life, Stathan had led a Jekyll and Hyde existence. By day, he ran an alternative healing practice and, by night, he spent time with a group of men who often brawled in bars and clubs. In the community, knowledge of Stathan's previous double life was neither concealed nor highlighted. All we, his fellow students, knew, was that he could be too functional, condemning, cut-off and heavy-handed. We were watchful of, and sensitive to, his management of those traits. We had no knowledge of why Stathan's early life had made him partly a healer and partly a fighter. Andrew had identified Stathan's latent violence, and our concern – identical to our expectations of every student - was that he took care of his negative impulses and gave only the best of himself.

On this point, giving the best of himself, I remember a unique event. Stathan is the only person I have seen break free of ego by physical effort. As described before, ego suffocates. It suffocates the soul, grips the heart, throttles the airways and paralyses the rational mind. At full strength, ego acts like a kind of seizure, turning people into wraiths. Usually, it takes time for this kind of paralysis to relax its grip but, in a men's meeting in the middle of a year-long period of intensity (Chap 20), Stathan physically battled his way out his ego's stranglehold. He successfully met like with like. He took his martial artist's practised use of force and applied it, inwardly, to overcoming his ego. Seeing his struggle reminded me of courtroom scenes, in which a previously dishonest witness decides to align with their conscience and then fights to voice the truth. In this case, Stathan, with gritty intention - that manifested as face contortions, disordered speech, and gasping and grunting - broke free from his ego's negative grip to let out his true feelings of frustration.

Working together was always a learning experience. This was especially true when we organised our big annual retreats. Suitable venues in Europe, India and America had to be found, and contracts negotiated. Many streams of practical preparation had to be coordinated: large amounts of money were involved; Andrew had to be happy with the teaching hall; the chairs had to be comfortable; the air-conditioning had to work, and do so silently; and, if the venue had a kitchen, it had to be inaudible. Managing these issues and the small multitude of people involved was Stathan's work, and he was masterful in the role.

In particular, students' expectations of consensus management have to be handled when organising a spiritual community. Many people want to have their say, but we soon learned the value of having just one recognised authority. Without that person, accountability fragments and inertia sets in. Stathan was skilled at holding sole authority. He did this by keeping his cards close to his chest and maintaining direct contact with Andrew. This made it hard for other students to undermine Stathan's overall control and while, in theory, he could have made big unilateral mistakes, this seldom happened. Would-be complainants were, on the whole, silenced by Stathan's efficiency.

As well as managing Andrew's public retreats, Stathan oversaw his personal security. Ninety-five percent of the time this just involved assessing situations and monitoring peaceful events. But, at city teachings, there was the possibility that unstable people might attend and, on longer public retreats, people occasionally became hysterical. Once, in the south of France, someone ran from the teaching tent, stripping naked, up into the mountains. Another time, in India, an unstable young American man walked through the audience towards Andrew's teaching platform wailing, "*I just want to look into your eyes.*" He had to be restrained. Peculiar behaviour was uncommon, but it was an ever-present possibility, and it was a godsend to have Stathan, a vigilant martial artist, overseeing this essential facet of Andrew's work.

Sometimes – albeit rarely - there were real dangers. On one occasion, Andrew's life was threatened. In the late spring of 2010, a disturbed man from St Louis, Missouri, USA, declared his intention to harm two named, spiritual teachers. Andrew's name was second on his list. Fortunately, the man was quickly caught and arrested but, for many days, an awful predatory threat hung over Foxhollow, and we were grateful for the security training and other preparations arranged by Stathan during the preceding years.

During twenty years as Andrew's student, Stathan changed from loner to leader. This change was the product of an interplay between his self-discipline and the standards he was held to by the community. Through self-scrutiny, he came to know his best and worst qualities, the strength of his ego, and his desire to participate in evolution. Guided by Andrew, the community provided a rising bar, an ever-developing standard of care for an overarching purpose. This demanding context called on the best in Stathan and, when he responded, he changed. He rose from the ranks and became head of the Amsterdam Centre and, in 2013, he was one of the five senior students who challenged Andrew's authority (Chap 23).

Andrew and Stathan had a strong friendship. I think Andrew was grateful for Stathan's competence and he trusted his practical advice. Andrew responded to the intensity of Stathan's character by making space around it, rather than fighting it. Over time, Stathan was victorious; his latent violence became just a memory.

Bernard

I had an unexpected experience when I first met Andrew in Bodh Gaya, in 1992. It came from observing the twenty-five close students – Sangha members – who accompanied him. By association with Andrew, they carried some of his aura, including the conviction that life can be experienced as radically positive. Their aspiration and active seeking for this positivity, together with their physical presence, strengthened Andrew's status as a teacher. Not only did I see Andrew embodying the goal, but I saw a substantial number of his students grappling with real spiritual challenges as they reached towards his realisation. As described in my Prologue, I was impressed by Andrew. But I was also unexpectedly impacted by seeing people like myself genuinely seeking for enlightenment.

Over time, I've become aware how encouraging it is to see someone similar to oneself aspire to, or attain, enlightenment. The achievement of a person comparable to oneself acts as an antidote to the ego's habit of creating distance. The ego creates distance by deifying a teacher while insisting upon personal hopelessness, thereby making enlightenment a noble but futile aspiration. In contrast, seeing the success of a peer raises the possibility of being enlightened oneself.

Bernard exemplified this phenomenon. At first, he was a student like me but, in my opinion, he became the most enlightened person in our community besides Andrew. For a long time he was just part of the pack, a member of our group of upper-core men who lived through Foxhollow's turbulent years, 1998 – 2002. Within that group there were shades of difference. Bernard was marginally more of a captain than a foot soldier but, functionally, we were one group with one name, engaged in one endeavour. This unity eventually broke apart (Chaps 20/21) and, among the many changes at that time, Bernard emerged as a leader. I will soon describe his transformation, but first I'd like to give a pen portrait.

Bernard, although American, had Portuguese roots, making his appearance and demeanour different from his American peers. He was of average height, with a trademark feature: a barrel chest. His substantial upper torso was - I thought - endearing; it reminded me of jolly giants from folklore and prosperous seigneurs from the Middle Ages. Given a 15th-century nobleman's breastplate, spear and pewter helmet, Bernard would have befitted the prow of Vasco da Gama's leading galleon. Consistent with this theme, he had a friendly, round face, happy smile, generous eyes and bushy, dark hair. His rounded appearance matched his warm personality.

Bernard was humorous and a good storyteller. When we arrived at Foxhollow, he worked as a schoolteacher, a job that clearly suited his character and, later, we saw how his interests in general philosophy and the science of education gave him an enhanced, meta-level understanding of the teaching profession. He was also a practical person, who willingly did his fair share of the community's less glamorous work. Lastly, I have an enduring image of Bernard: he didn't look like a track athlete, he looked more like a shot-putter, but he made enormous effort as a road runner, and formed a lovable picture huffing and puffing along the country lanes around Foxhollow.

I return to Bernard's transformation from platoon captain to enlightened man. I do not want to pre-empt the bigger story told in later chapters so, for now, I think it's sufficient to say that, in the first year of the new millennium, the established order of Andrew's men students broke down. In the process, Bernard hit a true spiritual low, when he was deeply alone and adrift from Foxhollow and the community. After his absence for some weeks, Andrew displayed an extraordinary letter from him. It chronicled an experience occasionally found in traditional scriptures, when a student totally surrenders to his or her teacher. I believe the experience takes the form of a transfiguration, when the student sees his or her teacher as the embodiment of the origin of life – as self-nature incarnate – and, in the intensity of that recognition, he or she immutably surrenders to the teacher's human form. This experience was the substance of Bernard's letter.

On the basis of his realisation and subsequent return to Foxhollow, Andrew soon made Bernard his personal assistant. It was this job that eventually catalysed another major change in Bernard. The position involved managing Andrew's communications, which Bernard did for a number of years in a calm, focused and diligent manner. Day after day, Bernard conveyed Andrew's messages, he absorbed Andrew's outlook, and came to feel the pulse of the community in the same way that Andrew did. He gradually acquired Andrew's desire for greater change, greater progress, and more independence from the community's key players. Bernard told us that one day he simply thought, "*What can I do to help?*"

While Bernard was absorbing Andrew's outlook, I moved from Foxhollow to manage the building of the London Centre. Shortly after it was finished, in 2004, Bernard came to visit. His purpose, like others before him, was to breathe life into the English men, who had again dropped back from the community's leading edge. At this time, I was part of that trailing group but, unlike earlier remedial episodes, which were akin to pulling teeth, Bernard's visit was memorable for better reasons.

His decision to engage in the community's development had changed him immeasurably. It had removed his student's conformity. He now brought a natural, gentle, observational and encouraging voice that, through its independence, called on one's own independent curiosity. This was something very new. Bernard brought Andrew's spaciousness and genuine desire for development, delivered through his own personality.

I especially remember our formal men's meetings, and how Bernard engaged with the London group's established hierarchy. I anticipated his engagement might be a sensitive matter, because Bernard wouldn't want to undermine the existing leaders, but nor would he want to compromise himself. What happened was that Bernard's independence softened each man's hold on his position in the group. The presence of just one man willing to speak openly, without an eye on his status, among men inwardly committed to doing the same, freed many from the established and rigid 'unnatural hierarchy' that had developed over time. Given the opportunity to speak independently, like Bernard, many men from different hierarchical positions did so. An interesting paradox then came into play, as some men started to conform to a new common standard: independence.

During Bernard's visit to London he - without knowing it - gave me a point of reference that I have cherished ever since. In a formal meeting, he talked about waking up genuinely thrilled about the future; both his own future and the future in its wider, cosmological sense. I saw the possibility of greeting each day with the same outlook, and I heard that possibility expressed as the real experience of a man who had once been my peer. It sounded so wonderful, and real and attainable. I knew it was the way I wanted to experience life, and I noted a well-known phenomenon: important forward movements can happen at random moments.

Bernard was not our teacher. He was not as responsible as Andrew for the community's evolution. But he adopted a portion of it, both by his creation of educational courses for new and existing students, and by his willingness to be a visible, torch-bearing example of spiritual success. His consistency was similar to Andrew's. Reliably, he embodied an unproblematic view that he shared with patience and good humour. As with Andrew, these uplifting qualities seemed to arise from an inexhaustible source, and they made Bernard an inspiring and remarkable person. He was especially remarkable because we remembered how he had been before.

I experienced the benefits of Bernard's spaciousness on a rainy evening in 2010. This short event occurred during a period of my life when I was spiritually withering away, working lifelessly at Foxhollow. Bernard's partner had been involved in a road accident, and he wanted to visit her in hospital.

But, some years before, based on some worrying driving incidents, Andrew had judged Bernard a danger to himself and banned him from driving. On this wet evening, the only driver available was me - in rough spiritual shape - and the only vehicle to hand was an ancient pick-up truck. From Bernard's point of view this shabby taxi and despondent driver would suffice and, despite him knowing that I was a woebegone fellow with whom others would not have engaged, we had a genuine conversation, untainted by either conformity to, or awkward avoidance of, the community's protocols.

Both Stathan and Bernard were once students much like me, who rose to be leaders in the community. Looked at from a distance, their ascents prove it's possible for relatively ordinary students to become inspiring figures. I suggest that, seen functionally, their victories speak as much for the culture that nurtured them as for their own obvious strength of spiritual intention.

Chapter 17

Money

The idea of including a chapter on money came to me as an afterthought; an indication, perhaps, of how money was low on our list of priorities. We were so thoroughly engaged in our spiritual meetings, practices, and evolutionary interests, that attention paid to money often trailed in the slipstream of a busy life.

I don't have an accountant's expertise, or sufficient information to compare EnlightenNext's finances to other non-profit organisations. You might be happy to hear this! But I can describe the community's relationship to money, EnlightenNext's sources of income, and Andrew's lifestyle. I would also like to use this chapter to refute Hal Blacker's assertion that Andrew financially exploited his students. Overall, I propose that money, while known to be - along with power and sex - one of humanity's big three stumbling-blocks, was not a weakness in our community.

Students

At Foxhollow we rarely talked about money, either as a problematic or motivating subject. For example, I can't recall any conversations taking place over dinner about an investment opportunity or someone's financial problems. Money was not a group interest, and it didn't have to be an individual interest. One could go for weeks without thinking about money, or touching it. We paid our expenses – rent, food, etc. - by monthly standing order and, unless we had a reason to go to Boston or New York, money could be out of sight and out of mind. Our method of paying group restaurant bills illustrates this relaxed relationship to money. First, everyone gave their calculated share. If the total was short, a second appeal usually sufficed. When eating out with Andrew, one person might generously pick up the tab, or we would pre-plan the payment. Occasionally, Andrew would pay for the whole meal. In short, we didn't, as a community, have an overly sharp-eyed relationship to money.

Within this freedom from collective financial concern lay a variety of individual circumstances. Some richer students were property owners, some were successful actors, some had inherited wealth. Poorer students included gardeners, cleaners and one violin-maker. On the whole, the job status of poorer students improved over time, and their deliberations about what they could and couldn't afford faded from general conversation.

The perhaps enviable situation at Foxhollow had some flaws, and its backstory was a little rocky. With the community's attention consumed by an enlightened project, it was possible for students to continue with bad financial habits and build up debts, either to credit card companies or to EnlightenNext itself. These rare cases were disappointing: it was undignified for everyone when an individual had to be coached back to health on what we thought was a basic responsibility. The situation regarding inter-personal loans was better. These had been a minor feature of the community's early years, when students scraping together money to attend retreats had borrowed from one another. This habit of living hand-to-mouth had died away before the community moved to Foxhollow, along with the potential for muddle that can accompany person-to-person financial exchanges.

Andrew

In my opinion, Andrew's lifestyle was not lavish. He lived with Alka in their comfortable but not opulent apartment. Andrew had his yoga studio, the Volvo we had given him, two gifted Sonor drum sets, and a fine wardrobe of clothes, again given by students over the years. His meals were carefully prepared and beautifully presented. My guess is that half of these meals were made especially for him and half were improved versions of what everyone was eating. Certainly, the trays taken to him and the tables set for him looked elegant. I think he and Alka occasionally flew business class but, mostly, they travelled economy. Given Andrew's leading role, none of these material benefits struck me as excessive.

Andrew didn't have expensive habits or hobbies. He didn't, for example, have a collector's obsession for rare artefacts, expensive watches, or vintage cars. Indeed, even the idea of him having the desires of a consumer feels alien to how we knew him. His job was to draw our attention away from personal concerns - be they emotional or material - by cultivating our interest in his teachings on Spirit and evolution. Our community's outlook was towards something that had no relationship to consumerism. The idea of Andrew craving luxury simply didn't exist.

Andrew's lifestyle, and students' attitudes to Andrew's lifestyle, exemplified the community's overall attitude to money. We recognised that good financial management contributed to the undistracted environment we valued, so we knew it was important for everyone to have sufficient money, including Andrew. Money was something to take care of, which meant having enough, but it was not a primary concern. We did not have a pecuniary eye on one another, or on Andrew.

EnlightenNext

EnlightenNext had four main sources of income. Firstly, it received rental income from Foxhollow's thirty-six apartments and from students living in other buildings on the property. Secondly, it made money from a number of educational activities. These included the international summer and winter retreats, a number of online and face-to-face courses, and an academic qualification taught at The Graduate Institute, Connecticut, USA (Chap 22).

Thirdly, students and other supportive people made donations. Core students made a monthly donation; the amount varied slightly between Centres, but it averaged $100. Wealthy students and supporters from around the world gave a lot more. The value of these bigger, irregular donations was not common knowledge, but I estimate that some of Andrew's highest-earning students – of whom there were four or five - must each have given EnlightenNext tens of thousands of dollars during their many years in the community. Occasionally, people gave very large donations; examples are the two that were used to buy Foxhollow, and another that funded the employment of the magazine staff and others between 1998 and 2002. As EnlightenNext grew from the handful of students who gathered around Andrew in 1986, the organisation inevitably called on the goodwill and resources of its members. Responding to this call, students sometimes took out bank loans – typically $4,000 repaid over four years - to fund particular projects, such as the building of the London Centre. Donations were willingly made but, over the years, the organisation's dependency upon them came to feel both onerous for students and financially unimaginative. In response, a full-time fundraising department was established.

Fundraising was EnlightenNext's fourth source of income. Two fundraisers were employed at Foxhollow. With the help of professional advisers, they organised events such as the annual twenty-four-hour global meditation marathon, sought sponsors for the magazine, and made partnership applications to American charitable foundations. The fundraisers' expertise developed over time and, in 2007, they crossed a threshold by raising one million dollars. This figure was surpassed in the following two years when – as reported in EnlightenNext's Biennial Report for 2008/9 – over $1.5million were raised each year.

Three further subjects relevant to this chapter arose in the course of EnlightenNext's history. I'd like to mention the calibre of the organisation's chief executives and, separately, the two types of tension that had to be resolved.

I admired EnlightenNext's chief executives. I felt my experience in the building trade had taught me to recognise competence, so, in the community,

I was reassured by the level-headedness of students chosen by Andrew to lead the business arm of our organisation.

Bill Yenner was EnlightenNext's first CEO at Foxhollow. He later wrote a book critical of Andrew, *American Guru* but, during our fluid early years, he provided a steady pair of hands. He built good relationships with neighbouring businesses and he established various matters of legal status.

Beryl succeeded Bill Yenner. She was warm, easy-going and decisive. She owned a gas station and adjacent convenience store in Colorado, which she managed from Foxhollow. Perhaps it was her experience with those businesses that made Beryl strong on human-resource matters: she hired and fired pragmatically, and had a caring eye on employees' welfare. I witnessed her tears of joy in 1998 when she achieved her dream: employment contracts and healthcare provision for Foxhollow's employed students. Unflappable and humorous, Beryl's early-morning routine included buying coffee from Lenox, and the sight of her car weaving its way down the drive is a fond, if incidental, memory.

Roy, a third CEO, had Teutonic genes wrapped in an American personality. He had a gift for straightening-out complex issues, and had co-written an authorised user's manual for the Excel programme. He was also a senior student, and one of the few parents at Foxhollow. Roy could have experienced his demanding roles – CEO, senior student and parent - as conflicting but, instead, he seemed to apportion his time efficiently.

Agnetha was an upper-core student, and EnlightenNext's chief accountant for fifteen years. She was Austrian, cheerful and previously a competitor in acrobatic rock 'n' roll dancing at world championship level. Ostensibly an unlikely accountant, she handled the financial challenges of an international organisation with calm efficiency. I was intrigued and impressed by the tranquillity she brought to her complex work.

I come now to the two different tensions. There was an eternal tension EnlightenNext had to resolve: between Spirit's innocent demand for immediate manifestation, and Matter's more 'lumbering' inch-by-inch progression. Andrew's appetite for forward movement - immortalised for his students in the phrase "*go, baby, go*" – expressed the impetus of Spirit. EnlightenNext's board of (dutiful) directors stood as the countervailing force of material limitation. This tension reminded me of an account I read as a young man, in Mary Lutyens's biographies of Krishnamurti. She described the practical demands Krishnamurti placed upon Rajagopal, his right-hand man. Repeatedly, Krishnamurti would make proposals in an effusive '*it's possible*' tone; Rajagopal would reply more wearily, "*Yes, it's possible, given time and money.*"

At EnlightenNext, this tension was successfully moderated. Andrew did push against perceived boundaries, but he was averse to financial risk and to debt. The board, on its side, was made up of sensible people and, moreover, it held the purse-strings of departmental expenditure. The conflict between Spirit and Matter was, therefore, successfully regulated by the structural strength of the organisation, and budgets prescribed by the board were adhered to.

The second tension, between two hierarchies, can be explained by a very short story. Students' first allegiance was to the teaching hierarchy: to positions held by *senior, core* or *lay* students. Their second allegiance was to the organisational hierarchy, of department heads, project managers, etc. In EnlightenNext's early years, someone with proven expertise and a responsible departmental position could be overruled by a student who was higher in the teaching hierarchy. This dysfunction, which resisted many attempts at correction, often undermined the authority of people appointed to get results. A solution came unexpectedly, when EnlightenNext employed members of the public. Their employment followed our recognition that people with years of experience in their field, who worked steadily from nine to five, were more productive than we were. With more relief than chagrin, we found ourselves conforming to the employment rights and job descriptions of our employees. This new obligation reined-in the spontaneous intrusions of upper hierarchy students and brought stability to the working culture of a now more disciplined and diverse organisation.

Exploitation?

I believe my account of the community's unproblematic relationship to money is accurate, but I am compelled – by two conditions external to the community – to pinpoint the few problems that did arise.

Firstly, I imagine some readers will have reasonable doubts. Money is known to be a primary and potent human value, more often troublesome than trouble-free, so I think there will be doubts about my account of the community's unblemished financial record. Moreover, the imperfect history of both conventional and alternative spiritual organisations, such as mainstream churches and the communities of various charismatic gurus, has created suspicion. The suspicion is that congregations and followers might have been exploited. Ironically, to allay prevailing doubts and suspicions, I need to acknowledge the blemishes that did exist in the community's relationship to money.

Secondly, Hal Blacker's 'A' List, posted on the internet, has nine entries under the title *Financial Exploitation*. His assertion of exploitation contrasts absolutely with my experience. Shortly, I will contrast Hal Blacker's negative account of an event with my experience of its creative and optimistic character.

By doing so, I hope to show that he has, indeed, *asserted* his accusations of exploitation upon the good intentions of Andrew and his close students.

I have already mentioned some minor problems: students' struggles to fund themselves, some messy inter-personal loans, and EnlightenNext's dependency – in the early years - upon donations. I should add one further matter.

Given the unpredictable nature of ego, it is perhaps unsurprising that money was occasionally involved in the precarious, ego-wrestling exchanges between Andrew and his students. As described before, Andrew was required to step into situations when all else had failed, when a student had retreated into a locked down state of mind. This meant Andrew had to work with whatever willingness was available and, sometimes, that willingness was expressed as an offer of money. The circumstances and details of these offers were not common knowledge, so I can only record what we, as students, knew, and the attitudes we held. We understood there were, at most, five or six ego-related offers of money in the twenty-seven-year history of the community; that not all offers were accepted; and that offers were students' initiatives, not responses to Andrew's demands. There was no sign of Andrew benefitting personally from these occasional offers, and we knew that they only came from his most experienced students. More importantly, we saw these stories involving money within our context. In that context, Andrew was not a remote figure; we were integrated with him in our joint venture and, while he had tremendous authority, he was not a distant autocrat. He was our much-loved leader, not our taskmaster. We were so unified in, and committed to, our venture, that any suggestion that we were financially exploited would have left us nonplussed.

It is against this backdrop of integration and trust that I read Hal Blacker's 'A' List, with its assertion of financial exploitation. In response, I am going to lay his account of an event alongside my experience of the same episode. By doing this, I think I can illustrate the contrast between his description and, perhaps, the experience of the majority of people present at the time, or, at the very least, my own experience.

Entries five and six on Hal Blacker's list relate to preparations made for the community's move from Marin to Foxhollow. I will give his account first, followed by mine.

"5. *In preparation for the move to Foxhollow, Andrew Cohen required every Marin County, California student (where his major center of operations was at the time) to contribute $1,000 for every year they had been a student (up to $5,000), telling them that those who did not comply 'would never set foot on the Foxhollow property.'*

"6. In preparation for the move to the Foxhollow EnlightenNext Center, students were required to make a full disclosure of their finances to Cohen and the organization, and to undergo financial 'counseling' as to how they would support themselves and the community after the move. In at least one reported case, a student was encouraged to lie to his parents in order to receive financial support so that he could pay rent to the organization after moving to Foxhollow."

Here is my account. I remember the meeting at which Andrew revealed his scheme to raise money for improvements to our newly-bought property, Foxhollow. The meeting took place in San Rafael, Marin, some weeks after a surprise party at which Foxhollow and its grounds had been unveiled. In the meeting were forty students, excited by the prospect of moving to Massachusetts. Andrew told us that he and the senior students had discussed the need to raise money for remodelling work and that they had reviewed the general state of students' finances. He announced their plan: each student would contribute $1,000 for each year they had known him. For a few students this meant $10,000, as they had known him since 1986 but, for most, it was about half that amount. I had recently arrived in Marin, so my figure was less than everyone else's, at $500. No one could arrive at Foxhollow before making their contribution, and students were required to show they could support themselves in Massachusetts. Coaching was mandatory for those who couldn't prove their solvency, because it was known that job opportunities in the Berkshires were scarce compared to Marin.

In the following days, I felt some sympathy for both the students who had to find large sums, and the students who had to improve their financial situation, but that feeling was overpowered by the community's prevailing positivity. Most of us had just been given an unexpected gift: the opportunity to live on an historic estate in the beautiful Berkshire hills. We were heading towards a new life that promised closer communion. Indeed, the recent party and financial meeting had already drawn us into a new form of partnership with Andrew and the senior students. We were now collaborating with them on a practical project. This was different from the usual mentoring relationship. We felt we were on the move, both geographically and spiritually. The future held tremendous promise: familiar routines were being enjoyably disrupted and, individually, we were being positively challenged. It felt as if we were on a rising tide and that the whole community needed to mature to meet our awaiting future. We were familiar with the concept of multi-faceted evolution - Andrew often talked about the Buddha simultaneously teaching at many levels - and here we were, in the midst of that phenomenon. It was happening, we were surging forward.

The idea of being exploited simply didn't exist.

Summary

The financial affairs of the community were well managed, and our collective relationship to money was unencumbered. Money was not a preoccupation. Individually, the picture was mixed. Some students struggled to fund themselves but, for most, it was not a problem. Andrew's lifestyle was not lavish and, while he pushed hard to get funding for projects which he thought were important, like the publication of the magazine, he was averse to debt and would eventually comply with reasoned advice. Within the twenty-seven-year history of Andrew's community, a few monetary exchanges with students did end either angrily or regretfully, but there was neither evidence, nor ever the suggestion, that Andrew was benefiting personally from those events. All told, I see EnlightenNext as financially competent and a good example of how, when attention is placed on a higher purpose, secular matters that are frequently potent and wrought with difficulty can assume their appropriate place in terms of importance. Perhaps the end result is telling: when EnlightenNext dissolved, there was no wrangling over money; there were no debts; Andrew received nothing; Harvard Divinity School was given the $800,000 that came from the sale of Foxhollow; and EnlightenNext London was left with £1.7 million to distribute as grants.

Chapter 18

Sex

As mentioned in Chapter 12, there was a pivotal moment in 1994 when Andrew, travelling through New York, sent a message to his students in Marin: *"I'm not returning until some relationships form in my community."* Andrew saw a sexual relationship as a natural part of human life and spiritual life. He thought his students were avoiding the complexity of sexual relationship and, to him, this was dissatisfying. Andrew knew that, traditionally, a spiritual community reflects the values of its teacher, and he wanted his students to reflect his values; hence his message. In this instance, his students responded, Andrew returned to Marin and, thereafter, there were many relationships in his community.

I always assumed American puritanism was the source of our rather monastic sexual culture; an assumption based on the striking contrast I saw between raunchy European advertisements, language and attitudes, and America's more moderate counterparts. But, in retrospect, I think that Andrew, while interested in the nature of sexual desire, was himself disengaged from it, and his community did – as tradition would suggest – adopt his relationship to the subject. An additional observation is that living in a highly demanding environment might have suppressed students' libidos.

Perhaps it was a combination of all three influences – American puritanism, Andrew's elevated perspective and his students' preoccupations – that produced our community's notably austere sexual ambience. Austerity, however, did not mean fear or frigidity. We acknowledged the power of sexual desire, studied our experience of it, and a section of Andrew's teachings was based upon our inquiry into sexuality. Always a stimulating subject, I hope you enjoy the following – inevitably male-oriented - three passages. One contains anecdotes illustrating community life, another summarises Andrew's teaching on sex, and the third recalls how Andrew responded to this vital impulse.

Lee Lozowick was a spiritual teacher also known as Mr Lee. On and off, he and Andrew were friends. Mr Lee was forthright, bearded, somewhat grungy, vulnerable and unfailingly real. Both men were musicians and despite some big differences - such as Mr Lee's five wives and his community's meat-eating episodes – he and Andrew admired one another and enjoyed each other's company. On a few occasions, Mr Lee and Andrew shared a teaching platform and, on one occasion, Mr Lee was invited to speak, alone, to Andrew's London students.

It's not unreasonable to suppose that Mr Lee saw Andrew's students as uptight. A direct comparison between the two teachers' communities would be reductive, but we heard that Mr Lee's students referred to us as "*the well-dressed ones,*" and that he touchingly admitted to feeling eclipsed after visiting Foxhollow. Perhaps, therefore, it was the puritanical composure of Andrew's students that Mr Lee wanted to disrupt, when he spoke to them in London.

Mr Lee's opening gambit was to tell his attentive audience that he hadn't changed his T-shirt for three days. This drew no response. Maybe students expected a punchline to follow. Instead, Mr Lee reached deeper into his arsenal. He asked which word our community used to refer to a woman's pudenda (my word), and he offered a string of common choices. Again, no response, but this time for a different reason: we had no such word. Indeed, our daily vocabulary lacked all four-letter Saxon words. They weren't consistent with our culture, we didn't express the lewd interest that might have brought them into use and, in truth, the established standard of our interactions, while not rigid or policed, generally excluded what we perceived to be the downgrading effects of swearing. (The year to be described in Chapter 20 was an exception).

Our customary physical greeting was as temperate as our language. It was a brief but firm hug, without kisses on cheeks, or back-rubs, or the lingering resting of one's head on another's shoulder. Smoochy, dreamy, eye-to-eye gazing was not our habit. At Foxhollow we moved as independent people, not holding hands or clasped arm-in-arm. Partners would not be seen canoodling on benches in the grounds. One would not stumble upon two unattached students kissing in an empty office or in the gazebo by the swimming pool, and I honestly doubt there was any casual sex between Andrew's close students. Even the words *casual sex* sound incongruous with our culture.

I recall a few digressions from this restraint. In 1992, Derek was a new core student. I soon have more to say about him but, for now, he was a London student and formerly a Church of England verger. Andrew encouraged him to disentangle himself from his co-dependent partnership with his wife, Celia. But, to the amusement of others, the verger was discovered to have – one might say – voluntarily 'defrocked' himself, with his wife, in the back of their car. In another breach of protocol, in 2008, two young, aspiring students brought forward their nuptial night and consummated their relationship some weeks before the arranged ceremony that would have set it within the community's formal structure. Later, an upper-core student from Chile (and his partner) did the same thing, except that he tried to brush the matter off with a nonchalant Latin shrug. These slim pickings are the few in-house digressions I can recall over my twenty years as a student. There will doubtless have been more that I'm unaware of, but I'd be surprised if they were any more sensational.

Two further incidents show how our sensitivity to language created a divide between subjects that could be spoken about and those that could not. In 1998, I was in London. My younger sister recommended I see a play, *The Vagina Monologues*. She had found it heart-rending. I felt that voicing the word *vagina* would cross an unspoken boundary and cause a stir in the community. So, without informing anyone, I stole away to the West End one Saturday afternoon. In fact, the play (critically both celebrated and condemned) was informative and moving, just as my sister had said. The experience of being in a theatre with 2000 women and 10 men was also memorable. But the title meant I couldn't admit to having seen the play. I felt that eyebrows would have been raised and questions asked. Conversely, in a separate incident, when my friend Lenny – big, tall, hunky Lenny – started a new relationship with Dafne in Amsterdam, there was much hilarity in the community over the story of how 'wrecked' they both looked at meditation in the mornings. These contrasting incidents show how we happily talked about sex from a certain distance, using agreed language, but drew a line at explicit discussion.

Another example of our community's 'interest from a distance' came during the preparations for a big winter retreat in India, in 1999. The eight organising students were having a logistics meeting on the patchy lawn of our extensive, rented ashram in Rishikesh. It was sunny and there were rose beds nearby. Camilla was in the meeting and so was I. Camilla has fabulous breasts, it's a simple truth and, as the mundane meeting rolled along and the sun beamed down and the roses scented the air, my eyes absentmindedly came to rest on her gorgeous cleavage. After maybe fifteen seconds, I raised my gaze and, without haste, resumed the semi-conscious, drifting perusal that had yielded such pleasant fruit. I met Camilla's smiling eyes. It was a transparent and intimate moment. I felt mildly embarrassed, but she seemed only to be amused. We understood the nature of my gaze and the conflicts that might typically have arisen from it, but we knew my offence wouldn't upset the beauty of the day.

The Promise of Perfection is the title of Andrew's teaching on sexuality. His teaching is not a manual for a good, monogamous sex life. Nor is it either a tantric teaching, promising transcendence through disciplined sexual activity, or a guide for people who want a life of unlimited sexual exploration. Instead, his teaching helps one achieve a free relationship to the strong feelings generated by sexual desire. These feelings can be divided into the desire for sex and the attachment sex creates.

Desire, in general, makes human beings feel alive. This is the starting point of Andrew's teaching on sexuality. In his book *Embracing Heaven and Earth* he says the following:

> *"It is important to become aware of the fact that when we want something or want someone, we experience ourselves as being intensely alive because it is then that we feel in touch with the drive within us to have. This drive to have – I want for me, I want for myself - is experienced by the ego as a positive thing. And when we think about whatever it is that we want – a new house, a new car – it excites us. And it is this very excitement that distorts our perception."*

He goes on to say that distorted perception produces a primary, misleading idea: we can be, or will be, fulfilled by finding something that is outside ourselves. Believing this idea perpetuates our entrenched human habit of seeking salvation through the acquisition of an external object. In the context of enlightenment, this habit is a problem because our attention is distracted away from the true source of our wellbeing: limitless, unproblematic, already bestowed, consciousness.

Sexual desire, typically experienced as exciting and urgent, wins all prizes for potency. Andrew says it is this potency, and the illusions arising from it, that make sexuality such a *"loaded issue."* He says people often cannot bear – by which he means simply have the experience, without avoidance or engagement - the strength and complexity of sexual desire, but that there is no simple, ready-made answer that will protect one from the seductive power of *"the most powerful illusion that there is."* An incident during a retreat in India – described below - in which Andrew set the sexual histories of two of his men students side by side, shows how the potency of sexual desire can be deeply distracting.

Cameron was a life-long playboy. He lived in Chelsea, London, drove a classic BMW and had an address book dating back to his time as a sannyasin with Bhagwan Sri Rajneesh. He was urbane. He wore wonderful shoes, per-fectly-fitting, faded jeans, and loose shirts with the cuffs turned back. He moved easily, spoke charmingly, was unruffled, and ran his own business selling Jacuzzis. On close examination, everything in his life was a pheromone, a come-hither beacon attracting footloose females from the world's jet set, and he once famously said, *"There's nothing in life as exciting as going to bed with a beautiful woman."* Seen in the context of a largely abstinent, spiritual community, his pronouncement - met with silence by surrounding men - was misplaced and noted by Andrew.

Derek (the verger) was a jolly fellow. He was rotund, barrel-chested and dark-haired. Every so often in life, one meets someone who closely resembles a different species of animal. These people can be seen as signposts: as evolution pointing to just one original, universal gene pool. Bird-like people are common, as are those with bug's eyes or horse's heads. Derek shared his genetic path with *Talpa Britannica*: the British mole. He was slightly blind, spoke in an agitated, whisker-twitching manner, and held his hands like forepaws. He had a selection of sleek, dark sweaters, and excess hair sprouting from his nostrils and ears. God must have enjoyed toying with Derek's genes because, in a magnificent final flourish to His synthesis of man and mole, Derek had had a career in civil engineering, as a tunnelling specialist. Unlike Cameron, Derek had had sex with only one woman: his own wife.

In the convivial atmosphere of a post-retreat men's meeting in Rishikesh, Andrew prompted both men to share their experience of sexual desire. Cameron was eloquent, and able to describe his very reasonable, it seemed, desire for more jet-set damsels, and his ideas for cultivating their participation. Andrew hammed-up Cameron's ideas, suggesting he could have a waiting room and a bell. In contrast, Derek could only lament his inexperience. Aged sixty, and restrained by a verger's morality, his future looked to be an extension of his past, especially now that he was a spiritual seeker in a community of monogamous, and mainly younger, people. Our hearts went out to him as he openly ruminated on his lot.

Andrew's point was that both men were caught in the same trap: they wanted more. Despite plentiful sex, Cameron was still not satisfied, while Derek remained in thrall to the idea that, if he had Cameron's experience, he would be fulfilled. Both men were enslaved, convinced by the thoughts and feelings arising in their minds. They were both still distracted by the intensity of sexual desire.

The other half of Andrew's teaching explores an equally powerful and – in our community's context - troublesome product of sexuality: attachment.

The Promise of Perfection reveals one of humanity's basic misconceptions – the idea that fulfilment lies in acquiring something that one doesn't already have - but this section of Andrew's teaching also shines a light on a more particular expectation: that perfect happiness can be found in a romantic partnership. Andrew's teaching is, therefore, also a response to the widespread difficulty people have when it comes to deciding which is more important to them: spiritual freedom, or a committed relationship.

Andrew says that sex creates attachment. He says that human beings have a biological, chemical response to sex which makes them want to form partnerships, and that sexual partnerships normally involve deep emotional and psychological attachment. In addition, this natural bonding process is magnified by society's promotion of the romantic partnership as an ideal, a destiny, and a primary source of love and happiness.

In the context of enlightenment this is a problem, because one wants to be emotionally and psychologically unattached, or free. It is independence that is sought, not dependence. And the double difficulty with romantic attachment - compared to other attachments, such as to an object or a place - is the lack of space: the inability to even question the merits of an established relationship. (Again, these observations were made in the context of enlightenment; I am not suggesting they apply elsewhere).

We saw this phenomenon many times at Foxhollow and on retreats. Couples from outside the community would arrive full of enthusiasm but, after a few days, they would look troubled. One could see them realise that Andrew's teachings called for independence, and then see them unconsciously conclude that their relationship was under threat. Before any intelligent inquiry had time to begin, they would often panic and run. This sequence – seen time and again – led us to understand that, for many people, an existing romantic partnership is frequently a non-negotiable matter.

In summary, it can be said that Andrew's teaching on sexuality offers no rigid, immunising strategy. He doesn't say do this or do that. He simply points to the power of the sexual impulse and the near-universal illusions that this impulse generates in the human mind. In short, he says freedom is found through being awake to what is going on. As with his teachings in general, he says that with clear perception – or self-knowledge - comes the opportunity for free, independent choice.

Andrew was not, in my opinion, a sexually-charged man. I thought his responses in this field, in many situations, were impeccable throughout my time with him. I have no memories of him making any comments or throwing any glances that would generally be disapproved of, and I would be surprised if anyone attending his teachings, throughout his career, heard him say anything lascivious or saw him make inappropriate gestures. Sex was simply not in the forefront of his mind, as far as I could tell, and he appeared to live by the same instruction he gave to his students, which was to give sex a low ranking on their list of priorities.

Neither was he a closed book or a rigid puritan. Questioned in his London teachings in 2011, about the viability of a polyamorous partnership, Andrew said he had no fixed ideas about what sexual behaviour would work for other people, but he predicted that, if he broke his monogamous relationship with

Alka, he would then see every woman he met as a potential conquest. On another occasion, a group of men met with him for a dedicated discussion about the dynamics in their relationships. Huddled in a pub in Belsize Park, London, Andrew asked his students how much sex they felt was enough (I think the answer was a moderate *twice weekly*). Giving his own answer on the question of frequency he said, *"Not very often, given the life we're living."*

The magazine team dived deeply into the subjects they investigated. Their method was to adopt the perspectives of the various teachers, leaders, writers and pioneers whose work they researched. At Foxhollow, we were usually told about the production of each issue of the magazine at its launch party so, over the years, we acquired a good sense of the journalists' stress and endeavour. Hence, I have a good idea of the depth of their investigation for Issue 43, titled, *Sex: the Good, the Strange and the Sacred.* That issue contains articles about David Deida's far-reaching, neo-tantric teaching, with its aggressively pornographic language; and the San Francisco community, *One Taste*, with its idiosyncratic, transcendent technique: ritualised masturbation. The magazine team researched the *Kama Sutra*, along with various graphic films showing transcendent sexual practices. Partly led by Andrew, they placed no limits on their inquiry but, when looking at especially explicit material, the men and women separated. That policy was thought to be consistent with the general distance we maintained from one another when it came to 'lower chakra' matters, as we termed them.

Lastly, I have a poignant memory which I believe captures the weight of Andrew's interest in the subject of sex and the nature of his responses.

In London, in 2006, a group of students was accompanying Andrew to the airport. He and I were walking in front, side-by-side along the platform at Paddington Station, towards the waiting Heathrow Express. In front of us walked an exquisitely beautiful woman. She was like an apparition, a figure gliding victoriously from the final scene of an historic Spanish saga. Elegant, kitten-heeled ankle-boots clipped evenly along the platform, while lace stockings - with snaking back seams – claimed my gaze and a knee-length pencil skirt outlined her perfect curves. A bolero jacket emphasised her delicate waist and formed a shoulder line that added power to her poise. Swirling around her neck, a black boa furthered her allure, while her cascading, dark hair was crowned by a blush, floral fascinator. I was entranced. Andrew turned to me with a smile and said, *"Ritzy lady."*

Chapter 19

The Women

I believe it would be hard to find a more valiant group of women than Andrew's women students. Clearly, in many walks of life there are individual, trail-blazing women, but our work with Andrew was done in groups. Therefore, my admiration for the women with whom I shared my spiritual life is based upon what they achieved together. They fought at the edge of human development, bearing Andrew's ceaseless demand for a new union in a new sphere, and I believe the value of their endeavour has yet to be recognised. The men and the women were always two arms of one student body and - as this book approaches its zenith - I'm aware that the strength of the women's intention played an equal part in our community's invocation of the Authentic Self.

Please be forewarned: some readers might be offended by the substance of this chapter. It might, therefore, be helpful to know that the next chapter, *The Men*, tells an equally tough story.

1. Enlightenment Is Not Empowerment

The women's story is worthy of its own book. It is extraordinary, especially when contrasted with current social narratives promoting women's equality. This is because the journey made by Andrew's women students took place in the opposite corner of the universe to today's interest in female empowerment. Enlightenment is about disempowerment: about dissolving self-importance and self-righteousness. It is about the discovery of gratitude. Gratitude for the gift of consciousness and the opportunity to witness a wonderful world. Enlightenment is about viewing one's experience with cool, responsible detachment, and about giving freely to the greater good. Ultimately, it's about submission to a higher power. These, I suggest, are not the central aspirations of the ideologies currently advancing women's secular status.

The values held by Andrew's community, therefore, contrasted with many of today's social attitudes. Our aim was to participate in the core purpose of Life: universal awakening. We wanted to be useful to evolution, and in our minds this goal was different from the goal of personal empowerment. To us, women's nature and women's history were part of the entire human condition. Those subjects were as open to scrutiny as any other. The preciousness that often accompanies social discussion of women's matters did not exist in our community, because we were in an enlightened context where notions of specialness were known to obstruct open inquiry. Instead, we held Andrew's view: that, despite their specific challenges, women were equally capable of building the new, enlightened faculty he envisaged.

This view was not disputed or policed, it was freely held and understood to be foundational to our work. Anyone entering our community, for example as a guest, would simply observe the view we held and either back away, or accept it. Our view of women as equally valuable to our work, and women's nature as equally open to scrutiny, didn't need to be spelled out: it was accepted, established and evident.

Understandably, women not in the community often found the scrutiny accepted by Andrew's women students difficult to comprehend. Perplexed, they would often ask Andrew's women students, *"Why have you chosen a male teacher?"* That question is reasonable coming from a gender-based paradigm in which womanhood is the primary identity, but it had little relevance for Andrew's students, who sought communion with the ungendered force of love and evolution. Questioners were again perplexed when Andrew's women students described the issues they were grappling with - habitual self-referencing, sexual competition, ancient mistrust, and unconscious undermining of one another – and the questioners often became bewildered when the women students went on to explain that their work was not merely to study these obstacles, but to become embodied examples of evolution beyond them. It was therefore not surprising if – when hearing of this engagement - people who were new to Andrew's teachings took a guarded step back.

Situations in which the women students spoke with intelligent, committed women from outside our community were fascinating to observe. Such conversations happened on retreats and after functions held at EnlightenNext's Centres. Common spiritual interest set a high standard of respect between the women, yet one knew that opposite ideas were often held. Frequently, there was an unbridgeable gap between those on a woman-centric spiritual path and Andrew's students, who spoke of their struggles to break free from that very same centricity.

Despite their differences, there were sometimes signs of common interest. Shared curiosity might arise when Andrew's women students spoke about the difficulties arising between them in their formal women's meetings. As mentioned before, these meetings were our most important forums, where we attempted to bring semi-conscious human habits into the light of day. All students floundered in this process, including the women, who battled for decades with the difficult female dynamics mentioned above. It was when

Andrew's women students spoke about the travails of their group work that they sometimes found common ground with other women.

2. The Character of Andrew's Women Students

What were Andrew's women students like, within this dedicated culture?

Physically, they dressed well, generally modestly, and didn't wear obvious make-up. They were mostly in good, athletic shape, although not Olympians. An incidental observation is that many of the women at Foxhollow were the same height, about 5ft 5in. Occasionally, one could look across to the coffee station and see eight women, of perfectly equal height, in conversation.

In character they were, put simply, rather formidable. They were independently minded, articulate and resilient. They were upstanding, committed and hard-working. They walked tall. They spoke powerfully and I had confidence that, if required, they could have stood their ground with the most accomplished women in society. They also seemed to manage practical matters, such as finances and travel arrangements, better than many of the men.

3. Intimacy

An interesting feature of our training with Andrew was the kind of intimacy it fostered. It was the character of this intimacy that determined the nature of our friendships and the feelings we had about social inclusion. I think this subject, intimacy, is particularly relevant to this chapter about Andrew's women students, but I will include everyone in the following description.

Without families to manage, careers to pursue, or problems with relationships to dwell on, some of the common subjects that normally catalyse personal intimacy were absent. Instead, intimacy came from our primary interest: the examination of our experience as grist to the mill of evolution. With personal preoccupations largely subordinated and broad territory to explore, avenues were open for interesting conversations to flourish between any of Andrew's students. It was rare to hit a self-conscious or awkward patch when talking with peers or those lower in the hierarchy. With people higher in the hierarchy the opposite could be true, but this would be because of one's own self-conscious response to their authority. In short, there were strong hierarchical divisions between students, but no divisive social groups.

Our brand of intimacy was not based upon personal loyalty, attraction, or affection. Of course, we enjoyed some people's company more than others, and had niche interests dotted here and there, but these pairings or particular passions were minor, extra-curricular enjoyments compared to the solid, central business of committedly forging forward as one group.

This order of priorities meant that, within the core student community, people were not excluded. There were no cliques, no long-running personal feuds, and no petty expressions of irritation. Choosing a seat at one of our round dining-tables – a moment of potential segregation – was eased by the knowledge that one was essentially included. My guess is that dining rooms throughout the world are socially-challenging places which raise questions like: *Who is sitting with whom? Whom do I want to avoid?* or, *Who will accept me?* But, in our community, commitment to a common cause filtered-out potentially injurious expressions of personal preference.

4. Equality

Please imagine a landscaped, Utopian city, built around a gladiatorial amphitheatre. The Utopian city represents the daily working environment of our community. The amphitheatre represents Andrew's work with his women students (and, separately, his men students). Broadly speaking, the two activities were separate; the spiritual work was contained within dedicated meetings, while the daily business of the community was conducted within an environment of dignity and equality.

Equal numbers of men and women were attracted to Andrew's teachings, from across the age spectrum of 18 to 75 years. I can say this with confidence. It was important information when preparing for retreats, so I took note. In fact, I came to think of the equal numbers, seen year after year, as profoundly significant. I imagined them to be a display; as if the driving force behind Andrew's teaching work was drawing attention to its own, genderless nature.

We were not concerned about gender equality in our working culture but, either by chance, or through natural distribution of ability, approximate equality arose. I don't recall a single comment being made about jobs being given to men or women. I once heard about disgruntlement in the magazine team over who was to write a prestigious article, but even that friction was not about gender assignment. As far as I know, everyone on staff was paid the same; certainly, there were no voices raised on the subject of equal pay. People seemed to be given jobs based on merit. We accepted that. Sexism in the workplace was not an issue. (I'm not suggesting these issues aren't at play in the world at large; I'm saying they didn't exist within the community).

We were one body. Our strongest sense of self was 'us', not 'me' the individual, or our gender grouping. So, the men saw the women as sisters, part of 'us', our team, our outfit, our unified community. The women were not seen as 'other' and, consequently, no one was weighing or measuring status. Even members of the magazine team - again, an unplanned group that was roughly gender-equal – who had an exotic life of travel and big-name interviews, were not resented for their glamorous opportunities. We were a community, with our eyes fixed on our collective work. Concerns about workplace equality didn't feature. Instead, equality appeared: a by-product of equal commitment to a common challenge.

Similarly, the teaching hierarchy was unregulated, but approximately equal. Senior students came and went over time, affecting the gender balance, but that balance was not a matter of general concern. A senior student was a highly-respected figure. We had more to do with our same-gender senior students, because we worked in gendered groups, but this didn't lessen the respect shown to all senior students.

Andrew expected the same from the women as from the men. He wanted all his students to do their spiritual practice diligently and to fully participate in formal meetings, obeying the instructions to "*have nothing, know nothing and be no one.*" He saw no reason why the women couldn't meet this requirement. Criticism of Andrew (Chap 24) has, strangely, arisen from his refusal to see women as less capable than men. Some women loved him for his willingness to suffer through hell and high water in his pursuit of a breakthrough for womankind; their letters, to him and to the magazine, proved this. Others now see him as punitive, and worse. As we will see shortly, there was a time when the community might have divided into higher and lower streams, but Andrew held out for the possibility of a unified, enlightened body. It's ironic to me that Andrew's willingness to fight against his women students' resistance has led to accusations of misogyny. He cared more than they did. He was fighting for spiritual equality, while his women students were (forgivably) caught in deep-time gender momentums. I will come to these soon.

Flying high above the observations made so far is the blazing example of Spirit itself. During our turbulent history - as people came and went, as groups rose and fell, as perspectives expanded and contracted - the community's need for certainty softened. Its culture became more pliable, less rigid and, as this happened, Spirit found new opportunities to burst into being. Unsurprisingly, Spirit did not show gender preference when it made use of these opportunities, as the following three incidents illustrate.

At the end of Chapter 13 I described how, in 1999, the Authentic Self first appeared in a group of core student women while they were on retreat in Les Cormettes. A second appearance came two years later through a mixed group of students, again on retreat in Les Cormettes. I was part of that group, and I remember how gender was of no concern. We had ears only for the voice of evolution, whoever it came through.

A third, more startling, humbling and bizarre eruption came in 2002. It started with the lay student women who lived at Foxhollow. Women were less likely to leave the community if they came to a spiritual standstill. Men tended to 'split' and were seldom seen again. But at Foxhollow, and in Boston and Amsterdam, quite a number of older women formed a lay student group. These women contributed practically, but they held back from a formal relationship with Andrew and, therefore, from participating in our core work.

The great force of evolution showed its willingness to travel through any medium by occupying the minds, hearts and souls of this group. A disorienting feature of our work at the time was the erratic appearance and disappearance of the state of consciousness we were seeking to invoke. In truth, while Andrew was trying to stabilise the invocation of this phenomenon, it was beyond his control. He would apply pressure to one group of students, by demanding their focused application of intention (usually this meant more formal meetings and direct exchanges with him), but the Authentic Self would surprise him – and others - by flourishing within another group in his community.

In this case, it was the lay student women who came alive. For no apparent rhyme or reason, they spontaneously became a radiant group of passionate adventurers, traversing their experience, sharing their learning and hungering for more collective inquiry. In an accelerating process – of growing love and fascination - that we later became familiar with, their current of unbounded, delighted curiosity spread to their sisters in Europe via revelatory international conference calls. In this way, the force of evolution confounded the community's assumptions. We had strong, perhaps limiting, ideas about each other's capabilities but, in this instance, the enlivening force we sought to invoke proclaimed its impartiality by occupying the hearts and minds of people thought to be unpromising vehicles.

During this episode, there was a riotous evening in the dining room. The familiar way to have an exclusive meeting was to group some tables together at the back of the room. Having done this, the lay women were on fire with joy and laughter as they experienced wild, unrestrained interest coursing through and between them. Their enthusiasm grew into a cacophonous, spiritual whirlwind. On this occasion, as is often the case with insensitive exuberance, it was annoying. It also, unintentionally, undermined our respected hierarchy because the lay students' liberated state overshadowed more senior students, who looked stranded. Nevertheless, this unregulated expression of the Authentic Self, which lasted a month, taught us two lessons: it showed the unpredictable power of Spirit to randomly infuse life into less-experienced students and, with more relevance to this chapter, it again showed that Spirit has no gender preference.

5. Andrew's Teaching on Women and Enlightenment

I think it is worth saying once more that Andrew's teaching on women relates specifically to enlightenment. It is also important to note that his observations on the challenges faced by individual women differed from his understanding of the challenges faced by his women students in their group work: the obstacles to transcendence were discovered to be markedly different in each case.

Women's Liberation was an important subject in his teachings. It was researched in depth, and treated with the same significance as subjects like Ego, Meditation, or Pride. For example, two issues of *What is Enlightenment?* magazine were dedicated to women's liberation: Issue 10, Winter 1996, and Issue 37, September 2007.

I appreciate that some women might doubt the usefulness of a man's commentary on the nature of women, or even his right to express that commentary. As stated in this chapter's introduction, our community didn't have these doubts. Even so, I would like to make readers aware of both my expectation that Andrew's perceptions will be judged by a variety of attitudes, and my hope that readers will find my necessarily abbreviated summary of his teachings useful.

Andrew's teaching on this subject is very simple. This fact gives me an opportunity to make a short digression to describe how his teachings generally work: how simplicity is essential in the process of transcendence. In this process, one is seeking to change, to rise above and no longer be controlled by conditioned impulses. This is not the same as fortifying oneself with knowledge. Seeking transcendence is a unique activity, incomparable to theoretical- or knowledge-based learning. Transcendence occurs through direct perception. It is perception, not knowledge, that is the agent of change. Here follows a description of how it often works.

In Andrew's teachings, one draws simple, pertinent observations from one's own experience and looks directly at them. One has to be willing to treat oneself as a guinea pig and use one's experience as the raw material for inquiry. This is easy if one cares about a purpose bigger than oneself; but, if not, it is almost impossible. Once engaged in this form of inquiry, one has to accept that it is an incremental process not wholly within one's control. As perception penetrates into experience, one enters into an unpredictable, symbiotic process in which small breakthroughs yield interesting insights and questions. There might then be a period of dormancy before a short cascade of connections appear, then more dormancy and further revelation. Gradually, a rich picture comes into view. Andrew used the sequence '*bear-with, understand, see-through,*' to describe this process, in which insights precede a breakthrough. The important result is that one owns a picture of reality, a picture that arises from an interplay between personal curiosity and bestowed insight.

Andrew's teaching on women has a simple observation at its core: women are physically smaller than men, and always have been. He says that, since the earliest days of our species, women have lived with the awareness that they can be physically overpowered by half the human race. Consequently, they have sought safety by controlling their immediate environment and, over hundreds of thousands of years, their methods of control – along with the fear of being overpowered - have become embedded within women's nature. Enlightenment requires one to be undefended and empty-handed. Understandably, parts of a woman's nature abhor that prospect, and this is where Andrew's teaching points to specific difficulties women have. Issue 37 of the magazine carries a conversation between Andrew and integral theorist, Ken Wilber. In that conversation, Andrew says:

> "I've noticed that the very notion of spiritual freedom is actually a concept that most postmodern women find harder to conceptually relate to than men do. Women seem to relate more to the desire for connection, wholeness, or fullness. But the idea of freedom, wanting to become free at an existential level, seems almost like an alien concept."

This is the first of four particular challenges that women face, in Andrew's view. Women are ambivalent about being empty-handed, to the degree that the notion of enlightenment is either unappealing or incomprehensible. Consciously or unconsciously, a woman's primordial need to protect herself inhibits her interest in transcendence.

The second and third challenges women face are easier to describe. Andrew and our community held the view that women use sexual power as a way of controlling their immediate environments. Sexual power is, I suggest, generally acknowledged to be one of the few tools that has been available to women throughout history, and one which is still used today with, perhaps, greater awareness. Andrew also observed that women were reluctant to speak openly. This observation came from our group work and is, therefore, a less acknowledged trait. But we held the view that women would '*shape-shift*' when under pressure, and refuse to be simple and direct about their experience. This was a problem, given that our work depended on descriptions of direct perception. Andrew said, "*I think women are asked to give up a lot more than men,*" and he saw their need to renounce these two forms of control – sexual power and indirect communication – as part of women's greater challenge.

During the course of our work, Andrew discovered a fourth obstacle, again a product of women's physical vulnerability throughout history. This obstacle seemed to be integrated within women's phenomenal stamina and resilience. During the forthcoming account of Andrew's confrontation with this part of women's nature, the women showed immense fortitude. Many of them were like indomitable boxers who would simply not give up; their commitment to Spirit was unbreakable, yet they never allowed it – Spirit - to consume them. This paradox – immense commitment coexisting with immense resistance - was partly explained by the discovery that women can retreat to a place inside themselves where they cannot be reached. In the same transcript quoted from earlier, Andrew describes this place as follows:

> "... *this isn't completely conscious, but women learn early on how to keep themselves emotionally and psychologically safe. For example, they seem to have an inner place they can retreat to when they want to protect themselves, where they just cannot be reached. And I can imagine this is a capacity that probably developed in women's consciousness a long time ago so that even if she could be physically overwhelmed at any time, even if they could have her body, they could never have her soul. All women still have this place of retreat, which for most men I know just isn't available.*"

Once again, while men were seen to have their own great challenges, women were thought to have '*more on their plate*' – more to give-up – in pursuit of enlightenment.

To illustrate Andrew's first and primary observation – that the idea of existential freedom is almost an alien concept to women – I want to tell a story about Miranda. She was a prominent figure in our community, who deserves special mention, so this account also fulfils that purpose.

I think an open poll of Andrew's core students would have selected Miranda as his foremost woman student. Before meeting him, she had lived in India for many years and been a committed meditator. In Andrew's community she held her senior student position easily, bearing responsibility with freewheeling, dynamic confidence. Like Ambrose, her partner, she came from an upper-class family, in her case Australian, and she assumed natural possession of her high status. Attractive and talkative, Miranda was an effervescent whirlwind. She

149

laughed easily, was affectionate and demonstrative, and related to everyone, as far as could be seen, with warm, upbeat motherliness.

Miranda was a figurehead, and she represented the very best qualities of a true seeker. Although not born an enlightened woman, or blessed by an unsought-for epiphany, she was, nevertheless, a woman who had reached for transcendence with exceptional dedication. It is revealing to see how she responded when Andrew spoke with her, pointing her towards emptiness.

He told us about his talk with Miranda at a meeting with his core students, in Marin in 1995. Andrew lived on Spring Grove at the time. In the context of her position as his leading woman student, he directed her attention towards the formlessness of Spirit, telling her that she needed to enter into, and then remain in, that formless dimension for the sake of other women in the community. Her breakthrough would be their breakthrough.

"Miranda literally burst into tears, literally burst..." Andrew told us, gesturing with opening arms to convey the suddenness of her response. The implication was that she found the prospect of dissolving into emptiness – the very destination she had so assiduously committed her life to - utterly terrifying. Andrew added, *"Of course, men are scared of this prospect, too,"* but not to the visceral degree illustrated by Miranda's involuntary reaction.

I could relate to what Andrew was saying. I imagined his conversation with Miranda had happened in his home, where I had experienced emptiness as something positive: *shimmering sanity*, as I described it in Chapter 13. Miranda's terrified cry exhibited – I thought - humanity's negative relationship to emptiness, when it is felt to be *absolute nothingness*. In myself, I felt more able than Miranda to hold both these interpretations within one view. With or without justification, I felt supported by something familiar: a momentum composed of men's frequent use of their rational faculty through history. I thought I experienced what Andrew was pointing to: the advantage men have, when relating to the experiences that arise when one looks towards the unknowable enormity of existence.

The journey to enlightenment is through one's own mind. Andrew repeatedly told us that one arrives at a natural, undramatised state. But, en route, the human mind generates threatening ideas. For women, one of these ideas is that *'if I let go of my defences, I might die.'* Our understanding was that, while men fear losing their identity and melting into a state of dysfunction, women have the added fear of physical death, a fear emanating from hundreds of thousands of years of physical vulnerability. Of course, this fear is a prospect thrown up by the ego, a fear that ensures self-preservation, but it is a powerful fear and one that is not lightly dismissed. As Andrew asserts in his teachings, women have greater obstacles to overcome in their pursuit of enlightenment.

6. Andrew's Confrontation with the 'Visceral No'

Andrew's teachings on women's liberation came from his interactions with his women students. He observed their responses to his guidance and gradually built a picture of the specific challenges they faced. The previous section gives a summary of what he learnt over nearly two decades. This section goes back in time to tell the story from which his understanding was gleaned. It does not trace, one by one, the origin of the four challenges described above; instead, it records the frictional, emergent nature of the interaction from which his teachings appeared. That interaction took the form of a confrontation.

My account of this confrontation is broadly chronological. The full story starts in 1988 and covers eighteen years. It came to an end, or changed markedly in character, in 2006, when Andrew gave the senior women responsibility for women's development in the community. This description covers the advent and substance of the toughest years: 1988-2001.

As I have said before, the women's story deserves its own book, best written by the people directly involved. But the following account fulfils the purpose of this book. By capturing the story's essence - the strength of the women's fortitude and something of their trials - and by describing the context held at the time, I can record the women's efforts and link those efforts to the community's invocation of the Authentic Self.

In 1988 a small incident - his women students over-preparing every detail of a restaurant meal - drew Andrew's attention to his wider experience of feeling suffocated by these students' need to control their surroundings. Two years later, when the emphasis of Andrew's teaching work started to change from individual to collective enlightenment, he saw that his women students were less receptive to this new direction than were his men. As his teachings gathered momentum, these two traits in the women – their need for control and their ambivalence about group inquiry - became problematic. They became inhibitors to the kind of open inquiry on which his vision depended.

Andrew's observations were the start of a lengthy war of attrition. In the first few years, he encouraged his women students to cultivate individual curiosity and collective trust, but with limited success. He came to understand that he was pitted against what he called a *'visceral no'*, or *'preconscious refusal'*. This resistance had nothing to do with individual character. It was not personal. In his view, it was a primal refusal to let go of ancient defence mechanisms and, instead, cultivate trust in life and in other women. This *visceral no* existed beneath women's relational nature and, in Andrew's women students, it undermined their ability to form a spiritually inquisitive group. Of course, Andrew could see that women would unite in a common interest or task, effectively and easily. But he saw a profound sense of panic in his women students if they were asked to simply be together, to relax in each other's company, and to see their experience as research material for spiritual inquiry.

I observed signs of this panic in my first years as a student. At that time, we would have men's and women's meetings on a Wednesday evening. Each week, I felt trepidation at the prospect of the meeting. I was afraid of failing. In our men's meetings, failure meant not participating, and I feared collapsing under the scrutiny of the forum, either by speaking feebly or not at all. However, I knew my peers had roughly the same experience and that we would not persecute each other. The women students appeared to have different feelings about their meetings. They went to them breezily, as if the meetings were another social event. But I always had a gut sense that they didn't actually want to join with their peers in our clearly defined type of spiritual inquiry; that, in fact, their breezy attitude was a mask, beneath which they felt fear. This proved to be true.

As the community's work developed, our meetings became increasingly important, and the women's ambivalence about working together began to stand out. In most other respects, there was parity between men and women students. All students harboured fear of the very freedom they were seeking. All students benefited from the community's gradual progress. But the women's *visceral no*, when aggregated in a group, manifested as a refusal to be vulnerable with one another: to trust each other enough to speak, in context, about what was real. Andrew implored them to *"come together in a higher consciousness beyond ego, beyond the personal sphere, beyond narcissistic self-concern."* But, apparently, he was asking his women students to rise above very deep resistance. From one point of view, this resistance was to enlightenment itself; to seeing their experience as an independent, sensory stream that was not self-defining.

In my view it's reasonable to say that Andrew was not an ordinary individual. None of us had become his students just because we liked him. We were drawn to what came through him: what he was connected to. We were united in valuing his embodiment of Spirit. That Spirit, originating at the beginning of time and ever hungry for self-knowledge, does not baulk when faced with glitches in human evolution. So, when Andrew was faced with the women's *visceral no*, the Spirit within him was never going to back down.

When Andrew first shared his observation of the *visceral no* with his students in the late '80s and early '90s, he hoped for an interested response, for investigation and insight, but nothing lasting came forth. It's probably fair to say that no one knew the scale of what was being touched upon. Andrew then pushed harder, but the response was still minimal and it tended to come in the form of declarations of love and devotion. This pattern, of Andrew pushing for real progress – which meant genuine interest and inquiry into the experience and function of the *visceral no* – but being given only assurances of love and devotion, was unsatisfactory to him. Nevertheless, it was – on the whole, and with notable individual exceptions - the state of affairs between Andrew and his women students when the community lived in Marin, and when it moved to Foxhollow in 1996.

At Foxhollow the community was more contained than in California, and Andrew was able to raise the stakes for everyone. This meant more spiritual practice, more clearly focused men's and women's meetings, and more demand from Andrew for independent interest in our work. The unmoving situation with the women, now in its seventh year, frustrated him, despite the insights he had gained from their difficulties. Meanwhile, random, individual breakthroughs by women like Selina and Hanna (a Swedish student, younger in the teachings) gave them raised platforms from which to see the women's group dynamics. They were able to contribute their insider's perspective to an emerging understanding. So, the community's first years at Foxhollow provided both further evidence that individual women could transcend the *visceral no*, and greater understanding of the issues active within the women's group. But there was still no unified progress.

Foxhollow's self-contained context, and the community's rising standard of individual participation, meant the women were under greater pressure. This resulted in many choosing to leave the community. Between 1998 and 1999, twenty-seven of Andrew's women students chose to leave (compared to perhaps two or three men). The frequent women's meetings, lasting late into the evenings, and general sense of the women '*not doing it*', made life tough for all the women students. If, on top of this, a woman was receiving feedback for not giving enough, or for being obstructive in the meetings, she might decide it was all too much, and leave.

However, understanding was slowly gained. One matter that came into view was the women's need to be seen as good people. Andrew gave specific instructions: on one occasion he said they should stop apologising to him, or anyone else, for their apparent failure. But an apologetic message with flowers was sent to him the very next day. In later years, Andrew repeated his instruction, but received the same response. Ironically, the women's need to be seen as caring and 'good' overrode Andrew's unambiguous command, making them disobedient, and eroding the effectiveness of their teacher's guidance.

Andrew applied further pressure. He felt that the women in relationships were affirmed by regular sex with their partners, and that this affirmation softened their sense of urgency about the need for a group breakthrough. So, throughout this confrontation, there were periods – each of many months – when the couples in the core community complied with Andrew's instruction and did not have sex. This abstinence reinforced the message that the sought-for union between the women had yet to happen.

It is fair to say that, for eighteen years, Andrew's women students were seen to have a problem, to be a problem, and to be less capable than the men of doing the community's core work. In an evolutionary perspective, which sees the human condition as a collection of powerful and conflicting impulses, one could say this judgement was misplaced: that the women were valiantly, on behalf of all women, attempting to transcend habits rooted deep in human history. In that view, the women are worthy of praise for eternity. But, as students, we were too involved in the process to see it clearly, so neither the men nor the women were able to hold that ennobling view. At the same time, Andrew, for the sake of what he was trying to achieve, could not afford to promote that interpretation; it would have reduced the pressure he was applying, and placed hard-won progress at risk. Without the existence of a meta-level perspective, it's true to say that the women suffered the shame of second-class status – regarding our core work - throughout the central years of the community's history.

Did the men gloat over the women's struggles and apparent lack of success? Outwardly, in terms of spoken responses or prejudiced actions, there were few obvious signs of such superiority: everyday dignity was maintained. (Please note: the men's maintenance of dignity was far surpassed by that of the women. Even in their darkest days, the women did not collapse into hopelessness). However, inwardly, the men did use the women's situation for their own benefit. It was always a relief to know that someone else was in Andrew's cross hairs, or to be in a meeting in which someone else had '*blown it*' and was under scrutiny. Likewise, one could walk around Foxhollow with a misplaced sense of freedom if one knew Andrew's attention was on a different group from one's own. Remembering my own experience, I believe the men gave in to this tendency to enjoy a false sense of advantage. We lived for a decade with unearned higher status, under less pressure than the women, and falsely believing we shared Andrew's wavelength. The next chapter will show how mistaken we were.

Continuing the story of this lengthy campaign, Andrew started to use the walls of the women's spa area – referred to as *the sauna* - to display letters, quotes and cartoons. The women's sauna was large and plush, with a twenty-person sauna, similar-sized steam room, showers, loos, a row of basins with mirrors and makeup lights, and banks of high-spec lockers. As I have said before, these spa areas (the men had one, too) had been built when Foxhollow was briefly a health resort. They were private spaces, reserved for use by core students and therefore off limits to lay students and guests. Andrew would select student's letters and have them enlarged on the photocopier and posted on the walls. He would vary the font size to emphasise the letter's implicit message, which might be positive or negative. He would also choose relevant quotes from other teachers, historians, or writers, and have them enlarged and displayed. Instructed by Andrew, Seth drew large, professional-quality A2-sized cartoons. These depicted expressions of ego by individual women, or symbolic scenes that represented the group's obstructive behaviour.

Over time, the sauna walls were covered in printed paper. To create more space, a free-standing display board was installed. The sauna became a living exhibition of Andrew's exchanges with his women students. It was used as a place of contemplation and had a unique atmosphere: reverential, ghastly, sobering, overpowering. It became the symbolic, physical representation of a mythic encounter, even as that encounter unfolded. Key moments in Andrew's confrontation with the women's *visceral no* could be identified by collections of letters, quotes and images. The legacies – good and bad - of women who had left the community were captured, again, by their letters and, sometimes, by Seth's cartoons. The sheer volume of communication, stretching over years, indicated the scale of the spiritual confrontation.

I appreciate that some readers might think of the sauna as something unwarranted, or cruel. If so, can I please say I am letting you into the heart of a lengthy and deeply-challenging process. The next chapter records the men's encounter with their deep resistance, an encounter in which their sauna was also used as an educational exhibition. Perhaps this knowledge, that students of both genders were given these visual reflections of their failings, might help readers understand that, in both cases, existential human objections to spiritual realisation were being confronted.

Returning to the story: more was learnt about women's behaviour in groups. Short-lived hierarchies came and went. A woman would find it within herself to rise from the ranks and assume leadership. Sometimes, a second-in-command would pair-up with this leading woman. But the new configuration would last only a few months. What seemed to happen was that the leading woman would have praise heaped upon her by the group. In time, the praise would elevate and isolate her, putting her in an unsupported position with an inflated sense of herself: a position from which she could only fall. The deference and admiration of ordinary members, far from being the support it pretended to be, undermined the leader. When the leader fell from grace, the uncomfortable presence of an independent voice was removed, along with the contrast between the leader and the group's rank and file. The group could then resume its declarations of good intent. Women, it seemed, formed hierarchies that were more fragile than those of men.

In his efforts to construct a hierarchy that would facilitate the group's development, Andrew put pressure on individual women. In his view, those at the top led the way for others and were either a hinderance or a help, depending on their willingness to '*live the teachings*', which meant subordinating the personal elements of their experience and becoming beacons of inspiration for others. Regarding the pressure Andrew applied to his leading students, I have written about the transformation of Selina's office into a paint-splattered, devil's dwelling. In another incident, Miranda was the subject of what is now (2020) held by many to be one of the most notorious examples of Andrew's allegedly abusive behaviour. A throne room was created, again in the basement, and – so the story goes, I wasn't there – Miranda was enthroned like a queen and a bucket of paint tipped over her head. I can only guess at the context of this event: Andrew was probably attempting to shift Miranda out of a resistant, shut-down state of mind. But I do know that American paint is water-based and that Miranda doesn't hold a grudge.

At times, Andrew openly questioned the demand he was making of his women students. He wondered if they were capable of making the breakthrough he saw as essential. During a winter retreat in Rishikesh, in 1999, when nothing was moving for the women, he raised the possibility of having a men-only core community. How serious he was about this was hard to know, but Andrew was not known for casual suggestions. Some men were attracted to the possibility, and one or two were even excited by it. I loathed the idea, partly because it edged towards – in my mind - an incarcerated, monastic life, but also because I felt that dividing from the women would be a sad conclusion to a spirited endeavour. Luckily, the division didn't happen, but the consideration shows how intractable the women's situation appeared to be at times.

In spite of the prolonged, resistant and painful nature of this conflict, the women – as I have said - conducted themselves with stoic dignity. In this they were helped by our commonly upheld standards of behaviour. Yet greater support came from another source: an awareness of the depth of their challenge. As the confrontation inched forward, year by year, progress was painfully slow. But awareness grew of the context in which the confrontation was taking place. We all learned that the women's challenge arose from deep-seated needs and habits, common to all women. This knowledge gave the women's situation great gravitas; it positioned the challenge at a depth that was far beneath the personal realm. Andrew's confrontation with the women's *visceral no* was not characterised by tears, anger or drama. Despite tough episodes it maintained, overall, the character of a noble engagement.

7. The Women's Meetings

While I am personally unable to describe the nature of the women's meetings, I am aware of the valuable experience acquired by Andrew's women students. To record and share what was learnt, I have commissioned two highly experienced, independent female researchers to conduct a qualitative research project. This will inquire into the purpose of the meetings, the issues encountered and the women's experience at the time. The research will consist of a minimum of eight individual, one-on-one, in-depth interviews. The result will be a 4000-word report available from June 2021 as a book, from Amazon. The title of the report will be *Invoking the Authentic Self: The Women's Meetings*.

8. Conclusion

It would be easy to overlook the successes of the women's venture. In today's society, the debate about gender equality is so charged that, almost instinctively, one recoils from evidence of difference. I anticipate many will judge Andrew's work with his women students to be misguided, purely because the outcome of that work does not uphold the idea of gender parity. However, setting aside secular assumptions and returning to the context in which the work took place, I see that Andrew and his women students achieved the following successes.

Andrew's women students are due great credit for reaching a robust, objective relationship to their experience. They built an observation platform from which they could perceive women's nature vis-á-vis enlightenment. They had to be pushed to do it but, nevertheless, it was constructed and maintained by their commitment and intention. Andrew often said that, in an evolutionary, spiritual context, every centimetre of progress is hard-fought-for and worth celebrating; the power of the momentums at play make tiny signs of progress important. While perhaps reluctant explorers, Andrew's women students made inroads into daunting territory.

The women students became experts in a specific aspect of women's behaviour: how women behave in groups under pressure. This expertise, I suggest, is rare, and likely to be needed in the future as women increasingly work together on the front lines of cultural development. I appreciate that the current criticisms of Andrew and his work make the women's discoveries difficult to share, but I think someone (not a man) should do it, because a wealth of useful information exists within the women who courageously participated in this endeavour.

Metaphysical pathways were cut by the women students. This aspect of their work is less tangible but, perhaps, more significant. Over nearly two decades they inquired into dense material, taking the light of awakened consciousness into new places, pulverising obstacles, and bringing order to chaos. If consciousness is seen as an undivided field of universal cognition, the women cleared and organised a section of that field and laid tracks for others. While this view might seem esoteric to some, I suggest that future inquirers into the same subject – women's groups and enlightenment – will, consciously or unconsciously, benefit from the progress made by Andrew's women students.

Their contribution to our community's invocation of the Authentic Self should also be applauded. Approximately a hundred women gave a decade or more of their lives to push the women's project forward. Their effort was integral to our community's work; it was part and parcel of the conglomerated push that sought to invoke the Authentic Self. Future chapters describe how the community's big breakthrough came through the men but, if that breakthrough is seen as a birth, and all activities leading to it are seen as preceding contractions, then the women's phenomenal effort should be acknowledged: they contributed more than half the labour.

One further consequence of the engagement between Andrew and his women students is obscure, but of vital significance to this book's story. It needs to be introduced in two parts. Firstly, as a matter of compassion, I want to say that Andrew's confrontation with the women's *visceral no* was costly for the women involved. It ended many women's spiritual search and, for the women who stayed, it was emotionally turbulent and profoundly draining. Yet, secondly, what the lengthy confrontation taught Andrew was vital to the success of the community's work. Seen in sequence, what Andrew learnt with his women students was preparation for his engagement with his men students; because, when Andrew realised his men students were not really with him, he reflected on his conflict with the women, saw how long and tiring it had been, and decided that his next unsought-for confrontation was not going to last so long. As we shall see in the next two chapters, his decision had critical consequences.

Chapter 20

The Men

Maslow's hierarchy of needs was mentioned in Chapter 14. It was not a reference we used in the community, but it will help me introduce this chapter. Maslow's hierarchy is drawn as a pyramid with five horizontal levels. The bottom level of need is physiological: food, shelter, sleep, etc. The next level is security: physical, emotional and financial. The top level (added later in Maslow's life) is transcendence: *"the need to give oneself to something beyond oneself."* Maslow asserted that human beings can move up the hierarchy only when their needs at each level are met. I want to highlight this feature of Maslow's hierarchy: while people are pre-occupied by their needs at one level, they have little or no attention available for the needs - or values - of the levels above. For example, someone whose attention is consumed by their need for friendship and intimacy cannot graduate to thinking about their need for self-esteem and status.

This chapter tells the story of Andrew's attempt to elevate his men students from one level of awareness to another: to raise them from their level - of self-satisfaction - to his level of commitment to a greater purpose. This graduation, as we shall see, is not a matter of intellectual grasp or academic study. Instead, as with Maslow's hierarchy, it is a graduation from one set of values to another.

At times this story is comical, theatrical and bizarre. We, the men, resisted Andrew's call and contracted into the safety of group collusion. Andrew's creative attempts to tease apart our collusion – half the content of the story - would look strange if seen out of context. But, seen in context, I think his actions portray a spiritual teacher's commitment to overcoming his students' deep resistance.

In part, the men's resistance to Andrew's call took the form of regression. This regression makes up the other half of the story. Denying what we knew, we became sleepwalkers, shadows of ourselves, bemused by events unfolding around us. Our regression and its accompanying amnesia made our situation surreal and, perhaps, doubly hard to understand. Please be forewarned.

I should mention three further points. First, the story begins with sixteen men in the group. Second, this episode in the community's history starts on July 16th 2000 and lasts for just under a year. Third, it includes two events of personal importance; these events usefully represent an esoteric element present in the confrontation, but I have also included them because they are precious to me.

Foxhollow, Year 2000: The Men's Recent History with Andrew

In Marin, Andrew had drawn the men closer to him. He had spent more social time with them and, in formal meetings, he had taken greater interest in individual progress. The closer relationship with Andrew gave the men confidence, and they relaxed with one another. This made their weekly meetings less competitive and more cooperative. The move to Foxhollow took a minor toll because not everyone made the journey and, even once students arrived, there were challenges: the tighter-knit community meant less personal time, and Foxhollow's physical perfection – feeling undeserved - took time to accept. However, once the men had acclimatised and welcomed some east-coast students, plus undergone a refreshing re-distribution of responsibilities, they started their new phase of life on a positive trajectory with Andrew.

Over the next three years, a beautiful camaraderie developed between Andrew and his upper-core student men. He liked to be with us, and we liked to be with him. Even in formal meetings, he did not hold himself aloof. Those meetings had a workmanlike, brotherly fairness about them, and a gentle, ecstatic, baseline union that felt heavenly. I might have anticipated such meetings nervously, but I never felt alone in them. Over time our men's matrix which, in our minds, included Andrew, grew stronger. We respected one another, and our commitment to a common cause gave us the invigorating and joyful experience of being a team.

I'd like to describe the elements of Andrew's teachings that I feel particularly appeal to men. By making this description I mean no disrespect to women; perhaps the same elements appeal to them. But, for myself, I feel his teachings vibrate on a wavelength that men easily attune to. These teachings are unsentimental, rational, precise, comprehensive, driven, linear and extreme. They have natural simplicity and refer to the kind of colossal, overarching authority that, I think, excites a man's sense of awe. What's more, his teachings encompass the timescale of the cosmos, while tracking earthly, anthropological progressions. My own feeling is that they exist beyond the orbit of convention; the adventurous part of myself loves them for that reason. These are just personal musings, but what I can say for sure is that Andrew's men resonated with his teachings.

In addition to this affinity, we benefited from the work of the great spiritual figures of history: those who had already identified and cut men's spiritual pathways. The work of bringing a man's ego into the light of day had already been done. Pride, Arrogance, Pretence, Narcissism, Cowardice; the big, classic issues for men were already known. Moreover, human anthropological development had, over eons, prepared us to work as a team; a great advantage as the community's group work became increasingly important.

The group enjoyed halcyon days, but it could not be used as a place to hide from personal responsibility. Andrew would go to war with individuals if destructive habits were not addressed, and our primary responsibility remained, as always, the management of our own mind. Individual men who failed to maintain this responsibility chose to leave the community. Broadly speaking, men chose to leave with the same frequency as women, except during the kind of exceptional episodes noted in the last chapter. This explains why, despite the men's and women's groups facing different levels of challenge, a gender imbalance did not develop in the community.

This story begins with the upper-core student men riding a wave of some momentum. We'd assumed ownership of a grand estate and divided it into departmental 'principalities'. We had settled into recognised, mutually-respected roles, each man the prince of his own domain. In our minds, our teacher was an elevated but, nevertheless, integrated member of our group. We were self-assured and we revelled in our chosen, haloed identity as 'The Men'. Everything seemed to be just great.

July 16th 2000, Guru Purnima Day

In eastern spiritual traditions, Guru Purnima Day reveres the guru. In the year 2000, it was still a day celebrated by our community. The men had planned a lunch party for Andrew at an unoccupied summer camp about ten miles from Foxhollow.

The women were not coming. Their exclusion was unusual for this focal event, a reflection of Andrew's dissatisfaction with their recent progress. News of their absence was unsurprising but, even so, I felt disappointed: the celebration would be less than it could have been. Meanwhile we, the men, were busy with our preparations and excited by the prospect of spending time with Andrew. Distracted by practicalities and the promise of the day, we accepted and forgot about the women's absence.

The venue, although well-maintained, was a collection of slightly eerie buildings. From many options, we chose one that had the utilitarian character of an English village hall. A few men had come from Europe for the celebration. We dressed for the occasion, laid out a beautiful meal, welcomed Andrew, and sat at one big table, twenty-five men in total.

The day seemed to pass successfully enough. Our conversation, always the main matter, moved between familiar subjects: world news, students' career successes, and stories of film stars met by the two actors among us. Andrew led our dialogue and gave brief responses to a few self-conscious questions about his travels. Later in the afternoon, he took an unprecedented nap. I was not sure what to make of this; was Andrew casting aside convention? Or bored? In the evening we watched a film, before returning to Foxhollow at around 10pm. The day appeared to have met expectations.

We were surprised to be called to a men's meeting the next afternoon and told by the senior student men – quite gently - that something vital had been missing from the celebration. It had been OK, passable and congenial, but afterwards Andrew had said, *"They're not really with me."*

After years of men's meetings, we were practised at identifying key subjects and responding to them with nuanced insights. We knew how to expand and contract a context, and how to build a discussion composed of varying takes on an emerging theme. After hearing the senior men's message, this machinery whirred into action. Some men recognised the mismatching wavelengths being pointed to, others said they'd had niggles that something was *'off'*, and a few confessed to not having had niggles but, instead, offered their immediate insights into the reasons for Andrew's dissatisfaction. At the end of the meeting, we felt our response had been satisfactory.

Foxhollow, 2000, August–December

There were probably further meetings in which the seriousness of the situation was impressed upon us. If so, these would undoubtedly have elicited further sincere declarations of concern. But what had real impact, three weeks after the event, was the posting of a large cartoon in the men's sauna.

As noted before, we happily made use of the two sauna and steam-room facilities that came with the property. The women's suite was decorated in subdued pinks, ours had a pale grey theme. In the last chapter, I described how the two saunas acted as interfaces for creative communication between Andrew and his core students. We therefore knew that the appearance of a cartoon in the sauna had great significance. It declared the existence of a problem. It placed the problem at our feet. And it announced Andrew's intention to solve it.

In size, the cartoon was one metre square. It depicted the Foxhollow men sitting around a fire, into which they were throwing Andrew's published books. Circling above the scene were the words Arrogance, Pretence, Cowardice and Disrespect. Skilfully drawn, it showed the Foxhollow men jubilantly engaged in wanton desecration.

In response to the cartoon, we withdrew. We withdrew from each other, withdrew from Andrew and withdrew from active interest in our situation. I simply didn't want to know. I didn't want what was happening to be happening. I had no interest in the reason for it happening. Outside our formal meetings, we avoided the cartoon's implications and either talked with discomfort about superficial matters, or stayed silent. In our meetings, to which the now watchful senior students came, we made more effort; but genuine enthusiasm was short-lived and the intelligence of reliably buoyant men was extinguished by the group's inertia. Our fortunes had reversed and our status had collapsed. Previously we were exalted heroes, now we were becoming calcified embodiments of denial.

The following three months were something of a war without gunfire. Andrew posted positive letters in the sauna from the few men who had brief insights into our predicament. One Dutch student, Geert, broke ranks. He saw the nature of the gulf between Andrew and the men, and courageously left the safety of our group to join Andrew in spirit. He remained aligned with Andrew for the next fourteen months, and his many handwritten letters, that clearly came from a different mind-set, became features of the sauna walls.

While we were confused by our fall from grace, uninterested in its cause, robbed of our status, and wary of each other, we were still bound together. Now our union was based on memories of better days and our common state of resistance. Withdrawn and forlorn, we were still very much a group.

Foxhollow, 2000, New Year's Eve

The head space of an individual rooted in denial is unstable, allowing both ridiculous and level-headed ideas to coexist. Despite the group's estrangement from Andrew for more than three months, I half expected he would receive us with open arms on New Year's Eve, given that it was normally a time of good cheer. Harking back to the parties of previous years, I thought the instruction we received – to gather at the meditation hall - might be the beginning of a turnaround: that all might be forgiven.

Our meditation hall was a detached building, the length of a tennis court but a little narrower. It had been built 100 years earlier by George and Marguerite Westinghouse as a playroom for their disabled son. The dark interior woodwork was finely crafted; it included a series of broad arches supporting the roof, and two narrow, almost miniature staircases at either end. These staircases led down to a basement of equal area to the hall, where we had installed a yoga studio and library. At eight pm on New Year's Eve, our group of sixteen men stood silently on one staircase; each tread supporting one man.

At the foot of the stairs a door opened, loud disco music was heard, and we were ushered onto the floor of a pulsing night-club. The astonishing transformation of the space erased all memories of what was there before. I surveyed the surprising level of detail: the low-level lighting, pictures, tables and chairs, barrel of beer, the inverted row of liquor bottles behind a full-scale bar, and the aproned and bow-tied barman. Swirling through this scene, in an eye-popping whirligig of cleavages, high-heels, boas and fish-net stockings, were Andrew's core student women, bearing trays of brandy.

I was uncertain how to respond but, primed by my earlier thoughts of a prodigal son's reunion, I decided to go with the flow, and drained my glass. Looking around for its successor, with an eye on the burlesque scene, I was alarmed to see many of my peers looking po-faced. In contrast to their solemnity, the women intensified their sensory assault by setting-off party-poppers, flinging glitter and blowing squawking, unfurling little party-horns. *"Don't take Andrew so seriously,"* they repeated to us, standing face-to-face, with raised, deadpan voices. As streamers fell, party horns squawked and glitter swirled in the turbulent air, I made some sense of the scene: *"Don't take Andrew so seriously"* was the obvious, ironic message.

It would be nice to record this event as a watershed moment but, despite its colourful content and memorable date, I can only say it was one further click on a ratchet. Having received the message, we did have the wherewithal to leave the party, convene a formal meeting, discuss the situation, and later clean up the mess. The party did not produce a group breakthrough. Instead, the increased demand for a meaningful response meant personal neuroses began to surface.

George was in his mid-thirties. He was a gifted mathematician, but socially odd. He often spoke with his eyes closed and the trembling intensity of someone whose voice cannot keep pace with their brain. George's oddness was balanced by his dedication to rational thought. This dedication meant he referred to Andrew's teachings as if they were proven mathematical theorems and, occasionally, George would surprise a men's meeting with his valuable, purely logical, insights. He was a strange man, but valued.

The sight of the women dressed as tarts had deeply upset George. He referred to them as his *"spiritual sisters,"* and decried the indignity they'd had to endure. Moreover, like a product of malfunctioning hypnotherapy, a link had been forged in George's mind between the women's humiliation and the party's glitter. The mere sight of glitter soon triggered George's trauma. Carried in our hair and on our clothes, it had dispersed throughout the manor house. Some diehard flecks had gone to ground in the deep-pile carpet of our meeting room. Hence, our post-mortem meetings, that should have been sober deconstructions of our predicament, were interrupted by cries from George as, reaching forward from his place in our circle, he spotted and picked out yet another tormenting speck.

Seen in the context of a year-long confrontation, George's response to the glitter can, perhaps, be seen as a hairline crack in the group's cohesion. But I should say that we, the men, didn't yet have that perspective. We were in the unknown. Nothing that was happening was recognisable, so we had no sense of being in a process; nor could we imagine an end to what we were going through. 'Things are bad and we don't like it,' was the extent of our perspective. Andrew, no doubt, had faith in a new dawn, but no certainty of its timing or even its arrival. In these circumstances, all either side could do was to keep going.

India, Rishikesh, January 2001

I was more than happy to travel to India and join the set-up team for Andrew's public retreat in Rishikesh. At Foxhollow, I was not a prominent figure faced with high expectations, but the preceding months had been relentlessly tough, and I welcomed some time away. Besides, I loved the familiar challenge of preparing the infrastructure of a westerner's retreat using Indian building supplies. Set-up typically took two weeks. Half of our team prepared the bedrooms of our rented ashram, while the other half - my team - built a water-purifying system and installed generator-powered electrical circuits for the teaching hall, outdoor kitchen and pathway lighting.

The retreat was attended by about 250 people. Slightly less than half were Andrew's core students. Most of those students started a separate, silent retreat, while five men from Foxhollow, including me, were to have meetings with Andrew's top student, Ambrose. The small configuration of five men was novel, I liked all the men involved, and my time in India had been a break from the strong sense – at Foxhollow - that there was a problem. I was re-energised.

My four peers were intelligent men in their early to mid-thirties. Govinda was Indian, an inscrutable Brahmin with seamless, upper-class composure. The others were American. Franklin, from Connecticut, was a graduate of Yale who, although self-doubtful, reliably exhibited his high-quality education. Tony, from Colorado, was tall and handsome, naturally buoyant, humorous and likeable. Holden was described by Andrew as having uniquely supple intelligence; he'd also been a mid-weight champion wrestler at his Oklahoma college. Tony and Holden held the highest status in our group, in part because they were editors of the magazine.

Embarking on our meetings, Ambrose reminded us that we represented the Foxhollow men and added that this was a do-or-die matter. If these meetings weren't successful, it would be the end of the road for us as Andrew's students. I'm not sure if we all believed this, but I most certainly did.

The meetings with Ambrose started well. We welcomed the opportunity to make a fresh start and were willing to take another run at the matter in hand: finding a new relationship with our teacher. With spacious encouragement from Ambrose, we described the context in which we saw ourselves, vis-à-vis Andrew, and talked about the challenge we faced. Our dialogue with Ambrose reached peak performance: our highest level of inquiry, developed in men's meetings over many years. My peers were, possibly, the most skilful proponents of this art: of gleaning contextualised insight from experience and then feeding newly-won perspectives into an ever-enriching loop of ascending cognition. So far, so good.

However, after a few meetings, and pushed by Ambrose to leap the hurdles we'd faced since Guru Purnima Day, we started turning in circles. Peak performance wore thin. Ambrose didn't relent, he wanted to hear something new. We started to flounder. Hitherto effective strategies now lacked traction, the feeling of a 'fresh start' vanished and, with only five men in the meetings, we became surprisingly transparent. As each man started to repeat himself, his modus operandi rose into view, exposing core dependencies. We became like robots exhibiting our dated programmes. Hitting, time and again, the same boundaries, we disclosed our strategies for getting-by, as follows.

Govinda could be seen to start all his contributions with the normally commendable phrase *"When I look into my experience,"* but his opening line now looked like a posh label on an empty tin. Tony's hitherto impressive oratory morphed into naked, effusive bluster, as, under brighter scrutiny, it looked merely clever and felt unreal. Holden looked at the floor and fell silent, his normal curiosity crushed, while Franklin, having milked dry his Yale confidence, looked like a stranded schoolboy. In my attempt to get-by I resorted to English verbosity, but Ambrose insisted we keep to the language of Andrew's teachings and so I, too, was left high and dry. Soon, each man's habitual form of response had failed him.

Drained of dignity, initiative and hope, we came to an emotional standstill and, halfway into the retreat, the heartbeat of these dialogues flatlined. We were then called to a meeting with Andrew.

The ashram buildings had flat roofs. On top of Andrew's apartment, a basic canopy had been erected. Beneath it were set out some chairs, rugs and cushions. This arrangement made an outdoor living space that overlooked a line of trees and the river Ganges beyond. Here, on the roof, we met with Andrew; he sat in a chair, we sat on the rugs.

The only precursor to what happened next was my appreciation of the unbroken perfection of the scene. The broad river, rushing over underlying rocks, was a sparkling torrent. A light breeze moved the warm air. Andrew appeared softly perplexed and in slight pain as he looked at us with incomprehension. Unusually, I found I could engage his eyes. The meeting started and, in the background of my awareness, the other men spoke to Andrew, their voices mingling with the sound of the river. My opportunity to speak must have arrived, I don't remember, but what came through me was a cry from the depths of the universe. There was not a glitch of resistance within me, this was a full-bore, full-volume eruption that moved too fast to control. I was choiceless: a bystander to my actions. Unsought for, and without prelude, I was taken over, at a cellular level, by an infinite power. I burst into tears and bellowed, "IT'S A FUCKING NIGHTMARE," while leaning forward and pounding the fist of my right hand onto the concrete rooftop. For a full minute my cries were variations of the original sentiment, equally unrestrained, while Andrew quietly commented, *"It is,"* and *"That's right."* Somehow my outpouring must have subsided, prompting Andrew, I presume, to bring the meeting to a close.

Over the following three days, I had my first full-blown experience of enlightened consciousness. I was immune to my wretchedness, immune to predatory thoughts, liberated from worry and able to love the world around me. I lived in a new-found dimension. The meetings with Ambrose continued, and I was able to respond naturally to the real situation. I could see the other men flailing helplessly, as if they were behind a barrier, or reaching out from Hades. It was crystal clear to me: they wanted to bring their shields with them, but shields were not needed in my world. I sat in meditation like the Buddha on an airfield, thoughts dive-bombing me like fighter planes, but they were powerless: I had effortless immunity. This delightful dimension did not seem to be fragile; mesmerised by its unexpected arrival and its beauty, I did not fear its disappearance. I was, therefore, unaware that it might collapse. In particular, I was unaware of the power of certain thoughts. In fact, it was just one thought that intruded into my enlightened state and dragged me down: *"How am I going to maintain this when I get back to Foxhollow?"* That thought had talons, it attacked my perspective and tore at my confidence. By raising doubts about the future, it planted fear in my fearless state and changed my world. My enlightened experience imploded and vanished. Panicking, I attempted to recover by imitating my earlier, naturally relaxed, condition; but Ambrose noticed the difference and challenged me. Once again enmeshed with my feelings, I re-joined my peers.

Our meetings with Ambrose disintegrated further. They lost all reference to the formality we normally upheld, and were clearly hopeless. At one point,

Ambrose said, *"If I were you guys, I'd be climbing the nearest mountain to fight for my spiritual life."* I took him at his word, thinking there was nothing to lose as life with Andrew was coming to an end. I left the retreat and spent two nights on an island rock, up-river. Not all dramatic actions have dramatic results; nothing significant came from my ascetic gesture. But afterwards – having been forgiven – I had an obligatory debrief with Ambrose, in which he let slip that, in our meetings with him, I was not a person of principal interest. Andrew and the senior students had been hoping to break down the resistance in Tony and Holden, thinking that, if the men with the highest status broke free and evolved, others would follow.

Ambrose's slip transformed my understanding of our predicament: I saw there was a hand on the tiller of this chaos. People cared about the outcome and were paying attention. Our hellish experience was not, perhaps, the doomed free-fall it seemed to be.

Foxhollow. Four Ghastly Months. February–May 2001

I still have the feeling that very little happened in the months after we returned to Foxhollow. My memories of that time are dominated by the dense, collective denial existing within our group. Our failure in Rishikesh had not helped the overall situation. My explosive moment had done nothing for the group as a whole, nor had it freed me from the negative gravity we dwelt in.

Like anti-matter, our response to every input was further contraction. We became a huddled mass of unspoken, collusive resistance, each camouflaging ourselves as an ordinary member of the group. In this state of avoidance, one only feels numb. This feeling, lacking variation, becomes a dull, monotonous continuum. In this shut-down state, we saw Andrew as a distant figure and heard his name as an unwelcome, painful reminder of a previous life. Excluded from the manor house, the hub of our community, we became mere shadows on the periphery of a civilization we'd helped to build.

In this condition, incoming information only adds weight to an existing sense of burden. And so, while the recollections below (there are seven, unnumbered, including an episode precious to me) might be interesting to a lively soul, please bear in mind that we weren't lively souls. Our aggregated, unyielding opposition to change neutralised the initiatives made on our behalf.

The sauna became a living collage of applied scripture. Andrew posted relevant passages from spiritual texts, he magnified and displayed his fellow teachers' comments on our situation and, on a daily basis, students' letters, both valiant and capitulating, were pinned to the walls. The film *Terminator 2* played constantly on a large TV; it was chosen by Andrew to illustrate the nature of ego, in the form of a bad-ass, indestructible, liquid machine-man from the future. Psychic accounts of astonishingly relevant dreams and intuitions, sent speculatively from concerned people around the world, were added to the paper patchwork. Gradually, all the walls, mirrors, locker doors and even the tiled surfaces of the steam room, were covered in commentaries.

Men were called from Europe to help with the situation. But, being no more evolved than the Foxhollow men, they had no impact. Indeed, they soon had to face the same issues in themselves. Separately, we had a few stormy meetings with the women. They, seeing we had feet of clay, were livid. For many years we had happily assumed we were beyond their state of core resistance, but now it was evident that we shared it, and were crumbling under the same pressure they'd managed to withstand. Our meetings with them contained some vitriolic moments.

Andrew had little direct contact with us during this time; instead, he sent instructions. One Sunday morning, we were told to list all his initiatives since Guru Purnima Day, and record our responses alongside. We did this as a group, using flip-charts pinned to a living-room wall. To the left of the charts hung an A2-sized drawing of Andrew, borrowed from the sauna. The drawing showed Andrew seated, cross-legged, on the floor. Glad to have something tangible to do, we began. The list of Andrew's initiatives grew while, in the adjacent column, we were forced to conclude, item by item, that we had not met his creativity with any of our own.

Continuing this account, of comparing Andrew's initiatives to our lack of meaningful response, I come to this chapter's second event of personal significance.

I had a moment of stillness, similar to the feeling of unity I experienced on the ashram roof. Geert, our man with the marker pen, encouraged me to speak. As I hesitantly started, I saw the drawing of Andrew miraculously start to move. I'm neither susceptible nor attracted to occult experiences of any sort - it's just not me - but, for two minutes, my awareness bridged two worlds. Speaking aloud, I described what I saw. As the figure of Andrew moved, each man in the room became – in a blend of symbolism and psychic association - a limb of his body. Appearing as one living, integrated and serpentine form, I saw each man's qualities as facets of Andrew's being. It was as if a metaphysical x-ray of our interrelationship with him had overlain and become unified with the physical scene in the room. I was more flabbergasted by this experience than consumed (as I was in Rishikesh), but I was again forced to accept that forces beyond my understanding were at play in our situation.

This experience released me from the group's myopia and amnesia, and I joined a small group of three men whose awareness was distinct from the collective gloop. For a few weeks I was, again, a liberated man. Within that period, I remember Andrew referring to a letter I'd written about my esoteric insight. Acknowledging the event, he gestured to the letter and said, *"You can't fake this kind of thing."*

Another of these seven memorable moments was when Stathan fought his way free from the group's negative force field. I have described this event before, in Chapter 14. Despite him being a martial artist with an enviable range of capabilities, our group's extreme condition of refusal had reduced him to a state of pale, alien translucence. His substance had gone. However, in an evening meeting he fought his way - using sheer grit and personal willpower - out of the group's suffocated state. For a while, he was also an independent man.

At one point, with just two hours' notice, our three leading men were dispatched to Australia for an indefinite stay. In Sydney, a group of twelve students manned one of Andrew's Centres and the three Foxhollow men went to join them. Their dispatch identified them as potential leaders. A measure of the deadlock at Foxhollow was that their departure and return, a month later, made no difference to the situation. Despite their efforts to become leaders, they were too bonded to the group to achieve or maintain independent standing.

Remaining forever in my memory with shivering discomfort is the experience of standing in a ring around Andrew's house. Months later, we heard he was consumed with frustration and desperate to make something happen but, at the time, I - and probably we - did not welcome our working hours being disrupted by his mid-afternoon instruction to drop everything and form a circle around his home. It was damn cold in the afternoon, and even colder as evening arrived. The men from Boston appeared, and the silent circle grew in size. The dark closed in and the cold rose from the ground. For some weeks, we'd had no close contact with Andrew and - in retrospect and theory - when he brought us hot food, there should have been more response to him than to the food. But there wasn't. Not one of us responded to the spiritual opportunity of the moment. I remember with regret how my personal discomfort was all I cared about. That said, and digressing momentarily, those hours of discomfort and the memory of my self-concern did eventually serve me. The physical hardship, and my regret at the missed opportunity, made one of Andrew's spiritual instructions unforgettable. After the event, he met with a few of the men who had been especially inert since Guru Purnima Day. Those men later relayed what he had said: *"If you could just find a grain of interest..."* His advice to them, delivered as both an imploring request and a teacher's instruction, has stayed with me ever since, helping to mobilise my initiative in situations where I have felt completely stuck.

I return to this chapter's storyline. Each Tuesday evening, I attended an evening class. At Foxhollow, we needed someone to hold a Massachusetts contractor's licence, to certify our building work. It was agreed that I would pursue the qualification, despite the messy situation with the men. These evenings, as you might imagine, provided me with a few welcome hours away from Foxhollow. After one class, in mid-April, I switched on my pager, saw there was a message waiting and, en route back to Foxhollow, I pulled into the *Stop and Shop* supermarket, where there was a pay-phone. Standing alone in a deserted parking lot, I was informed that the men had been told to leave Foxhollow instantly, without possessions, and that my eleven expelled peers (four men had dropped out of the group since New Year's Eve) had booked into *The Pilgrim's Inn*, in Lee.

Lee and Lenox, The Motels, Late May/Early June 2001

It was hard to know how being 'thrown-off the property' affected us. One would think those words would invoke panic or despair. But neither my feelings about our new circumstances, nor the behaviour of the other men, indicated deep disturbance.

I concluded: *"This is the end of my spiritual road,"* and was surprised to feel so neutral about arriving at such a momentous point in my life. My mind started planning a new future in England and working through the steps necessary to close down my life in America. Even thoughts of my spiritual teacher did not upset the bland equanimity I felt. Strangely, my mood was even lifted a little by the novelty of the scene - the smoky motel rooms and fenced-off pool - and I was curious about the reactions of my peers.

Their reactions were not easy to see, because we were trained to '*hold formation*'. This term, occasionally used, meant that each man put the interests of the group before his own. It was, therefore, not our habit to speak about our feelings unless it helped to clarify a discussion or inquiry. Blurting out frustrations, expressing despair, crying, or lashing out in anger would have broken our common standard. This standard was not enforced - we didn't have military bearing – but, between one another, we would talk only about common concerns, not personal sentiments. So, my scrutiny of the other men didn't reveal panic, despair, or rage. If anything, it seemed as if our state of emotional lockdown had merely been relocated, from Foxhollow to the motel.

In the same way that my mood was lifted by the motel's novelty, some miscellaneous matters needing the group's attention brought fresh air to our joint predicament. While the name - *The Pilgrim's Inn* - suited our homeless state, we lacked even a pilgrim's basic supplies. We had one wallet, one car and no spare clothes to share between twelve men unaccustomed to ascetic life. It might be an apocryphal tale, but I heard that someone was despatched to buy a bundle of underpants from *Walmart*. I didn't hear the inside story regarding the procurement of these underpants – I was away during working hours, managing holiday rentals at Foxhollow - or ever get to wear the nylon garments, but this tale serves to introduce a surreal quality, that came and went during this period.

Tony, an entrepreneur by nature, had the gumption to write to Andrew and ask for help. Andrew sent back a stack of his books, gift-wrapped. His implicit message was *Live my teachings*. Shortly after, Andrew sent a document that was, to us, extraordinary. It was a list: a creative criticism of each man. Nakedly truthful, I felt it had the qualities of an anatomical Renaissance sketch. Tony *"had an ego higher than any mountain he could ever climb,"* Franklin was *"a cosmic goofball,"* and Andrew wrote this about me: *"Tim cares, but never enough to change or really make a difference, so what difference does it really make?"* Tony generously noted that Andrew's critique of me, last on his list, was the only one with positive content.

The Pilgrim's Inn was close to a big highway going to Boston. A gas station nearby sold confectionery and the motel's reception had a drinks machine but, otherwise, there was little to eat. We decided to move motels and go to the *Comfort Inn*, located between Foxhollow and Pittsfield. We received word from Foxhollow that the name of the new motel was not a favourable sign and, again illustrating just how discombobulated our situation had become, we agonised over the influence the new name might have on our prospects, before agreeing to move.

The *Comfort Inn* lived up to its name. It was newly-built, the rooms didn't smell of smoke, and – joy of joys - ingredients for breakfast were laid out each morning in the foyer. There were small pots of yoghurt, mini-packs of cereal and little cartons of orange juice. Guests duly opened the packets and peeled off the lids as they pieced together a practical start to the day. Being residents, our group had the same right of access to the pots and packets but - unlike other guests - we then stayed on the premises. For an hour or two, the foyer was then a place of animalistic tension, as we eyed the remaining food while reception staff watched suspiciously from their booth. By mid-morning, pot by pot, the breakfast table was stripped bare.

We had nothing to do. One-on-one conversations eroded our sense of unity. Everything that could ever be said in a group meeting had been said a thousand times in the past months. We were tired of hearing the same phrases, we had run out of vocabulary and, more to the point, anyone's declaration of interest or care, having lost credibility through fruitless repetition, was disbelieved. We had reached a standstill.

Andrew sent Beryl to take us out for a drink. Warm, smiling, humorous, huggable Beryl, bought us all a beer. She asked after us, took an interest in the arrangements at the motel, heard the underpants story, and chatted about world news and sports results. She asked if we'd like another beer. By this time some of the men had caught the gist of her message: did we want a life of superficial chat? They led the way by refusing her second offer, and we left the bar soon after.

The motel rooms had two double beds. Our requested extra cots, or camp beds, occupied much of the spare floor space. Soon after Beryl's visit, mid-morning, a truck arrived at the motel entrance and twelve huge flower arrangements were carried through to our rooms. These blousy bouquets were suitable for a hotel's entrance and, with three positioned in each bedroom, they dominated what little space we had. Andrew had sent them, the message cards said, *"with love."* The arrival of the flowers and Andrew's message had minimal impact on our bovine state of awareness. We registered their arrival, but they stimulated little emotional response. From habit, we knew we should get together and write a message, which we did but, bogged down in the quicksand of our resistance, we lacked the energy for either despair or hope. The flowers merely reminded us of the world we once knew so well.

By this time, the motel staff were looking upset. Motels, as everyone knows, are not for living in. Twelve subdued men milling around the parking lot, or sitting inertly in the lobby, don't improve first impressions for other customers. We were well-behaved but incongruous guests: abnormally present and oddly silent. The massive, but soon drooping, bunches of flowers, our only belongings, did little to rescue our reputation. Instead, they fed the feeling that our welcome was withering. The *Comfort Inn* became less comfortable.

Our rooms backed onto a gravel path that ran between the motel and a boundary fence. One evening, soon after the arrival of the flowers, we heard rustling, cooing and whooping sounds outside our windows. Looking out, we saw nothing. Minutes later, the sounds resumed and, in the twilight, we saw what appeared to be four Arab vagabonds. They wore the most peculiar garb, and had their faces wrapped in rags. One looked like a camel trader, another a mummy from the pyramids, and the last two resembled desert tramps. In fact, they were four of our fellow upper-core students, babbling incoherently. They came into one of our rooms and, still in character, a semblance of a meeting took place. Although incomprehensible to me at the time, this was another message from Andrew: *Look how insane this whole situation is.* Our response to our peers' play-acting was, as usual, to send Andrew a message of gratitude.

Perhaps twelve days into this episode, I was milling around the motel's driveway. So was Bernard. Without speaking, he and I began to walk together. It was a nice evening and Pittsfield, about two miles away, became our assumed destination. We started to talk freely, commenting upon our freaky situation and some of the odd behaviour of our peers. Irreverence caught hold, then gathered momentum until, for the major part of our return journey, we were doubled over with gut-wrenching, weeping, face-aching laughter. With agreed codes of behaviour long-gone, and any sense of responsibility thrown to the wind, we tore the group and its situation to shreds in search of every ounce of humour we could find. Perhaps we were releasing tension, or maybe this was a small sign of the fractures that were about to appear. It's hard to know. Whatever purpose this breach of protocol served, neither of us ever mentioned it, to anyone else or each other.

Throughout the nine months since Guru Purnima Day, we had always responded to Andrew in the same way, by sending flowers and a message. Our messages were written with great care but, in essence, they all said the same thing: *We know we're bad/unworthy/at fault... but we love you and we do intend to change and become real players in evolution, we really do.* A simple record of events would read as follows: Andrew sent us a precise description of our spiritual profiles, we sent him a message. Andrew sent Beryl to take us for a drink, we sent him a message. Andrew sent us huge bunches of flowers, we sent him a message. Etc. Perhaps it is not surprising that these life-memorable, peculiar and possibly incomprehensible nine months of estrangement came to an end when someone decided to do something that would disrupt this pattern.

After living for almost two weeks at the *Comfort Inn*, there were raised voices early one evening. Tony, in particular, had had enough. We were banned from Foxhollow, but he was going to live in the adjacent woods. He was serious. Despite anyone's protests or practical objections, he was not going to spend another night in the *Comfort Inn*. Three men shared Tony's intention, their plan was communicated to Foxhollow, and all four men left the motel. Their actions broke the group's cohesion, authority devolved, and each man became responsible for himself.

Tony and his three colleagues were intercepted en route to their new habitat. They were directed to start an austere retreat at Foxhollow, meditating and living in the meditation hall. The remaining eight men chose different paths. George and one other man chose to leave the situation, and the community. Others moved to a different motel until they had individual epiphanies and were instructed, one by one, to join the retreat. Bernard, later to be Andrew's most enlightened student, was the last to return. I took advantage of the group's fragmentation and went to live in my Foxhollow office. I was permitted to be there during the day and, for a week, I hid at night. Divorced from my heart I was an automaton, mechanically doing my work while bearing the dull ache of egoic denial. Sitting in meditation one morning, my heart rebelled. Spontaneously and desperately, I went and sat on the flat roof of the bunker (a garage), level with the windows of Andrew's first-floor apartment. Time had collapsed for me; there was only the brilliance of the day and the seamless sense of *now*. Roy, a senior student, soon came and asked me what was going on. In tears I said, *"I love him."* I was then told to join the retreat.

The storyline resumes a short way into the next chapter.

Reflections

As noted previously, earlier in my life I read Mary Lutyens' biographies of Krishnamurti. Towards the end of his life, he commented on his followers, lamenting, *"Not one person has fundamentally changed."* In this chapter's introduction, I refer to Maslow's hierarchy, and his assertion that people can only graduate between levels once their needs are met. What we see in this chapter is, I suggest, Andrew making evolution happen. Krishnamurti was, famously, a hands-off teacher, disappointed by his results. In Maslow's system, people are dependent on progressions that take time. In Andrew's work with his men, I think we see something different: direct human engagement.

The historic value of the men's story becomes clear in the next chapter. Here, at this point of reflection, it is also valuable to see it as a magnified encounter with ego. At the start of the story we, the men, had already transcended men's more obvious egoic traits – like competition and pontification – but we had formed a strong group identity that looked inward. We were self-satisfied and proud. We felt happy and thought we knew everything, so we weren't looking upward and outward, we weren't reaching to meet a greater power, or seeking to be useful to a greater purpose. Andrew felt this, encouraged us to change, but was met by fierce resistance. We burrowed into ourselves, hunkered down, contracted, and feigned ignorance. Andrew's job was then to tease apart this tightly-wound ball of resistance.

John Cleese is a well-known English actor and comedian. He was one of the Pythons. His daughter recently said that, when she threw tantrums as a child, her father would go down on all fours and act like a gorilla. That piece of theatre was, I thought, an excellent response to irrational human behaviour. It made me think of how Andrew used theatre – as is evident in this chapter - when dealing with his students' egos.

Thinking of my own experience of irrational protest and stubborn refusal, I'm aware of the unpredictable duration of those episodes. No one knows whether, or when, someone is going to see sense and emerge as a more mature person. The story told in this chapter illustrates the formlessness of such episodes. It has no predictable, final breakthrough. Nor does Andrew employ a well-known masterstroke. Instead, the men's trajectory has some of the characteristics seen in Helen Keller's transformation: it mirrors her bewilderment, her mentor's stoicism, everyone's helplessness, and the desolation that preceded her big moment.

This reference to Helen's pivotal discovery provides a good stepping-stone to Part 3 of this book.

PART 3

The Authentic Self

Chapter 21

The Authentic Self

July 30th 2001 (hereafter *July 30th*) was the most momentous day in the history of Andrew's teaching work. After fifteen years, in which hundreds of students of varying capability and longevity had given heart and soul, an extraordinary fusion occurred in a men's meeting at Foxhollow. This chapter describes the nature of the intelligent force that revealed itself in that fusion: the force which our community named the Authentic Self.

Groundwork

It will be helpful to review quickly the main events of Andrew's teaching career leading up to July 30th.

Aged sixteen, in 1971, Andrew had a powerful experience of cosmic consciousness. In 1986, with the help of his Indian teacher, Poonja, Andrew's years of committed seeking culminated in his powerful enlightenment. Soon after, in Europe, people left their lives to become his first passionate but temperamental students, and Andrew's teachings on individual enlightenment took shape. In 1990, Andrew suffered a painful split from Poonja, just as the emphasis of Andrew's teachings started to change. He now drew attention to the greater enlightened potential he saw existing between his students. After seven years of development in California, his community moved to Massachusetts where, divided into men's and women's hierarchies, Andrew pushed his students (hard) to become selfless participants in joint, formal inquiries. He sensed that these unified forums would invoke a higher form of enlightenment.

I loved our community's pioneering spirit. Stories from the years before my time were packed with colourful twists and turns in which Andrew's first students - heroes in my eyes - had archetypal status. Their struggles with issues such as sex, superiority, immaturity and self-consciousness seemed – to me - like the solo battles narrated in the parables of scripture. When I met Andrew in 1991, this spiritual turbulence was still active: his teachings were profoundly changing, his split with Poonja remained a sore subject, and his students' ability to maintain an enlightened perspective was unreliable. Energised, rocky and wild, the 1990s were filled with the promise of enlightenment, and flavoured by the fruits and failings of human endeavour. Andrew and his community, unrestrained by the rules of a lineage, rode without reins, saddle, or stirrups.

Clinging to the mane of evolution, we were not so much walking a pathless land as careering headlong into an unmapped future.

Andrew's enlightenment was the source of our inspiration. Our community looked inward – it could be said - towards him and his realisation, learning as he did, afresh and anew. Hence, it was when we began to look outward, after July 30th, that we discovered blueprints existed for the manifestation Andrew sensed was possible. Most notably, Indian philosopher Sri Aurobindo (1872-1950) had predicted the possibility of what he termed *Supermind*. A quick look on Wikipedia will find his beautiful conception of *"a plane between heaven and earth,"* or *"a force leaning down on earth's consciousness."* Some people might attribute primary importance to the predictions of a posthumously-applauded man like Sri Aurobindo. But, supporting Andrew's status as a truly independent teacher, I want to point out that we strove to build the edifice that Sri Aurobindo merely imagined. As a builder, I'm more inclined to applaud the fellows who dig trenches in the mud and lay wiring on freezing afternoons, than to attend a drinks party celebrating the architect's vision. Sri Aurobindo's conception, while divinely inspired, doesn't include any assembly instructions. It was our community that, with cracked fingertips, cement-ridden hair and arthritic knees, spent fifteen years building the physical infrastructure that received the Authentic Self.

While on an impassioned roll, I'd like to offer my own simple description of what our work was all about. We didn't use Christian language in our community but, as a vicar's son, I see the Authentic Self as the Holy Spirit. The New Testament, with statements such as *"The Holy Spirit descended upon them,"* or *"was among them,"* or *"appeared between them,"* describes a force that, given the opportunity, permeates the consciousness of a group. In the New Testament, the Holy Spirit seems to descend when the disciples are vulnerable: when they are shocked, amazed, or devastated. In my view, Andrew cultivated that same condition of vulnerability - or spiritual openness - in his students. Eventually, they were able to receive, more reliably than the disciples, this same intelligent force: The Holy Spirit, or Authentic Self. This, I emphasise, is my retrospective, personal view.

Arrival

At the end of Chapter 20, all the upper-core student men, bar two, had found their way back to Foxhollow and been put on a full-time retreat. We meditated and lived in silence in our meditation hall. After ten days, some changes were made: the retreat schedule was formalised, a few men from Europe arrived to participate, and Jason and I were told to resume our work managing the property. Our removal from the retreat, which seemed to be a matter of practical necessity, meant that we did not participate in the important meeting soon to be described.

It was now June. The weather was lovely and the women students, some men students and the lay members of the community observed the men on retreat from a distance as they followed their schedule, moving in silence between different locations on the grounds. As June moved into July, Foxhollow became very peaceful. The presence and routine of the twenty men on retreat imbued the community with reverence, and letters from the men - posted by Andrew in the sauna - expressed corresponding insight and gratitude.

By all accounts, what happened in the July 30th meeting was unexpected. Seemingly from nowhere, a cosmological force burst into the men's meeting that evening. Letters posted the next day were like fireballs of uncontained energy. They described the arrival of a metaphysical creature, similar to an awoken dragon, that writhed with serpentine ferocity while whipping its wings and glaring at its stunned recipients. The men wrote about reaching a critical mass that exploded, of an energised presence - a living whirlwind of higher intelligence - coming among them. Their letters described it as *"off the scale of any previous event,"* as a tornado, a forest fire, the beating heart of what our community had been seeking. It *"consumed ignorance,"* *"burnt separation,"* and was *"overwhelming and compelling."* It drew the men irresistibly into its wild, ascendant nature with *"evolutionary urgency."* This wasn't a measured event with time for self-reflection; it was a breakout, the intelligence of life let loose. Spirit arrived among men who were barely ready to be its witnesses but, even while shocked into reverence, they were able to recognise their experience as a defining moment; one that would soon divide the history of our community. July 30th became a watershed. Thereafter, we entered a different phase of life.

I first knew of the meeting the next day, when Stathan came into our workshop. He wanted to build a temporary monument. That word, along with *shrine* and *altar*, had never been used by our community, so his desire was extraordinary. Stathan said that the men had immediately told Andrew about the meeting. Andrew had sensed the event had occurred; he was pleased, but unsurprised. His instruction to build the monument reflected his recognition of the moment. While this was happening, more remarkable letters conveying the nature of the meeting appeared in the sauna. Each was unique, but carried the same tone of gratitude and awe.

The men's retreat continued, and letters from further meetings confirmed that the revelation was continuing to unfold. After some weeks, practical changes were made. Jason and I, along with two other men, became lay students. We had not shown any desire to move from our peripheral positions to become involved with the men's retreat, so we were not surprised to be demoted.

Our lack of interest might seem strange, but it was an example of students' fluctuating relationship to the challenges of this period. Another example, perhaps more surprising, was when two leading men left the community. Geert was one of them. He had been a consistent force-for-good since Guru Purnima Day but, despite being warned by Andrew about this specific possibility, the intoxicating, exhilarating nature of the Authentic Self had gone to his head. He had probably – drawing from my knowledge of what happened throughout the history of the community - taken the power of enlightened awareness for himself and, instead of remaining an empty-handed innocent vessel, assumed that his experience was an expression of new-found personal attainment. He had become superior and arrogant. As with many before him, his desire to be more important than the force that informed him led to his exit from the community.

The arrival of the Authentic Self was not smooth; it was wild and unsettled, and it continued to shake and rattle our community for many years, as coming chapters will show.

Experience

Our experience of the Authentic Self was not consistent. Its full-blown arrival on July 30th was a distinct, tumultuous event. The encounters of later months and years were more regulated. I have chosen to use subheadings to help clarify our different experiences of this phenomenon.

The First Emergence

As described above, the Authentic Self was ferocious in the July 30th meeting. It had an esoteric quality which invited mythic descriptions. One account compared it to the stretching of divine, new-born muscles. Too unknown to be confidently explained, we nevertheless guessed that the explosive appearance of the Authentic Self was an exhibition of its power and, perhaps, the final flourish of its birthing process. It's hard to be sure. But the character of that July 30th meeting seemed consistent with the disturbance surrounding breakthroughs of any kind – be they technological, social, or scientific – and, in our eyes, the magnitude of the meeting made sense of our ten years of intense preparation.

Immersion

I can offer this description of being immersed in the Authentic Self, drawn from my experience, over many years, of meetings in which there were twelve people or more:

It feels like a heavenly blood transfusion. For a time, one is occupied, cleansed, refreshed and fortified by a compelling force that is understood to be the intelligence at the core of existence.

This force draws on one's curiosity until one is wholly engaged in its movement, agenda and instructions. One's identity softens and one's sense of separation fades. Individuality becomes a quietly pulsing, functional element in a larger organism, as the margins of oneself gently merge into a greater whole.

Distinction between self and other also melts. Endearingly, friends' faces look similar to one another and, surprisingly, they appear to be subtle duplicates of one's own. Also, sharing the same thought stream, one can anticipate the words of others and, absorbed into a natural flow in which speaking and listening are barely distinct, ownership of either action is felt to be immaterial.

The Authentic Self lives up to the time-honoured reputation of God, or Spirit. It is all-knowing, all-seeing, all-powerful and everywhere. It completely occupies the conscious realm as it works on its singular agenda: Self-Discovery. "See Me, know Me, so that I might know Myself," it communicates, while purifying each individual to become an agent for that one eternal purpose.

Fundamentally, the Authentic Self educates. It teaches the individual about himself or herself, each person about each other, and the group about its composition. It also, rapaciously, seizes the precious opportunity to build self-knowledge. Unknown to itself until seen through the eyes of others, it commandeers the awareness of its hosts, then reflects upon its own nature with divine delight.

Retrospective Descriptions

Reports of the Authentic Self came mainly in the form of letters written to Andrew after formal meetings. Over the years 2001-13, he would have received hundreds of such letters (now archived in Lenox) written by students brimming with passion as they describe their common experience of the same enlightened vortex. In this respect, the letters are remarkably similar and, frankly, while their unfettered transmission undoubtedly feels authentic, it can also make them overwhelming and hard to absorb. I have noted this phenomenon before in this book, when recalling how perplexingly difficult it could be to take in Andrew's unrestrained responses; they came from a different dimension that was hard to keep pace with. Therefore, I have chosen to give just one example of this genre of letter, synthesised by me from letters read by Andrew on his website. You might notice that the characteristics of the Authentic Self – its transformative, sacred, contagious and independent qualities – are each represented.

> *"Dear Andrew,*
>
> *Last night in our meeting of twenty-five men and women we found ourselves face to face with a consciousness that was wild, churning and chaotic. It was totally disarming, disorientating, absolutely engaging and completely thrilling.*
>
> *"We entered another dimension where the mysterious relationship between the individual, the group, and this cosmic, animating force, became endlessly fascinating and ever self-revealing. We found ourselves in a vast, eternal space that rendered our notion of personal significance completely obsolete and we saw this bigness as our destiny.*
>
> *"We were all completely together in this uncontainable force as it expanded without instructions, pulling ever more people into its field, moving faster than any of us could keep up with yet holding us all as one body. There is NO LIMITATION to this miracle and we have no idea where it is taking us, but it undeniably has an agenda and is demanding that more and more people dare to leap beyond self-interest and be consumed by it.*
>
> *"The situation felt so uncontained, we were all leaning in, evolving, responding, seeing transformation occurring before our eyes. It felt like the essence of what it means to be a human being was starting to reveal itself and we were in awe of the evolutionary significance of our own lives.*
>
> *"My own experience was of being so completely taken over by it that at times I couldn't relate to any solid sense of myself at all. And this morning I'm still thrilled by the feeling of infinite potential*

unleashed between us last night. What a miracle after all these years that evolutionary enlightenment is coming into manifestation and your efforts have finally led to this seismic explosion and leap in consciousness.

"I had no idea it was possible to love life this much. I wouldn't be anywhere else or anyone else in this world.

"With a blown mind and an unconflicted heart, Pat."

First Decade

The turbulent years before July 30th were characterised by extreme pressure and resistance. In comparison, the following decade was a time of peace and prosperity. Andrew was now confident that the Authentic Self was a real entity. He had also breached his students' reluctance to be leaders, giving him people to work with. The engraved stone monument marking July 30th symbolised an arrival point and a shift in emphasis: the community now sought to strengthen its ability to invoke the Authentic Self reliably.

The next chapter describes the many material successes that justify my use of the phrase *a time of peace and prosperity*. But the Authentic Self was not a force to be brought under human control. Nor were all of Andrew's students ready to act as recipients. The Authentic Self had arrived through a group of men who had been softened and made receptive by a year-long sequence of extreme events. Understandably, the rest of the community lagged behind, while some of the ground-breaking men, unable to maintain an expanded state of mind, dropped back into self-concern. So, the community still needed to develop, and our experience of *peace and prosperity* was only relative: it did not mean we lived a comfortable life.

Over the next decade, we experienced more of the Authentic Self. Students at the top of the hierarchy were now far better informed, they knew the level of intention needed to make our meetings work and they were unafraid of what would arise. Instead of being self-preoccupied impediments, they became motivators and catalysts. Their new-found capabilities supplemented Andrew's transfusion of curiosity into the community and, while the invocation of the Authentic Self remained an emergent, hit-and-miss matter for many years, a useful number of students now worked hand in hand with Andrew, furthering the community's maturity.

This developing expertise was employed in many teaching situations. For annual ten-day retreats, Andrew developed a hierarchical arrangement of groups, each with its own mentor. Over the course of the retreat, these groups became interlinked rings, each sufficiently selfless to experience the Authentic Self. His women students also had many episodes of the same contagious experience, most notably in Montserrat, Spain, in 2006 (Chap 22). Meanwhile, worldwide conference calls of 50-100 students also entered into this focused communion and, in EnlightenNext's American and European Centres, weekly public events attempted to create the same field of inquiry, with some success.

I'd like to make special note of how the ability to receive the Authentic Self was passed on to younger students. They benefited from three influences. Firstly, Andrew learnt how to fine-tune student groups; he became expert at placing students in groups conducive to their development, both on retreats and in the smaller, weekly holon configurations. Secondly, the community's standard of participation rose. In the same way that mainstream moral standards put people under positive pressure, so students benefited from the expectations of their peers. This meant that students made more effort in their formal meetings. Thirdly, younger students were influenced by their experience of the Authentic Self. That experience fuelled their passion for the life they had chosen. Experiencing the gentle, informative intelligence of the Authentic Self allayed students' deep fears about the implications of a spiritual life, while boosting respect for the work of our community.

Students' Meetings: Two Useful Questions

Guessing that some readers might still be puzzled by the content and character of students' meetings, I have formulated and answered two questions: *What was talked about?* and, *How were meetings different from social conversations?* Because my answers take attention away from the Authentic Self, I have placed them in the Appendix.

The Authentic Self: an Example of its Potential

The event described below takes place in London in the late summer of 2003. By that date, I was living in London, managing the construction of Enlighten-Next's future Centre.

I should advise readers in advance that I played an important role in this story, and it might look as if I have selected it for that reason. The truth is, I had no alternatives. Firstly, it was the only event, that I know of, in which the Authentic Self untied a cultural knot. Secondly, to be able to tease out the subtleties, I had to use a situation in which I was deeply involved.

At that year's summer retreat in Les Cormettes, eleven students of average rank had been grouped together. In the second half of the retreat they came alive, inspired by the Authentic Self. I was one of the group's older students, along with Herma, a long-standing Swiss student, and my Irish friend, Brody. Together with eight younger students, we blossomed on the retreat and returned to London flying high on the wings of Andrew's evolutionary perspective, unified by the curiosity flourishing between us.

Andrew hoped we could impart our spiritual impetus to other students. He suggested students from Foxhollow and Europe travel to London, and that London students who had not attended the retreat also join the event. As numbers rose, the gathering soon became a ten-day, post-retreat symposium of over sixty people.

For many reasons, we were not a homogeneous group. The Foxhollow students were surprised to find themselves in London, and they did not wholly look forward to learning from the students of a smaller Centre. Some European students, disappointed by their performance in Les Cormettes, were suffering from low confidence. Meanwhile, the London students who had not been in France were shocked: an event they thought was over had arrived, still active, at their door.

To add to these shifting sands, the authority framing this symposium was loose. It was a big event, but Andrew was not nearby, and we were told the senior students would not be attending our meetings. Moreover, Herma, Brody and I - the leading students, but only by dint of spiritual lottery – were untested in our role. All told, the gathering had an experimental air, as if our band of impassioned novices – the fired-up group from Les Cormettes - had been let loose to see what it could achieve.

To seat everyone in the meeting room of our Belsize Park Centre, we formed two concentric rings, one seated on chairs, the other on floor cushions. This arrangement, when populated by a large group of students of varying dispositions, conjured the potent atmosphere of a tiered amphitheatre.

I'm sure some of the Foxhollow delegates and mustered Londoners must have found our evening meetings torturous, but I remember them as thrilling. Our tight seating circles acted like the walls of a reactor: by containing our unregulated energy, they created an unfamiliar and invigorating vortex. The presence of new leaders enriched this vitality: their novelty disturbed expectations, and opened hearts and minds. In this atmosphere our dialogues, fast-paced and risky, generously accommodated errors. This, in turn, encouraged experiment. Young, and free from adult eyes, the leading contingent of this mixed group was delightedly autonomous.

Before reaching the heart of this story, I need to refer briefly, again, to the community's commentary on national characteristics. I have been told this commentary looks old-fashioned in light of today's social mores but, in the community, we thought cultural background was both humorous and significant. Importantly, certain national behaviours were seen negatively; for example, Australian casualness, French dramatization and Dutch stinginess. The Germans were especially burdened by their reputation for heavy-handed rigidity.

I return to the story. Brunhild was a gentle, sweet-natured woman. She later became Andrew's leading woman in Germany, where she upheld her position alongside two strong countrymen. But, at the time of this symposium, she was timid and unrecognised. In one of our meetings, I was watching her efforts to join the turbulent dialogue swirling around our self-fashioned amphitheatre. Freed from the community's hierarchy and buoyed by the high spirits of my small group, I was able to have an overview of proceedings, and could see Brunhild struggling with various burdens. She carried her own low self-esteem, as well as her low rank in the eyes of our assembly. But, more significantly, I could see her crushing sense of shame for being German.

The Authentic Self does not push one into involuntary action, nor is a magic shield provided to help with confrontations. Observing Brunhild's pain, I was given only a burning form of clarity. I saw her situation precisely, and I was presented with a choice between acting, or not acting. My options were to fall forward, or hold back. I was emboldened by my knowledge that I would be falling into the Authentic Self; into the same intelligent stream that informed my view.

Knowing my words would fly in the face of our community's view of the Germans, I took a breath and spoke about the wealth of the suppressed German culture, about the Germans' philosophical strength, their incredible music and their powers of organisation. I saw the position of the German nation through the eyes of the Authentic Self: how their talents were needed for evolution and how the world was a poorer place with the Germans cowering in shame. Through those eyes, I was not interested in soothing Brunhild's personal suffering; I wanted to release the wealth of her culture, and I saw her as the conduit for that to happen.

My words settled the assembly. Despite mixed states of mind, we were all capable of hearing important truths and respecting well-intentioned risk. Brunhild and another German woman, Lora, a once wealthy artist, gratefully used the now receptive forum to speak about the guilt they had felt for many years, and their fruitless attempts to correct their faults. Other Germans joined the inquiry, while the rest of us held back so as not to intrude. For perhaps forty-five minutes, they laid bare their experience, using the guiding nature of the Authentic Self to bring inhibiting ideas, thoughts and feelings into the light of day.

This meeting had interesting qualities. Like an orchestral conductor, the Authentic Self drew relevant information forward on cue. Individuals sensed the right moment to contribute and, in tune with the overall flow, their realness engendered realness in others. Confidence grew. This prompted participation and made the unknown a place of exciting self-discovery. Sparking off one another, an up-draught of contagious curiosity developed that appealed to students' most deeply-held values. Just as an awakening individual experiences revelation, so the Authentic Self brought new information into view while holding open the expanded context. By revealing a true picture, it set our minds at rest and freed our attention. Liberated, the group could understand - and revere – both the view that emerged and the beautiful, symbiotic process that revealed it.

Here was an example of evolution in action. Or, as Sri Aurobindo put it, *"a force leaning down on earth's consciousness."* At the time I remember feeling I'd been shown the future. Now I see the event as a carefully placed notification, or calling-card, left by the Authentic Self for posterity. Sceptics might ask, *"Was the entire German nation immediately liberated from global disdain?"* Of course not. The significance of this story is that human beings worked together with a higher intelligence. They were not just aspiring to be guided by higher intelligence, or excited by the prospect; they were working in partnership with the energy and intelligence at the heart of the universe.

To Be Continued...

The knowledge that Andrew's community dissolved in 2013 might lead one to assume that the receptive faculty described above has been lost. Quite reasonably, one might think that, as students scattered, they took pieces of the faculty with them. However, I think an intriguing question counters such a hasty conclusion. That question is: *What brought the Authentic Self into being?* Maybe the work of Andrew's community was conceived and executed by human beings, in which case, Andrew was the principal progenitor. But, conceivably, he and his students were shaped, conditioned and manoeuvred by a greater force. This question is further examined, along with others, in Chapter 23, *Review.*

PART 4

Development and Dissolution

Chapter 22

Development

True to its title, this book is about the invocation of the Authentic Self. It was never my intention to write an exhaustive record of everything that happened during the community's twenty-seven-year lifespan. So, while this chapter covers a period of almost equal length to that which came before July 30th, 2001, I have elected to give only a concise summary of what happened in the twelve years that followed. At the end of my summary are two personal reflections that, I believe, help to convey the community's changing character in the later years of this period.

Internal Work

The internal work of the community built on the success of July 30th. Andrew now knew how to create the conditions that would receive the Authentic Self. His knowledge, combined with the men's experience of the preceding year, meant that a nucleus within the community was now confident of the existence of the Authentic Self, and of its ability to invoke it. The next task was to impart that knowledge and confidence to Andrew's wider community. As mentioned in the previous chapter, this occurred in our regular weekly meetings, and during short and long retreats.

With more students confident of success and willing to bear responsibility, Andrew no longer had to be the sole source of vision and discipline. The creation of small, self-monitoring peer groups – the *holon* groups also mentioned previously - helped with this partial decentralisation. Holon groups were self-monitoring; they made students responsible for, and obligated to, each other. As individuals became more responsible, the common standard of care for our work strengthened. This, in turn, developed trust in one another and respect for our forums.

In particular, engaging with ego - previously a big feature of community life and a drain on resources - became less necessary. Students mastered their negative tendencies. Their growing ability to prioritise collective success over personal predicament freed up time and attention, which then became available for the community's internal and external development. Gradually, the community matured and became more effective.

In 2006, during our summer retreat at the Spanish monastery of Montserrat, Andrew's women students experienced an event similar to that of July 30th. In an account of this, existing in Issue 37 (pp 78-84) of the magazine, the women describe how a profound tension existing between them, that they hadn't realised was there, dropped away, and how they then experienced a new-found state of transparency and ecstatic communion. In that article, they also speak about discovering forces within themselves – I'm using their words here - that are not typically seen as womanly, such as independent agency, and freedom from identification with feelings. For those who might be interested, the article includes a page listing the *Ten Challenges of a Liberated Woman*. This is a form of avowal compiled by Andrew's women students in this period of development. (For copyright reasons, I cannot include it in this book, but it can currently be seen at *actualisedaily.com*)

On November 25th, 2005, an important event occurred that later became an annually-celebrated milestone. Soon known as Declaration Day, it marked the point at which Andrew felt the specialised receptive faculty developed by his community had become strong enough to justify public announcement. He invited his worldwide audience to attend a weekend gathering at Foxhollow. Together with 150 people - a mix of close students and his wider community - Andrew led a review of the creation and significance of *'intersubjective enlightenment'* (our alternative, in-house term for the Authentic Self), and he asked if people were ready to bear the consequences of *"going public"*, whatever those consequences might be. We had no idea of what the public announcement might bring. In fact, there was only positive public response followed by a new phase of broader cultural engagement by the community.

Declaration Day then became one of our four annual holy-days. The others were: July 30th, for obvious reasons; Andrew's birthday, in October, which honoured him as our teacher and the spiritual importance of the teacher-student relationship; and March 25th - Freedom Has No History Day – that marked Andrew's pivotal first meeting with his teacher in 1986.

While the upper levels of the student hierarchy matured, many new students joined. In 2002, the Practitioner membership programme was launched. This created a worldwide network of over a thousand people, who used Andrew's teachings to inform their lives in mainstream society. At the same time, the core students (one rung beneath the upper-core students) became a more effective and tightly-knit, worldwide group of about sixty people. Individuals from this level of the hierarchy now occupied prominent positions in the magazine team and the editorial, fundraising and marketing departments.

To conclude this résumé of the community's internal work following July 30th, I should refer readers back to the previous chapter, to the section titled

First Decade. In that section, I describe how Andrew increasingly employed our ability to receive the Authentic Self in his public retreats; and I explain how that ability was passed to younger students.

Organisational Structure

In this first decade of the new millennium, attention was paid to the community's organisational structure and function. Currently (2020), with the reputation of our work discredited, I think it would be unfair to risk the reputations of the consultants we employed, by listing their names. But several high-profile American individuals and institutions were brought in to advise EnlightenNext on restructuring, rebranding, and fundraising. One result of this was the renaming of the organisation in 2008. *The Impersonal Enlightenment Fellowship* became *EnlightenNext*.

Organisational growth also came in the form of bricks and mortar, with three Centres opening in Europe. In 2003, a new French Centre opened in Paris, followed by the impressive London Centre in 2004 and an extended Danish Centre in Copenhagen in the same year.

Some structural changes in the organisation were successful. At Foxhollow and EnlightenNext's other Centres around the world, new members were added to the governing boards and CEOs were reshuffled. Other efforts to make structural change didn't wholly succeed. One example was our attempt to make working practices more efficient. This started with a series of weekend, in-house symposiums. They were well-intentioned, but - as business consultants will know - attempts to streamline an organisation can be thwarted by the existence of rival hierarchies. These certainly existed in our situation. Andrew's spiritual function was to bring an unregulated, universal power into manifestation, whereas the remit of our consultants and top brass was to create a regulated organisation. At times, the goals of these two parties didn't align. I can represent this long-running dynamic as a metaphor. While our flirtation with the advice given by business consultants was enthusiastic - to the point that we declared our commitment to a new future - that flirtation did not, ultimately, affect our strong marriage to a spiritual narrative. So, despite sincerely-offered, professional advice, the spiritual agenda of EnlightenNext retained its matrimonial status.

Outreach

EnlightenNext had five active avenues of outreach during this time: Andrew's developing reputation as a teacher; the increasing recognition of the magazine; two books by students; the launch of various education programmes; and a number of multimedia interface events with the public.

As well as EnlightenNext's developing online presence, Andrew's website – representing him as a teacher - evolved in this period. In addition, two of his books were published: *Living Enlightenment* in 2002 and *Evolutionary Enlightenment* – later translated into French, Danish and Portuguese - in 2011. He was a speaker at the Parliament of the World's Religions in 2004, in Barcelona; and again, in Melbourne, in 2009. A year later, he was one of many renowned figures teaching at Moscow's International Transpersonal Conference. Between attendances at this type of collaborative gathering, Andrew travelled the world, teaching and leading retreats. He was also, of course, editor-in-chief of the magazine, and his community's spiritual authority, inspiration and guiding hand.

In 2008, *What is Enlightenment?* magazine was renamed *EnlightenNext Magazine*. It won a number of awards in this period: The *Folio Golden Eddie Award* for best spiritual magazine in 2000; *Webby* awards for best spiritual website in 2006 and 2007; and *Gold* and *Bronze Folio Magazine* publishing awards, for content and design respectively, in 2009. Translated editions of the magazine were also published for the first time in Holland and France.

Michael Wombacher published his book, *11 Days at the Edge*, in 2008. It records the spiritual context, and his experience, of Andrew's 2005 summer public retreat in Tuscany. Carter Phipps's book, *Evolutionaries; Unlocking the Spiritual and Cultural Potential of Science's Greatest Idea*, was published in 2012. These were the first books independently written by students while within the organisation.

Education programmes were designed and developed by some of Andrew's senior students. These programmes included a certification course, authorising mostly younger core students to enrol participants and teach a specified curriculum based on Andrew's teachings. Different courses were available for people who had joined the Practitioner membership programme mentioned above. These courses made use of conference-call services. Between 2004 and 2010, an academic course was taught at *The Graduate Institute*, Connecticut, USA, by Andrew's students holding doctorates. Graduates of this programme gained an MA in Conscious Evolution, accredited by the State of Connecticut.

Voices from the Edge was an international speaker series staged by EnlightenNext in America and, especially, Europe. It began in 2004 and ran for three years. It hosted forty-three lectures by Nobel nominees, scientists, leading thinkers and cultural critics. Also popular were the two-day virtual seminars broadcast from Foxhollow in May 2010 and 2011. Over ten thousand people, from seventy-five countries, signed-up for these events, which comprised interviews on the subjects of *The Transformative Power of an Evolutionary Worldview*, and *Leadership at the Edge of Culture*. Several social media platforms were used to facilitate real-time, interactive engagement between participants and the magazine team that conducted the core interviews.

Sandwiched as it was between the community's gritty experience of the late nineties and the shock of the Dissolution in 2013, one may be tempted – in a broad view of the overall story - to overlook this relatively calm, twelve-year period of development. Perhaps this chapter, being only a swift summary, strengthens that temptation. I'm aware that my description doesn't do justice to the progress made on many fronts, but I think it does convey something of the scale and status of the community's work.

Similarly, this chapter's brevity might invite the assumption that students were living a tranquil, bountiful life. Compared to previous years this might be true, but I should say that, behind the various successes I have listed, students – including me - were engaged in their regular activities: daily spiritual practice, physical practice, twice-weekly meetings, and practical work such as organising retreats and teaching trips. At a personal level, even during these less contentious years, our lives were very busy.

Reflections

So far, this chapter has largely been a list of achievements. I'd like to add some warmth by including two evocative memories. One recalls an incident that occurred in the middle of this period of development; it looks back at preceding years. The other, of an event that happened towards the end of this time, looks forward and hints at the future.

In 2006, we held a big party in Denmark to celebrate twenty years of Andrew's teaching work. As I've said before, party planning was a forte, and this event was suitably choreographed to include performances, speeches, live music, gifts and messages. The venue was a pavilion on the outskirts of Copenhagen. Its surrounding grounds were like those of a country-club: flat, with softly-illuminated paths winding through knee-high shrubs. Inside, the pavilion reminded me of a double-height ski chalet; it was pine-panelled, with sloping ceilings, a stage and, facing that, a mezzanine balcony. The split-level venue was soon filled by the noise of a vibrant party. Nothing went wrong but – mid-celebration - Andrew spontaneously stopped the proceedings and declared that he could happily forget the previous twenty years. Touchingly, he managed to communicate the profundity of what had been achieved and the toll it had taken on him and on us all. Standing in the middle of the decorated hall, with the party silenced, and without preparation, he said that the best years lay ahead. It felt as if we'd been interrupted by a message sent from another dimension. With Time briefly on hold, Andrew said that, given its nature and objectives, the spiritual life shouldn't always be as tough as it had been over the last decade.

My other memory is of travelling back to Foxhollow with Andrew after a local performance by his band, *Unfulfilled Desires*. This was in the summer of 2010 when, in terms of student strength, I was a floating ghost. My younger sister had died in December 2009 (Chap 7) and – feeling devoid of spiritual intention - I was living peripherally at Foxhollow, adrift from myself and others. On the evening I'm speaking about, despite my impoverished spiritual state, Andrew invited me to travel with him and the band's manager, Joan, in his car.

Thinking back to this car, an Audi A8, and comparing it to Andrew's previous Volvo 850R, I see how the character of these cars might mirror different periods of the community's history. I see the Volvo representing the community in the late 1990s, and the Audi representing the community over a decade later. I doubt anyone else would read much significance into the comparison, but I think it has some usefulness and charm and, if not, the conversation in the car – described later - might restore your faith in me.

The Volvo was black and it had a turbocharged engine. It was given to Andrew in 1996 by his students, to mark the ten-year anniversary of his teachings, which coincided with the community's move to Foxhollow. The gift of the car was an expression of his worldwide students' gratitude. The car's lines were straight, it was low at the front and high at the back and, with its slightly tinted windows, it resembled a gleaming black wedge. I also remember how the suede seats held one firmly in position.

The Audi was a slightly older car. It was a luxurious, top-of-the-range model, given to Andrew in 2008 by a student who'd bought herself the latest version. Andrew innocently told me that, with four-wheel drive, it was deemed by others to be a better car, for safety reasons. Design-wise, Audis of that period had distinctive rounded corners and their rake (angle to the ground) was sedately horizontal. I remember this Audi's colour was pale, metallic silver, and that its leather seats were slippery.

Andrew's gleaming black Volvo, with its slicing shape and gripping seats, was a perfect representation of the piercing nature of Spirit as we experienced it in the late nineties. The more rounded, sumptuous and cruising character of the Audi captured, in my mind, the softer, less driven state of affairs, thirteen years later. These are just my personal musings on the changing character of the community. Perhaps the conversation in the car was more significant.

Andrew and Joan were engaged in strong, albeit jocular, argument. There was allegedly - many students would say provenly - a mould problem in the manor house at Foxhollow. At great cost, expert services had been called in to remedy the issue. Worryingly, the invisible mould, said to be propagating in wall and floor voids, had split the Foxhollow community. Some students claimed total mould-intolerance and refused to enter the manor house, while others said the problem was entirely phantom. Joan was sure the mould was real, while Andrew leaned towards thinking his more health-anxious students were making a meal of the matter. Their vigorous exchange occupied our journey home.

The presence of the mould needs to be set in context. Firstly, while the community was proud of its ability to inquire at the cutting edge of human development, it was also open to the idea of being undermined by dark, spiritual forces. Our study of ego, and engagement with it, had taught us to watch out for strange, negative intrusions. This watchfulness was not a strong part of our culture, but it did exist. Therefore, the very existence of the divisive mould raised questions about its significance. Secondly, throughout the community's history, bad health had been the only condition that removed students from Andrew's auspices. In good health, we were always held responsible for our actions, whereas, if we were ill, Andrew's authority would soften, and he'd show concern. Seen in the context set by these observations, the issue of the mould, be it real or unreal, looks like a breach of Andrew's hitherto watertight authority.

The matters I have highlighted - the Audi's bland design, Joan's argumentative vigour and the insidious manor-house mould – might generally be thought of as minor issues. I would normally agree but, when compared to the community's culture in earlier years, they become significant. In the late 1990s, these matters would not have arisen: the Volvo's design was exciting, Joan would not have argued and, somehow, the mould would not have been there. The youthful spirit of that decade would – I feel - have repelled such incursions. So, I tentatively include these recollections as early signs of things to come: of Andrew's authority being challenged from different quarters.

Addendum

I would like to make special mention of the closure of the magazine in 2011. This was a big disappointment for Andrew, the editorial team and the community as a whole.

The magazine had been the applauded, public face of Andrew's work as a spiritual teacher. It had raised the community's status in spiritual circles and provided a window into the work of our community. The inquiries conducted in each issue had enriched Andrew's teachings and, thereby, the breadth and vitality of his students' perspective. The magazine had showcased the work of many extraordinary people and, through its in-depth, one-subject-per-issue formula, it brought accessible, synthesised spiritual knowledge to a wide audience.

While writing this book, I have frequently referred to my set of magazines. I have worked in their shadow, literally and figuratively. Forty-seven issues make an impressive stack, and my knowledge of each issue's journalistic rigour and spiritual depth has often - sometimes depressingly - reminded me of my novice writer's status. More importantly, I see the collection as a resource that should not be overlooked and, for this reason, I have included an index of titles, subjects and key interviews in this book's Appendix. For your information, digital copies of the magazine can be viewed on Andrew's website: www.andrewcohen.com

Financially, the magazine always needed support through sponsorship or donation. Each issue cost $250,000 to produce. Some large, private donations sustained it for many years and, once that money was spent, great effort was made to find more sponsors. But, ultimately, the prudent choice to discontinue publication had to be made. On Wikipedia, under Andrew Cohen's name, this decision has been listed by someone as evidence of EnlightenNext's financial difficulty but, as far as I know, there weren't any difficulties – such as debtors - and the decision to end publication was simply a matter of responsible financial management.

Chapter 23

Dissolution

Why did the community dissolve? I imagine many people's interest in this question will surpass their interest in the Authentic Self. Certainly, it has been the first question asked by friends about this book's story. My reply has been that the dissolution can be understood from two very different points of view. It can be seen as the product of a personal failing; an interpretation strongly promoted by a group of ex-students. Or it can be seen as an evolutionary upheaval; a possibility I examine in my upcoming Review.

My intention in this chapter is to describe the dissolution as factually as possible, in sequence and with only one short digression. I have two reasons for wanting to tell only the bare story. Firstly, by omitting comments and explanations, I hope to offer readers an opportunity to draw their own conclusions about the dissolution's cause. Secondly, I do not want to create an alternative focus for this book. I should explain this second point. I think an unravelling analysis of the dissolution would take attention away from this book's central subject: the invocation of the Authentic Self. That is something I want to avoid.

Aiming to give a factual account, I have placed some information - that might appear to steer readers' opinions had I placed it within the narrative – in a postscript.

When the dissolution started, I was living in London. I had left the community two and a half years before. At that earlier time, as mentioned in Chapter 7, my sister's death had deeply upset me and disturbed my commitment to the community. My grief had reconnected me to my heart but, as I emerged from bereavement, I sensed something had changed. I now felt greater loyalty to my personal future – albeit undefined – than to the future I saw in the community. I did try to reintegrate with the community, but my heart had moved on. So, eight months after her death, I chose to leave. I then experienced two horrible years of withdrawal. I won't dwell on that time; I'll just say it was, literally, gut-wrenching: I carried a lifeless void in my stomach. The dissolution of the community coincided with the end of that withdrawal and the beginning of a miraculous turnaround in my experience. I'd taken some risks, pursued some threads of interest, and was beginning to make spontaneous, independent use of Andrew's teachings.

I was amazed and thrilled – I have chosen both words carefully – to find autonomous interest in an evolutionary perspective blossoming within me. Because of this gift, which is how I experienced it, news of conflict between Andrew and his senior men aroused more curiosity in me than surprise. I felt connected to Andrew and his teachings and, therefore, aware of his deep desire – a desire seemingly alive in the teachings themselves - to reach more people. I sensed his frustration with the community's slow progress, especially in the UK. On the other hand, the senior men – whose actions, as we shall see, triggered the dissolution - were once my peers, and I also sensed their possible frustrations. Indeed, I had my own memories of feeling constricted within the community. I had felt I would be '*forever in training*', and I had felt cooped up in the confined culture that had existed – and, as far as I knew, still existed - in the London Centre. As news of a conflict filtered through, I felt in tune with its possible causes, and I was more curious than judgemental.

My situation at the time means that my knowledge of what happened is not first-hand. But there is an upside to my onlooker's status. I was not embroiled in the powerful emotions that circulated. Nor did I do anything I later regretted, or take an entrenched, strident position. I was largely untouched by the trauma. Here, after assessing the value of my conversations with people involved, and having reviewed the written material available, I feel I can, with integrity, describe the critical moments and salient features of the episode.

On September 25th, 2012, an informal ceremony took place at the London Centre. Its purpose was to mark the start of a committed relationship between Mansoor, an upper-core student, and his girlfriend, Scarlett, an interested lay student. Typically, these events were organised by the couple and Andrew would give a short talk - about the nature of a sexual relationship in a spiritual context – before he raised a toast to the couple's future. A party would follow.

This ceremony was similar, but it had an added feature. To be there, Andrew was making a dedicated journey from Europe, and he agreed with Mansoor and Scarlett that an event with fifty guests would make his journey worthwhile.

The ceremony started, with the agreed-upon fifty guests in attendance. However, Andrew was not happy. For some time, he had been frustrated by the London Centre's lack of impact upon the UK's culture. This lack was not disputed, but there were different views on its cause. Noel, the Centre's leader, and the other upper hierarchy students, felt incapacitated by the demands of running a large building with few resources. Andrew thought this was an excuse. To him, the leading team was unadventurous, and its conservatism was the cause of the Centre's poor performance. He came to the ceremony with months, if not years, of accrued frustration. Now, he was unhappy about the guests' lack of relevance to the work of the community. Fifty guests had been invited, but many were friends, family, or lay students, all of whom had only a passing interest in Andrew's work. At his dinner table, he vented his annoyance.

This was a bridge too far for the upper echelon of London students. They had invited the agreed number of guests, but Andrew was not content. His conspicuous expression of annoyance catalysed *their own* months, if not years, of resentment. They felt Andrew had been putting them under unjustified pressure and now he was acting rudely. They took the unprecedented step of calling him to a correctional meeting.

The combined weight of the four students – including Noel - was enough to deliver their message to Andrew: *you were out of order.* Andrew forcibly put his case: *there's still nothing happening here.* But, eventually, he recognised that his students had a point, and accepted their complaint about his behaviour. Two details of the meeting filtered through over time. One was that Andrew felt the meeting ended congenially, the other was that *Noel had never been so angry.*

For two reasons, I need to digress to describe Noel. Firstly, he was an important figure in the community, who deserves mention in this book. Secondly, his anger with Andrew following Mansoor and Scarlet's ceremony was entirely out of character and, given his high status, the existence of his strong feelings could be seen as a hairline crack in the community's structure: the very first sign of the dissolution.

For twenty-four years Noel was, without question, Andrew's most stable student. He had never collapsed. Unlike all other students, with their chequered histories, he had had the resilience and integrity to be a consistent lieutenant. He had met Andrew in the late eighties, and they shared some baby-boomer values. He loved the music of the sixties, disdained stuffy traditions, was politically left-leaning, and had a Buddhist background. Acutely intelligent, he had a fine eye for the presence and use of irony, and a sense of humour that could be termed 'English Absurd' or 'Pythonesque'. More of a scholar than a rebel, Noel was too fastidious to be a firebrand and, for that reason, he lacked command in front of audiences. I am not scholarly, so I didn't share Noel's modus operandi, but our interests overlapped on a different matter. In a short but unforgettable conversation, I remember his joyful description of an underlying English characteristic: pugnaciousness. As he spoke about this hidden quality, of readiness to fight, he looked like a different man: there was a rakish glint in his eye. Since then, I have felt grateful to Noel, for unearthing this treasured quality with such memorable, piratical passion. He was drawing attention to a valuable part of himself and myself.

Returning to my account. In the worldwide community, there were five senior men students at this time. Noel had the greatest longevity, Bernard the greatest influence. Karl and Stathan were leaders of European Centres, and Holden had worked closely with Andrew on the magazine. Sharing near-equal attainment, these men formed an established peer group that had been functioning steadily for some years. Their group was the top-ranking holon in the community; it was composed of an all-star cast: students who had the most experience and held the greatest responsibility.

Andrew's nature as a teacher was to push forward. His eyes were on the future, and he was always prompting and cajoling his students to keep moving. His demand applied equally, if not more, to top students. Responding to Andrew's 'evolutionary tension', the five senior men arranged one of their occasional face-to-face meetings (which, for clarity, never included Andrew), away from community responsibilities. The gathering took place in England in February 2013. While Noel's recent and unprecedented anger might have caused a hairline crack in the community's structure, this senior men's meeting produced a definite fissure.

In two respects, the meeting was like Mansoor and Scarlett's ceremony. Firstly, it took place against a backdrop of discontent. Secondly, no one had bad intentions. However, this meeting was far more potent. It comprised Andrew's top students, meeting in the clearly-defined context of his teachings. Moreover, they carried stronger tensions than were present at the ceremony. The first came from their awareness of the low-level dissatisfaction that had existed in some departments at Foxhollow for a few years. It had one theme: Andrew's unwillingness to give his close students, and their initiatives, room to grow. A second tension arose from the men's position in the hierarchy. Being on the front line, in close, permanent communication with Andrew, they were the first to receive his unrestrained expressions of frustration. Indeed, just before the gathering, Stathan and Holden had been strongly – and, in their minds, unjustly - criticised by him. In the meeting, adding to this mix of background tensions, was Noel's recent and unprecedented anger.

Once together, the men shared their experience. The extraordinary correctional meeting in September, having broken new ground, created the conditions for unguarded exploration. Breaching established community protocols, they experienced a new union as they brought forward hitherto unspoken concerns. Autonomy arose within them and they reached a common vision. They saw a need for structural adjustment in the community and they formed a pact to achieve it. They committed to stand together and confront Andrew about what they now felt was his inappropriately authoritative manner. Their concerns included Andrew's lack of support for students' independent interests, as mentioned above, and his occasional personal remarks - about appearance, for example - which had been acceptable in the past but which were now experienced as disrespectful.

Normally, Andrew was informed about the progress of important meetings. But now, with the men's pact in place, he was deprived of this communication. He sensed rebellion.

During February and March 2013, Andrew was at Foxhollow while the senior men were located across Europe and America. At first, Andrew rejected the men's request for a meeting. He was enraged by the implicit challenge to his authority, and he attempted to break the men's unity by sending Ambrose as his envoy to speak with them. Andrew's tactic failed: the men remained steadfast in the face of Ambrose's attempts to re-assert the chain of command. In fact, they went one step further. They cut communication with Andrew, creating a stand-off between them and their teacher.

The situation deteriorated. While the confrontation was kept secret from the wider community, it expanded to include the senior women students, and an undreamt-of situation developed. Throughout the community's history, the upper hierarchy had been united in one perspective, but now, in late March and early April, divisions appeared. As senior students took sides and stood their ground, relationships became fraught.

Positions held by Andrew and the senior men then reversed. He, weakened by failed attempts to exert his authority, finally agreed to meet with the men. But, with the strength of the student-teacher relationship challenged, and personal respect eroded by the stand-off, the men now refused to meet with Andrew. Repeatedly, he implored them to hold the meeting, without success. Instead, the confrontation moved to a higher level, when the senior students arranged a gathering in Portugal, to which Andrew was summoned.

In mid-April, a group that included Andrew, the senior students of both genders, and some EnlightenNext board members and staff, gathered in Lisbon. (A city chosen to equalise travel).

Andrew had been told only that the meeting was to deal with the crisis, so he was surprised when, on the first day, he was presented with a legal document detailing the surrender of his position as CEO of EnlightenNext. (His position as CEO was distinct from his role as the community's spiritual leader). Bewildered - by the speed of recent events and now the unexpected demand to give up his position - Andrew compliantly signed the agreement.

The ten people in the following meeting had different desires for the future. Everyone wanted to remain connected to the work of EnlightenNext but, regarding their relationship with Andrew, only a minority wanted to continue with him as their teacher. The majority wanted a remodelled relationship in which they had autonomy. On a separate matter, everyone except Andrew agreed: Andrew should take time off to review his function as the community's sole figure of authority, a role he had performed without dispute for twenty-seven years.

With both the structure of the community and the student-teacher relationship in question, emotions swirled. Some senior students were angry, and intent on revolution, while others maintained their normal equanimity. Meanwhile, Andrew was reeling, unable to reconcile his anger towards the unexpected insurrection with his excitement about recent positive developments in his public influence as a teacher. He had just completed his best-ever European teaching trip, and his latest book was out in Denmark, France and Portugal. His press coverage was growing, and he knew his teachings were coming through him with unprecedented fluency. He was reaching so many people; for him, the equitable, collaborative future proposed by his students – if, indeed, they still were his students - held no appeal.

That evening, Bernard accompanied Andrew to fulfil an online teaching commitment. Afterwards, finding their silence unbearable, Andrew suggested they have a drink. Recovering a degree of their former close relationship, they were able to talk more openly, and Bernard gave Andrew his honest advice: Andrew should take time off, both for his own sake and for the benefit of everyone else. He should comply with the wishes of the majority. Touched by Bernard's sincerity and - one would guess - some human contact with his much-loved senior men, Andrew agreed.

Convening the next day for a second meeting, people were astounded when Andrew announced he would be taking a sabbatical. Despite the group's consensus the previous day, no one believed Andrew would accept its recommendation. Yet he had acquiesced. Three agreements were then reached. Andrew would take time off to think about his role. In six months' time, the group would reconvene to plan the future. And, during Andrew's sabbatical, the senior students would lead the community. These agreements, however, were short-lived.

Even as events were unfolding in Lisbon, news of what was happening was leaked to ex-students in California. From there it was passed to Foxhollow, where the core students were – for a slightly complex reason - primed to react. Here is my view of their predicament.

Core students were talented, dedicated and accomplished people. I observed them as a happy crew, more joyful and bonded in friendship than the ego-wary students of earlier years. Coming from the cream of their generation, they were laden with academic and other qualifications, and were remarkably capable.

But I think it's fair to say that their situation was not perfect. Over the years, as the community had developed, students of different generations had been confronted by different challenges. These challenges were real obstacles, they were not trials that could be duplicated to temper other groups. For the core students this meant that, being without their predecessors' ground-breaking opportunities, they were always going to be less weathered than their elders. In our context, being less weathered meant having less gravitas, less presence and less natural authority. So, the core students were well-qualified by the standards of mainstream society, but their status in our community was supressed by their relative lack of experience.

Moreover, while core students' positions in relation to their elders were unsatisfactory, so were their positions with regard to those beneath them in the hierarchy. Lay students had worldly freedoms, they could choose their level of spiritual practice and their attendance at retreats, they could take holidays, and they weren't scrutinised by their peers. These secular benefits were not available to core students.

In summary, core students bore responsibility and lived austerely, but they didn't hold positions of notable authority. I think it's fair to say that, lacking recognition, they held some forgivable resentment for being overlooked.

Into this tinderbox of underlying and unspoken dissatisfaction, via the unofficial Californian source, fell the news from Lisbon.

One student living at Foxhollow gave the following description. *"It was as if the electrical charge maintaining an atomic structure had disappeared. Protons, neutrons and electrons collapsed into a heap. Without its familiar central authority, the community's cohesion crumbled. Order turned to chaos."* Even before the Lisbon group returned, students at Foxhollow were packing and leaving. Cracks and fissures appeared: hierarchy was ignored, commitments abandoned and loyalties forgotten. Tremors from the implosion reached the community's European Centres, which also began to fall apart, and sensation-alised reports in English national newspapers fanned the flames of a destructive wildfire. *"Rome is burning,"* and *"Something unstoppable has begun,"* were other descriptions found in students' emails from this time.

Some senior students ignored the Lisbon agreement. They left Foxhollow and left the community. Meanwhile, the remaining core students were angry. They were angry with their exclusion from critical developments, angry with the deserting senior students, and angry with Andrew, who was no longer himself. After just ten days, most of the core students had left Foxhollow. With the organisation's administration in disarray, hundreds of outlying practitioner students were left without communication. Meanwhile, other senior students tried to hold the fragments of a crumbling fort - the paid staff and a few remaining students - together.

Shocked and panicked, Andrew was seeing twenty-seven years of precious progress dissolving. Foxhollow was nearly empty, the worldwide Centres were closing, most of his close students had fled, and his future - recently so promising - looked desolate. Concern for his financial welfare reappeared in his awareness and, when he voiced his concerns, some students felt betrayed by what they saw as his descent into petty-mindedness.

From the moment Andrew compliantly signed away his authority, something inside him had changed. His enlightened consciousness had begun to drain away. It was replaced by the personality he had before his enlightenment, before he met Poonja. Self-preoccupation and self-concern returned. A student at that time said of Andrew, "*He was speaking like one of us,*" and, years later, Andrew said, "*It wasn't me speaking, I was doing what I thought everyone wanted me to.*" It was in that discombobulated state that Andrew left Foxhollow, bound for India, in late June.

On July 18th, Hal Blacker, founding editor of *What Enlightenment??!,* a blogsite critical of Andrew Cohen and his organisation, posted his now-famous 'A' List. On the same day, it was reposted, 'at the editor's request,' on *integralworld.net, a* website dedicated to 'critical discussion' of integral philosopher Ken Wilber's work. I will let readers draw their own conclusions about why Hal Blacker publicised his list at this time.

Alka and Miranda, with the help of local former students and Enlighten-Next's employees, spent the next six months disposing of students' scattered belongings and restoring Foxhollow's dignity. To sell Foxhollow's equipment, they organised local sales. They also found buyers for the books and furniture, and homes for EnlightenNext's small forest of house plants.

By December 2013, Foxhollow was effectively closed. Alka later wrote:

> "*Indeed, it was a labour of love, choiceless really, knowing that I was closing down for all of us and for the love, dedication and one pointedness with which we built our lovely home in Foxhollow and for what it represented. I wanted to honour that and honour and respect what Andrew and we all have put into it. So yes, that gave me the fortitude to do it despite all the gamut of feelings and emotions that arose. I also wanted to leave there knowing that I did everything from my side and not leave with any regrets, but at peace. And I am happy that it is so.*"

Dissolution

In March 2014, nine months after Andrew left Foxhollow, three ex-students opened a closed-group Facebook page called *WhatNext?* As its title suggests, the original purpose of the page was to see what could follow the dissolution but, once established, it also acted as a communication platform for anyone who had been involved with Andrew. From its inception, this Facebook page has been the only freely-accessible common reference-point for former students and, at first, it brought together many people from different periods of the community's history.

The page has 450 members. Of these, 279 are ex-students who had left the community some time before the dissolution, and 86 are recent students, by which I mean people who were students at the time of the dissolution. The remaining 85 are unknown to me and probably made up of more peripheral people who, for example, attended Andrew's retreats.

Taking a broad view of the last six years, participation on the page has been mostly by ex-students who, in their day, were from the middle and lower sections of the student hierarchy. Ex-senior students have also been active, but less so; the same is true of recent, lower hierarchy students. Almost entirely missing from the page has been the top half of the more recent hierarchy.

This analysis might seem unimportant but, in the community, we knew each other thoroughly and for us, hierarchical status, maturity, weight and perspective were interrelated. Track record and credibility were linked. We were acutely aware of both, and - as I believe most human beings do – we remembered people's past performance. I appreciate the counterview – that because people can change, they should not be boxed, and that, in today's western society, all voices are equally valued – but I want to remain true to the context held by the community. In that context, some voices were more important than others.

WhatNext? began as a place of joyful reconnection. The warmth expressed by reuniting ex-students was palpable, and a common theme was the spirited abolition of old divisions. However, a month after the page was opened, different attitudes towards Andrew, his teachings and our life in the community began to appear. Had it all been misguided? Opinions differed and exchanges became more heated. Like a swelling ocean wave, intransigence appeared on the forum and, within a few months, the page was dominated by partisan voices, intolerant of alternative opinions.

WhatNext? then became a typically reactive social media site. Its voracious appetite for accusations meant they became increasingly harsh and personal. Soon, they were directed only at Andrew. Moderate voices withdrew as, uncensored by its founders, the page provided free rein for people to label

Andrew a narcissist, psychopath, sociopath, etc. Rallying beneath the refrain, '*It must never happen again,*' members on the page jumped to adopt Hal Blacker's parallel narrative: Andrew had been, and was, an abusive teacher and the leader of a corrupt organisation. Thereafter, *WhatNext?* has remained the domain of former students who adhere to, and promote, this interpretation.

Silence played a role in the destruction of both Andrew's reputation and the credibility of our community's work. *WhatNext?* became a place of such heated criticism that anyone daring to suggest there had been a baby in the bathwater (the metaphor often used) feared being set upon. This meant that respected student voices were mostly silent. In the wider world, Andrew's friends and peers, while privately supportive, were also in a state of fearful withdrawal. One of his friends put Andrew's experience within a wider context, saying there was "*a general witch hunt of spiritual teachers*" active at the time. To me, there are two explanations for students' and supporters' silence. I believe, as mentioned, all individuals were intimidated by the vitriol being expressed. I also think that, once Andrew's situation was drawn into the reputation-destroying machinery of social media, his peers were, effectively, unable to speak on his behalf.

A remarkable feature of the *WhatNext?* page is how few people it took to dominate an environment. Of 450 members, only about 100 have ever posted on the page and, of those, the truly assertive, critical voices have numbered about twenty-five, with only eight or ten active concurrently. I think these numbers provide an interesting example of how a few people, empowered by their belief in a simple, solid narrative, can influence an empty-handed larger group.

One might reasonably ask why the larger group was empty-handed. Given students' commitment and fortitude while in the community, their passivity seems remarkable. I'd like to suggest that, among other factors influencing their situation, they were rendered helpless by their lack of a narrative. In the community, we were united in Andrew's teachings, in a shared interpretation of our experience. We were accustomed to looking upwards, towards the narrative of evolutionary enlightenment. I suggest the shock of the dissolution destroyed the credibility of that reference, leaving much of the community empty-handed and open to persuasion. In the coming chapter, I attempt to provide a new narrative by introducing a perspective in which the dissolution, and students' experience of it, are seen as evolutionary events.

To close this section, I would like to describe my experience – now, seven years later - of trying to make sense of the dissolution without referring to a meta-narrative. I hope this will show how difficult it is to explain the dissolution by reason alone. I'm also hoping that the absence of a reasonable explanation will encourage interest in the alternative interpretation I offer in my coming Review.

I find my mind moves in a circle as I look at the actions of the senior men, then Andrew's responses, then the background conditions. It's hard for me to see enough destructive intent or reprehensible behaviour to account for the sudden collapse of an organisation composed of deeply committed people. The senior men initiated events, but their request for a meeting was reasonable; they did not imagine it would lead to the community's dissolution, or want it to. Andrew fiercely resisted the men's request and possibly, had he agreed to the meeting, the story would have turned out differently. But: he could have defended his authority more assertively; he capitulated quite quickly; and, in Lisbon, he was compliant. In the body of the community, there were grumbles and resentments, but none that were strong enough to be the cause of a full-scale meltdown.

Weighing actions against outcomes, I find it hard to match cause with effect. Some conditions in the community were imperfect, but were they imperfect enough to cause the dissolution? More satisfying, to my mind, is the idea that a number of forgivable actions combined to act as a trigger, a thrown stone that set off an avalanche. Approaching the next chapter, the big questions for me are: *What dimension of Reality might have been triggered?* And *why?*

Postscript

Some of the following information supplements my account of the dissolution. The remainder helps to bring the community's overall story up to date.

- *No one has ever suggested that the senior men intended to bring down the community. About 18 months after the dissolution, I met with Noel who said, both defensively and with an element of schoolboy's awe, "We didn't mean everything to fall apart."*

- *It was within Andrew's power to dismiss the senior men when they formed their pact.*

- *I have heard of only one student privately predicting the dissolution. That prediction was made on the basis of unsustainable finances. Otherwise, the dissolution was not predicted.*

- *No significant spiritual figure, group or organisation has spoken out in either support, or condemnation, of Andrew.*

- In America, EnlightenNext's remaining money, including proceeds from the sale of Foxhollow, were given to Harvard Divinity School. In the UK, a substantial sum from the sale of EnlightenNext's London Centre is being distributed as grants to public applicants.

- EnlightenNext's Centres in France and Germany have continued to function under new names. Worldwide, the senior students have, by and large, taken their experience in Andrew's community and combined it with their own interests, for example in politics, adolescent education, spiritual teaching and business coaching. To a lesser extent, the core students have done the same.

- Andrew went to India, where he did charity work and suffered a near-total mental collapse from which, with Alka's support, he slowly recovered. In April 2015, he issued an open letter to his former community. In this letter, he apologised for the unnecessary suffering he had caused his students, while upholding the successes of the community's spiritual work. WhatNext? participants were not satisfied by what they called his apology. In 2017, with the help of a few benefactors and supporters, Andrew started teaching again. A petition attempting to stop him teaching was signed by a 60/40 ratio of disaffected students and the public. It almost reached its target of 250 signatures.

- In 2017, Conscious2, an online platform offering a variety of spiritual products, made and broadcast a six-part documentary series about Andrew, entitled How I Created a Cult. Generally judged to be of poor quality, it was soon withdrawn.

- Andrew is now teaching at his own retreats and, by invitation, in India, America and Europe. He also teaches online courses based upon his teachings.

PART 5

Review

Chapter 24

Review

In this book I have tried to write a fair-minded account of the life and work of Andrew Cohen's spiritual community. At times, I've felt the need to explain our outlook and what we were doing and, at others, I've thought it necessary to push against prevailing social attitudes. Broadly speaking, I have tried to cover the important subjects and provide an accessible description of a niche spiritual endeavour.

In this chapter I am taking a risk. I have learnt a lot since I left the community ten years ago: my own journey has provided me with some extraordinary revelations; the process of writing this book has been highly educational; and my three-year friendship with Andrew that came after the dissolution, as well as being unexpected and joyful, was instructive. Using what I learnt as a student, and what I have learnt since, I want to take the risk of interpreting this book's key subjects through the lens of Andrew's teachings. In other words, I want to review the salient points of the story from the point of view of an emergent, evolutionary force.

I recently went to an art gallery on London's South Bank. Approaching one installation from the side, it looked like a towering jumble of rusty gardening tools. Some were scattered on the ground, while others were suspended mid-air, or propped against one another. Moving to view the assembly directly from the front, I saw how the tools were ingeniously positioned to form an enormous, beautiful, iron face.

Evolutionary spirituality takes an unusual view of human life. What makes this view unusual is the reassessment of what is important. I think it's fair to say that, in most people's awareness, creative power is felt to be located within the perceiver. The individual's thoughts, feelings, analyses and conclusions are assumed to be the important activity. But, in evolutionary spirituality, importance is relocated. It moves from the activity of an individual's mind to the activity of evolution. What is now most important is the activity of an evolving universe. This relocation of importance means that life is no longer seen through human eyes. Instead, life is seen from the perspective of - as Andrew termed it - *the force of love and evolution*. Often in this chapter, I personify this force, calling it *the Creator*.

If one imagines the face of the art installation to be the face of the Creator, it comes alive and acquires soft, engaging, living eyes. These eyes look back at oneself, the perceiver, with immeasurable depth. Creator looks at created. There's no power-struggle in this, it is not a tussle; the eyes of the Creator simply communicate its eternal, infinite nature; beaming to the perceiver a message of love and evolution: *I need you to be yourself, to live your life, to give your gifts, to play your part in my emergence.*

To someone with particular spiritual values, who seeks authentic self-expression, this message resonates with their deepest desire. The nature of the Creator and the aspiration of the created are felt to vibrate on the same frequency. The micro-movement of individual yearning is experienced as part of evolution's macro-movement and, by responding to that yearning, an individual becomes part of an unimaginably positive, cosmological awakening.

In this communion, one feels uplifted and propelled. One becomes an agent of divinity, informed, equipped and energised by evolution. Problems become mere specks of flotsam drifting within a universal upheaval, and common human worries lose their strength and wither away. No longer is someone tethered by our species' doubts; he or she is now able to see life through the eyes of the Creator; eyes that can narrow down to understand complexity, or pull back to see the broadest picture of creation.

A review of my motives for writing this book will, I think, clarify the book's purpose. I *wanted* to write this book, I *had* to write it, I felt I *should* write it, and I was *curious* to see what would come of writing it.

I was not short of motivation. I welcomed the challenge of organising a complex story, and I thought that learning to write would equip me for the future. I also wanted to right what I felt was a wrong; I felt the negative, prevailing interpretation of Andrew and his work was selective, so I wanted to put forward an alternative, comprehensive account. Simultaneously, I felt strongly for everyone who had chosen Andrew as their spiritual teacher; I'm aware that choosing a spiritual teacher is a profound event, and I wanted to uphold the decision of many hundreds of people. Lastly, I am deeply grateful to Andrew, and to the force that propelled him, for setting me free; so, I welcomed the task of writing this book as a way of showing my gratitude.

It was also a choiceless matter. I had to write it. My investment in my vocation - nearly thirty years of my life - lies bound within the story of Andrew and his community. I am not alone in this. The spiritual credibility of approximately two hundred people is currently locked in negative ice. For myself, for my peers and - if it doesn't sound too grand - for the benefit of our species, I had to do something to start a thaw. Placing an honest account of the community's work into everlasting print struck me as a powerful, practical beginning.

My experience of the Authentic Self made me feel I should write this book. I regard myself a pragmatic person. As I look at the world's problems I see, chief among them, the difficulty human beings often encounter when it comes to working together. Often, it seems, the issues faced by our species are more relational than technical. I have no doubt about my experience of the Authentic Self, of harmoniously inquiring with others, or of the synthesised intelligence that appears when human beings are aligned. I felt I should write this book, to publicise the community's successful construction of a specialised receptive faculty, and to record how that faculty was built and the extraordinary form of intelligence it received. I felt instructed by both that intelligence itself, and by my conscience, to make known the entity that appeared and the fortitude required to invoke it.

I am curious to see what this book will do. In fact, regarding its future, curiosity is my only option. This is because both the book and its potential readership have assorted qualities, which, together, make it nigh-on impossible to predict the book's reception. Its subject, enlightenment, is a challenging one; yet the story told in this book is, I believe, captivating. Adding to the book's contrasting qualities is the fact that I am a passionate, but novice, writer. Meanwhile, its potential readership is also of varied character. I anticipate a mixed response from the former community, but I cannot know how the book will be received by a wider audience. On the one hand, it might be of no interest. But on the other, with the book's roots drawing from rich, spiritual soil, it might have broad appeal and bear surprising fruit. With its charged origin and unpredictable future, I am curious to see whom the book will reach and what effect it will have.

Andrew is this book's central figure. I believe it is both interesting and useful to review his character and his role from the point of view of evolution. I think I have a unique perspective to share. As a student, I knew Andrew as a teacher. After the dissolution, I knew Andrew as a friend. I knew him at the height of his transmission and, later, I saw his recovery from a near-total breakdown. I believe I understand him quite well.

I experienced the student-teacher relationship as being unlike any other. I am convinced my peers would say the same. At its most powerful, my heart's longing for unfettered expression, my desire to be at home in existence, was embodied in, and represented by, Andrew's physical form and spiritual function. My passion to know God resonated with his love of God and – at the best of times - I felt not a trace of separation existed between us. Conversely, he could appear – in my mind's eye - to be my enemy. Whenever I felt victimised by my experience, and judged my victimisation to be more important than the community's work, the very thought of Andrew would generate dread. At those moments, I knew I was undermining the work of our community and that he would disapprove of my capitulation. My experience of the student-teacher relationship, therefore, had little reasonable middle ground. It oscillated between extremes. It wasn't a steady-state experience in the same way that many relationships are and, for that reason, I think it is hard to describe. Perhaps Andrew's representation in this book has also had this unusual, hard-to-define quality.

I was astonished when, eighteen months after the dissolution, and after visiting him in India, I became one of Andrew's few close friends. At first, he had closer friendships with other ex-students who, I felt, valued the analytical element in his teachings more than I did. But when they dropped away, I was surprised to find myself Andrew's principal ally. A strong part of my experience at that time was the arrival of my unorthodox Christian love (defined in the Appendix). Its arrival added to an extraordinary range of developmental currents that circulated within me and, separately and differently, in Andrew. He was gradually finding his feet after the comprehensive collapse of his worlds, inner and outer, and the bombardment of vitriol he had received, and was still receiving, from ex-students. He was like a soldier recovering from shellshock. Meanwhile, I was in a state of utter gratitude. I felt my growing strength had two sources: Andrew's teachings enabled me to stay calm in the midst of these surreal developments; and, emanating from my surfacing love of Jesus, I felt an invincible commitment to what I saw as the true story of Andrew's life and the dissolution. In fact, central to my view of the dissolution and its aftermath, was my awareness of Jesus' cry from the cross, *"My God, My God, why hast thou forsaken me?"* His utterance stood strong in my consciousness, making me realise that even great spiritual figures can lose their enlightenment in extreme conditions.

During our friendship, Andrew was fun to be with. We were like brothers, sometimes enjoying drinking Guinness together, and otherwise sharing, via Skype, our experiences of living different, travelling lives. He did not assert his previous authority; he was genuinely and touchingly grateful for my support. At one point, I told him that my father had been an Anglican priest, and I described my Christian love and the perspective it gave me on the dissolution. (More on this later). Andrew was amused; he said my affections and thoughts weren't a problem. I knew my arising Christian interest was incongruous to the context of Andrew's teachings but, nevertheless, I was surprised by his response. What I experienced as a burningly relevant construct in human consciousness seemed to mean little to him. It reminded me that, of course, not everyone values the Christian story. More relevant, perhaps, to understanding Andrew and his role in evolution, is what came from his dedicated efforts to transcend his predicament.

Inwardly, as far as I could tell, Andrew accepted his circumstances, past and present. He didn't fight them. At times, I could tell he was reeling from the intensity of his experience, but he dealt with that within himself. As I knew him, he didn't lash out at his detractors, or rail against his lot; I didn't see him do anything reprehensible. Outwardly, he applied himself carefully and diligently to his recovery. It is not for me to disclose the many and varied efforts he made to understand himself and his downfall, as he described it. But I can say that he took the accusations levelled at him seriously, and he spent time and money inquiring into their possible origin. As is perhaps often the case, from dedicated effort in one direction came an unexpected breakthrough from another. It came in the form of a statement made spontaneously by Andrew after a ten-day, immersive-healing event. I believe his statement pinpoints a formative episode in his life that, in part, prepared Andrew for his career as a spiritual teacher. I think that this episode can be seen as the improbable – even preposterously improbable - source of his teachings. The statement Andrew spontaneously made was, *"Everything comes back to my brother."*

Andrew made this statement after he had taken a great risk and immersed himself in a form of inquiry incongruous to his expertise. It came at a time when he was still disorientated by the dissolution, but beginning to find some stability. I emphasise, it was *his* statement. Here, I want to take a risk and share my thoughts on the relevance of what Andrew said. I think his words are key to understanding his role in life.

As a boy of three and four years old, Andrew was bullied by his older brother. In Andrew's autobiography, he euphemistically writes: *"My older brother of five years was very resentful of my presence in his life."* As Andrew's students, we came to know of his brother's methods of schoolboy persecution. The details of this are not mine to share. Andrew very occasionally, but openly, referred to them, and he told us of their consequences. He had had trouble learning at school and his parents, seeing something was wrong, had sent him to a child psychologist. This was information we, Andrew's students, knew. It was neither highlighted, nor hidden.

I believe it is well known that elements of people's development can freeze at points of trauma. I want to suggest that Andrew's treatment by his brother left him with both a child's innocence and a degree of immunity to the suffering of others. I also suggest that, seen in a sequential, evolutionary view, these effects were preparation for the role Andrew later performed.

Innocence is, perhaps, an unusual trait in an adult but, the more I came to know Andrew, the more I could see the presence of innocence in him. As a teacher, his transmission was unrestrained by knowingness. He could teach with measured precision when required but, often, he just let his teachings spontaneously come through him. His method of inquiry was interactive; with his students, the public and his peers, the form of learning he most enjoyed was face-to-face dialogue. Personally, I knew him as someone who didn't bear grudges and who would approach strangers with innocent curiosity on all sorts of matters: their menu choices or travel destinations, for example. I think many people recognise the function of innocence in spiritual teachers, and see how their essential qualities of authority, spontaneity and originality spring from a child-like state of mind. It is this that makes them spiritual conduits. I suggest that Andrew's innocence, a product of his brother's persecution, was key to his charisma, his success as a teacher and the birth of his modern-day teachings.

More controversial, perhaps, is Andrew's muted interest in other people's emotional landscape. This second effect of his brother's treatment, if true, lands in a minefield of secular expectations. Yet, despite those surrounding dangers, I contend that this feature of Andrew's character was even more vital to his role as an evolutionary spiritual teacher than was his innocence. I suggest that secular expectations of a spiritual teacher are, consciously or unconsciously, based upon prevailing Christian notions of compassion; that the primary quality looked for in a spiritual figure is one of empathetic care for people's feelings. In religious or other circles, this kind of care might be valuable. But Andrew was pushing something new into manifestation. His genre of spirituality was enlightenment, and not just the enlightenment of individuals, but the enlightenment of groups. Enlightenment is transcendence, the elevation of identity from thought and feeling, to consciousness. This graduation is extremely challenging: the human mind is very powerful, and its transcendence comes with enormous implications. All Andrew's students struggled in this process. His job was to assist their graduation. It helped that Andrew was a little immune to his students' trials and tribulations. He would never have shaped us, his students, into the receptive faculty that received the Authentic Self had he not been resilient to our protestations. His muted interest in our feelings was, I suggest, essential to his role.

Andrew is not, as his critics claim, an abusive man. Nor is he a pastoral figure. His empathetic qualities lie somewhere between those two extremes, but definitely on the right side of a dividing line between trustworthy and untrustworthy. I am quite a sensitive man; I care about people's feelings, including my own, and I know when I feel unsafe in someone's company. I know what it's like to be worried about someone making insensitive remarks, or fragmenting my attention with their chaotic demands. I recognise mild forms of abuse. With complete integrity I can say – even while acknowledging that this is subjective - that I have never felt unsafe in this way in Andrew's company.

I'd like to propose an alternative explanation for some ex-students' accusations of abuse. I believe they seek to alleviate the suffering that comes from giving up the spiritual journey. After leaving the community in 2010, I spent two and a half years in a terrible state, believing I'd destroyed my opportunity for spiritual success. I couldn't sleep, and I was convinced I had stomach cancer. Worst of all, there was no depth to be found anywhere in life, and no prospect of ever finding any. I was in an enforced, nihilistic-hell realm, feeling it would last for ever; and this was without the effects of turning my heart – as others clearly had - against my teacher. It is not hard to imagine how ex-students, suffering the same disconnection from their heart's desire, may have seized on the community's dissolution and the seeds of the abuse story as a means to assuage their profound pain. Accepting and promoting the abuse narrative would have relieved their suffering and positively re-evaluated their spiritual status. If the community had been misguided all along, they could be proud of their choice to leave.

An evolutionary perspective, or the view of the Creator, puts an existing situation and its backstory within one frame. It shows the origin of a situation. In Andrew's case, one can see the dendritic pattern – the branching lines of cause and effect – that led him to be a spiritual teacher of a particular type. There are many other significant features of Andrew and his story that I have not been able to include here, most notably his supple intelligence, but I hope I have laid out enough of the picture of Andrew's life to show that his gifts as a spiritual teacher came, partly but significantly, from his suffering.

The above paragraphs looked at Andrew's life in detail. Now, moving to look at the Authentic Self, the view greatly broadens.

I refer to two sentences written recently in this book. Describing the experience of the Authentic Self in Chapter 21, I have used the line, *Unknown to itself until seen through the eyes of others* and, in this chapter's iron-face metaphor, I write *Creator looks at created*. I want to use these sentences as a starting point, to initiate a consideration of the relationship between human beings and an immortal, creative force.

We had a refrain in our community to describe our place in life. It was, "*We are in a process greater than ourselves.*" To explain this we would say, "*We are the products of an evolving universe, perceivers of that universe and participants in its awakening.*" In my experience, the effect of this refrain was to put my identity on a carousel. Instead of thinking of myself as a static, fairground observer, I found my identity became mobile, that it became freer and able to locate itself in any of the positions listed above: *product of, perceiver of,* and *participant in.* I think this idea of being integrated within a three-stage, circular flow can be used to consider the higher relationship between Creator, human beings and Authentic Self, as follows. The Creator made the human beings (in this case Andrew and his students), who formed a receptive faculty, through which the Creator, in the form of the Authentic Self, came, both to observe itself and fine-tune its human recipients. When imagining this higher, circular flow, I think it is interesting – almost comical - to see the interdependence of two participants that have very different sizes and lifespans: The Creator, infinite and timeless; dependent upon human beings, who are finite and short-lived. Despite their dimensional differences, both seem to need each other. The Creator needs a relationship with humankind, to know itself; human beings need a relationship with the Creator for the same reason. In this perspective, the following question might seem unnecessary, but I think it is still valuable to ask: Who was the progenitor of the Authentic Self?

I see two possible progenitors. Either Andrew and his students were the primary creative players, or they were the minions of the Creator. If the work of the community is seen as human-driven, it will be weighed and measured against human expectations, values and motives. So be it. But the context of this book is not human-centric. Enlightenment is its context, and enlightenment depends upon the subordination of human-centricity, or self-importance. I think it would, therefore, be sensible to subordinate the importance of Andrew and his students and propose that the force of love and evolution was the progenitor. How does the community's history look in the light of that proposal?

I believe the energy of evolution provided the beginning, the middle and the end of the community's story; evolution was always the wind beneath our wings. As described in the last section, Andrew's early life can be seen as his preparation for his future role. Then, when he was sixteen, he was given his first, unsought-for experience of enlightenment; an experience which drove his spiritual search thereafter. Next, Andrew's full enlightenment can be seen as his surrender to a cosmological force. His students, soon drawn to his transmission of enlightenment, were sustained by both their experience of awakening - of evolution in action - and their desire to be further immersed in that process. From observing his students came Andrew's vision of the Authentic Self; witnessing their interactions, he saw the potential in their purposeful communication. Meanwhile, his teachings changed; they became aligned with the evolutionary impulse. As teacher, teachings and students came together, and the obstacle of ego was fissured, the Authentic Self – in fits and starts - appeared through unpredictable apertures until, on July 30th, it arrived full-bore. Shortly, I will show how it's possible to see the dissolution as an evolutionary phenomenon. Given this sequence of events, I think the story of the community can be seen, from beginning to end, as the work of an emergent Creator.

If the community's work was inspired and steered by the Creator, it is not unreasonable to think that the Creator captured what was learnt for future use. Quite possibly, in ways beyond current human comprehension, the community's progress – made over many years of emotional grappling and cognitive development - was stored in some sort of memory bank, or noosphere. If the idea of some form of capture is accepted, another question arises: what might be the future role of the Authentic Self? I can suggest two answers, based on what has been revealed so far.

The first draws from the central story of this book. The invocation of the Authentic Self started with Andrew's vision of an enlightened group. He predicted that the spiritual transmission of a group would be a '*forest fire*' compared to the '*burning matchstick*' of an enlightened individual. The enlightened field created by an individual is evident in history; it is clear that a *burning matchstick* enlightens the world around it. Regarding a *forest fire*, I believe this book records some features of this new type of enlightenment; it describes the brighter beacon and - more importantly – the contagious nature of what an enlightened group can invoke. We called this phenomenon the Authentic Self. It is the rapacity of the Authentic Self that makes it so significant: its capacity to draw people in and infuse them with liberated consciousness. This is why Andrew originally made the comparison between group enlightenment and a forest fire. Invoked by an enlightened group, the Authentic Self can speed up the process of universal enlightenment.

My second suggestion for the future role of the Authentic Self draws on my account of the 2003 symposium described in Chapter 21. In that account, the Authentic Self conducted a liberating review of German shame. Perhaps other inhibiting cultural constructs could, likewise, be disentangled and disarmed? Examples might be Motherhood, The Legacy of Slavery, Scientific Materialism, The Protestant Work Ethic, or The Chosen People. I suggest these examples tentatively but, certainly, one can see how big, rolling momentums - including national habits like English cynicism – are currently trapping people and causing them to live lives of reduced scope. It is not hard to see how, ultimately, a faculty capable of taking divine intelligence into deeply established, compressed and potent preoccupations in civilisation, could accelerate both mankind's evolution and the universe's awakening.

Attempting to look at the dissolution of Andrew's community through the eyes of the Creator, I come to this chapter's biggest idea. Perhaps the dissolution was not a negative event; perhaps it was an evolutionary upheaval.

A timeless, resource-rich Creator, looking at Andrew's community twelve years after the birth of the Authentic Self, might have seen a situation with some redundant elements, yet great potential. Here was a strongly hierarchical, spiritual community that had, some years before, successfully performed its role as incubator of the Authentic Self. Within that community were many highly-trained students, somewhat constricted. Not constricted, but perhaps now underutilised, was a spiritual teacher whose mission had been accomplished. Seeing this situation, the Creator – having driven evolution for eternity and being committed to its task - might have decided to act.

Shortly, I describe the developments that could still follow the dissolution. But first, I want to take some time to validate the idea that the dissolution might have been – from the point of view of evolution - a positive event.

As acknowledged before, at certain points in this book I have had to push against prevailing social attitudes. Now I am challenging the widely-held assumption that the dissolution was caused by human failing. Knowing the strength of that assumption (I have never heard it questioned), I feel I need to strike two blows. I want to do this by referring to two phenomena, drawn from different fields of human interest. The first phenomenon comes from the field of statistics; it establishes an umbrella idea, or principle. The second phenomenon relates directly to the *spiritual* context of the dissolution; it is the central event of western civilisation's spiritual narrative.

The work of Nicholas Taleb supports (unintentionally) a fresh look at the dissolution. Taleb is an author and professor in the field of statistical risk management. His 2007 book, *The Black Swan*, has been described as one of the twelve most influential books written since World War Two. He writes as follows:

> *"What we call a Black Swan is an event with the following three attributes: First, it is an outlier, as it lies outside the realm of regular expectations, because nothing in the past can convincingly point to its possibility. Second, it carries an extreme impact. Third, in spite of its outlier status, human nature makes us concoct explanations for its occurrence after the fact, making it explainable and predictable.*

> *"A small number of Black Swans explains almost everything in our world, from the success of ideas and religions, to elements of our own*

personal lives. Almost everything in social life is produced by rare but consequential shocks and jumps: all the while almost everything studied about social life focuses on the 'normal', particularly with 'bell curve' methods of inference that tell you close to nothing. Why? Because the bell curve ignores large deviations, cannot handle them, yet makes us confident that we have tamed uncertainty."

Taleb points to the fact that cataclysmic events are more significant in determining the course of history than are periods of steady development. I'd like to show how some features of the dissolution perfectly fit Taleb's Black Swan criteria and, thereby, suggest that the dissolution – seen in the community's context - was one such cataclysmic, formative event. Firstly, the dissolution was not predicted. Secondly, it was extreme: the community collapsed rapidly and students' attitudes to Andrew reversed suddenly, absolutely and almost universally. Thirdly, ex-students and others later spoke about the dissolution as if it had been predictable.

A review of Andrew's life also supports the possibility of the dissolution being an evolutionary, or Black Swan, event. Indeed, his life looks like a series of such interventions. In his developmental years, he experienced major upsets: his brother's treatment of him, his mother's departure and his father's death. Then followed his teenage cosmic visitation, his enlightenment and his split with Poonja. From his enlightenment came three new spiritual constructs: a new teaching, a worldwide community and the Authentic Self. Placed within the sequence of Andrew's extraordinary life, the dissolution – I suggest - looks less like a man-made disaster and more like another evolutionary turn of events.

I now come to the second phenomenon I've chosen to support a review of the dissolution. From my point of view, this second phenomenon suits my purpose perfectly, yet it comes wreathed in unhelpful, sensational associations. The phenomenon centres on the crucifixion of Jesus, but I want to pull back from the drama of that event and single-out the principle it exhibits. Positioned at the epicentre of western civilisation's spiritual heritage, the crucifixion story has two facets: humanly, it is a story of anguish, doubt, betrayal, injustice, mob-rule and abandonment; historically, it is widely seen as an event that elevated, and is still elevating, civilisation. The principle appearing from these two facets of the crucifixion narrative is this: a devastating event can be the origin of a new emergence.

One lesson I have learnt on my spiritual journey is that seekers must, in part, be scavengers. One cannot afford to be a snob or a purist; vital lessons can appear at any time, from any source and, in one's struggle to transcend limitation, one needs to recognise and seize upon truth regardless of its presentation. Andrew taught his students something similar, but more regulated; he implored and instructed us to look for, and live from, spiritual principles. Hence, while I recognise that a storm of emotions, assumptions and objections might accompany my reference to the crucifixion, I am, like a scavenger, interested only in the principle – stated above - that it illustrates.

Attending Andrew's teachings used to deliver a recognisable feeling experience. It is the same experience one can have when walking out of church on a Sunday morning. I imagine this is true of other religious services. It is the experience of transcendence. After spending time contemplating life's big questions, one is drawn into an expanded, positive field of awareness. It could be seen as the positive side of the experience of being overwhelmed, in which one is raised above normality to delightedly discover spacious sanity, natural curiosity and gratitude. This experience was ambient at Foxhollow. Andrew exuded it, and so did his close students. His books and the magazine also carried these transcendent properties. This enlightened quality of experience is real, valuable and worth fighting for. That is why I have risked referring to the crucifixion. I imagine the reference will divide opinion and, possibly, court accusations of evangelism or sacrilege, but what that reference won't do is collapse under scrutiny. There, at the source of one of the world's great spiritual traditions, established and irrefutable, stands an example of the mayhem that often precedes and surrounds revolution.

Many developments could still follow from the dissolution of Andrew's community. Each deserves a full explanation but, not wanting to overload this chapter, I will be succinct. The student-teacher relationship could – in its broadest context - be examined and improved. With the benefit of many intelligent people's hindsight, the value of the relationship and its specific function could be more tightly specified, making this form of education more attractive to modern society. Next, the Authentic Self could be invoked by others. The dissolution of the community effectively de-branded this spiritual phenomenon, setting it free for others to invoke and employ. Regarding Andrew, I venture to suggest an evolved role might await him. He used to say, *"There's always further to go,"* and the question *How does a powerful teacher evolve?* is an intriguing one. A further development might involve former students cutting new pathways. I believe little is known about the process of graduating from the auspices of a spiritual teacher, so an opportunity exists for former students to both lay tracks across virgin ground and, for the benefit of others, record their experience of doing so. Lastly, the dissolution provides space for former students to find their spiritual vocations. I know this is happening to some degree but, if an evolutionary interpretation of the dissolution became the established narrative, I think the earlier confidence of many former students would be re-established and their consequent creativity would benefit the world.

'Return to zero.' This was a phrase briefly used by students to represent enlightened consciousness. Looking back at the community's structure while wearing my builder's cap, I see the necessity for our strong hierarchy. Like the structure of a reactor, it was needed to contain the evolutionary forces we were engaged with. Our work was a form of fusion: first, ego had to be split from awareness; then, many people's awareness had to be focused upon a common subject. This work required both self-discipline and hierarchical control; forms of authority which, over time, shaped a monolithic structure. In a very simple view, it makes sense to me that that monolithic structure would need to be demolished before something new could arise; true to the community's understanding, it had to return to zero. The dissolution, I suggest, can be seen as that return to zero, and, thereby, as a significant, evolutionary opportunity.

At Foxhollow we were safely ensconced, focused on our spiritual work and out of the public eye. The dissolution flattened our monastery's walls. Many students turned against their teacher, and the community's unifying meta-narrative disintegrated. Our shining enterprise, which seemed invincible to us, became a publicly-witnessed failure. This book, in small part, takes this process further. It places embarrassing, ego-handling practices and Andrew's troubled childhood before a wide audience. It would be easy for bystanders to mock some elements of the story. The exposure is, in part, humiliating.

Without doubt, intelligent inquiry is one method of spiritual development. But the softening of one's rigidity through humiliation is another. As I have said before, my student experience of holding my head in my hands and saying to myself, *"How could I have done that again?"* was very familiar; I came to see it as par for the course, as integral to my pioneering spiritual life. I gained this view from the community's work. From our lengthy, painful engagement with ego, we came to understand that ego humiliation was related to humility; this meant that, while humiliation was never exactly welcomed, it was eventually – on the whole – received with composure and treated seriously.

The dissolution can be seen as intense humiliation, as the stripping away of the community's dignity and the imposition of shame. Yet, intriguingly, if this humiliation is proportionate to the humility that should follow, a more permeable interface with the force of love and evolution should arise. My episodes of burning embarrassment as a student were a small price to pay for the sensitivity I gained. Perhaps, likewise, the community's humiliation could turn out to be for the greater good.

To end with, I think US President Theodore Roosevelt's famous 1910 quote – which became known as *The Man in the Arena* - beautifully places humiliation within the context of brave endeavour.

> *"It is not the critic who counts; not the man who points out how the strong man stumbles, or where the doer of deeds could have done them better. The credit belongs to the man who is actually in the arena, whose face is marred by dust and sweat and blood; who strives valiantly; who errs, who comes short again and again, because there is no effort without error and shortcoming; but who does actually strive to do the deeds; who knows great enthusiasms, the great devotions; who spends himself in a worthy cause; who at the best knows in the end the triumph of high achievement, and who at the worst, if he fails, at least fails while daring greatly, so that his place shall never be with those cold and timid souls who neither know victory nor defeat."*

Finally

I didn't know what to expect when I went to see Andrew in India. It was a year and a half after the dissolution, and I hadn't seen him for nearly three years. I could only speculate on his state of mind and his feelings about my visit. Faced with the unknown, my mind couldn't settle; it restlessly scanned a broad spectrum of possibilities. However, I had one sustaining, rock-solid belief, which functioned as a motto: *The world cannot afford to lose Andrew's experience.* Sitting front and centre in my awareness was my knowledge of his enlightened engagement with thousands of people over almost three decades; I was acutely conscious of the rarity and value of Andrew's accumulated expertise.

I now feel the same about the experience accrued within Andrew's community. I hate to think of it going to waste. Hence, one of my hopes for this book is that it will disseminate the rich learning experience I had in the community. My final chapter concluded with an evolutionary view of events, but I want to say that I am not insisting upon that interpretation as the most credible view. Rather, I would like to point out that many different views, in many different fields of life, make sense from the standpoint of the holder. Socialism, Capitalism, Feminism, Materialism… each view looks well-reasoned to the people who support it. At the same time, different views lead to different lives. And this is my point. An evolutionary view leads to an evolutionary life. It's one option among many.

Writing this book over the past two years has been the greatest challenge of my life. I have lived in a state of constant review. I now look back on my time in the community as a period of training, of immeasurable value, which I have no desire to resume or repeat. Looking ahead, I have ideas for further books, and I'd like to create a self-inquiry course that implements Andrew's teachings. I have one thought about the community's future. Logically, I think an affiliation is what should develop, an expanded network of practitioners, working independently, yet informed by Andrew's teachings. An affiliation would have all sorts of possibilities: joint ventures; a forward-thinking task-force; and annual gatherings to share successes and cross-fertilise people's learning. That, to me, would be an arrangement that would provide a framework for individual enterprise and a vehicle for the teachings to evolve. But it is not, currently, my intention to bring such an affiliation into being.

Andrew once described me as *"thoroughly square,"* and, on another occasion, Noel said I had *"the chivalry of a bygone* age." Both are examples of the no-nonsense, humorous and blunt reflections that were common currency in the community. I wouldn't argue with either - they were affectionately meant but, more to the point, they now exist within the context of my immense gratitude. I love the effectiveness of Andrew's teachings. I love their precision and, especially, the way they teach one to look for, and refer to, essential, everlasting principles. My favourite amongst these is the principle that self engenders self, or *authenticity begets authenticity.* By living a true life, we give true life to others. This book has been my idea, my composition, my voice. It should, therefore, according to this principle, evoke authenticity for its readers. I hope so.

My time in Andrew's community has liberated me from worries about myself and worries about the future. It has furnished me with enough self-knowledge to know my direction of travel. In these circumstances, I've felt the writing of this book was the least I could do.

Appendix

The Five Tenets

The following short descriptions are this author's interpretations. Full versions of the tenets can be found in Andrew Cohen's books, *Embracing Heaven and Earth* and *Evolutionary Enlightenment*. His five tenets work in sequence; they build upon one another. They are tools that enable an individual to see through the often-powerful activity of the human mind.

1. Clarity of Intention

"Keep your eyes on the prize," Andrew often said. His first tenet saves one from the weakening effect of wanting many things, of spreading oneself too thinly. Because the human mind is immensely powerful, transcending it takes tremendous energy. This means that the desire to be free has to be consciously placed before all others; the first tenet reminds one of this necessity.

2. The Law of Volition

This law states that with awareness comes choice. Although human beings often claim helplessness, the second tenet holds that within our ability to see ourselves lies the potential to act independently of what is seen. This recognition is an antidote to self-victimisation because, as this tenet states, like it or not, we have a choice. The tenet makes a great demand: anyone who wants to be free has to accept responsibility for their response to everything that happens to them, be it in the past, present, or future. Andrew stresses that this level of responsibility is a huge challenge.

3. Face Everything and Avoid Nothing

The third tenet instructs one consciously to adopt an enlightened relationship to experience. This means not being despairing, shocked, jubilant, or impressed by the activity of one's mind. In essence, this tenet says, *"Look at what arises in your experience, but don't assume it defines you."* As the mind pitches and tosses, this tenet helps one to remain calm and curious, and to hold one's conclusions lightly.

4. The Truth of Impersonality

This tenet says, *"Notice how every element of your experience comes from the fabric of shared human experience; see how impersonal, or common, it all is."* Seeing this commonality affects one's awareness: it integrates one with the undivided field of Life. Conversely, individualising one's experience – *personalising* it - leads to the sense of being separate and a 'special case'. The truth of impersonality counters the human tendency to create a unique, and often hopeless, drama from one's experience. Thereby, it leaves one able to make use of proven laws and truths.

5. Care for the Whole

The last tenet interfaces with enlightened consciousness. As one sees through one's experience, one makes contact with a limitless form of awareness that is not self-centred. This dimension of awareness *is* enlightenment, and it has its own agenda. The fifth tenet prepares one for an enormous change in motivation, from wanting something for oneself, to giving of oneself to a greater cause.

The Six Principles of Evolutionary Enlightenment

The six principles are quite complex. They come as three pairs. Each pair exhibits an interplay between different impulses. These impulses are both human impulses and the impulses of an evolving universe. The nature of each interplay – described under the headings below - is different in each pair. Also, as with the five tenets, the six principles form a sequence; they build upon one another.

The six principles are naturally-occurring interplays that become visible as one's awareness is freed from personal preoccupation. They are discovered to exist at the interface between human intention and the force of love and evolution. Therefore, as they appear in awareness as naturally-interacting impulses, they improve one's understanding of life's complexity. In short, knowledge of, and reference to, the six principles strengthen one's participation in evolution.

(Words in italics are taken from Andrew's books).

Purity of Motive and Integrity of Action

The two impulses of the first pair of the six principles are mutually supportive.

At first sight, these desires look foundational to any level of civilised life, so it's important to know that – in the context of the six principles - they refer to our highest impulses and aspirations.

Andrew describes purity of motive as *wholesome passion*, as our sense of *connection to a higher purpose*, and as *the compulsion to create the future*. Purity of motive is inherent in our felt sense of the *Self that lies beneath small-minded concerns and conditioned impulses*. Integrity of action means obedience to pure motive. It is the *heroic spirit* that enables us to follow through on our pure motivation. Having the integrity to act on our pure motivation aligns us with the force of love and evolution.

Autonomy and Communion

The two impulses of the second pair of the six principles might appear to be mutually exclusive but, in the context of evolutionary enlightenment, they are seen as complementary.

Autonomy is authentic independence. It is our care for, and commitment to, our individual talents and personal destiny. It is our willingness to stand apart from the status quo on behalf of our true vocation. Communion is the state of non-separation, of being *unified with others in the pursuit of authenticity*. Communion with others is an integral feature of the undivided, self-seeking matrix of existence itself. Autonomy and communion fuse when they are held in awareness with equal value. That juxtaposition produces a new potential. The co-existence of *thrilling autonomy and blissful communion* creates a new, dynamic field. That new field of awareness, stronger than either of its components, has the potential to accelerate evolution.

Evolutionary Tension and Natural Hierarchy

The two impulses of the third pair of the six principles are contrasting, yet complementary.

Evolutionary tension is the desire to grow. It is the force pushing and pulling human beings towards their highest potential. It is the creative impulse itself, and the beating heart of enlightened awareness. Whereas evolutionary tension is energetic, dynamic and formless, natural hierarchy has shape. *It is a structure of human relationships, an arrangement of knowledge and competence, that is formed from actual differences between people's levels of development.* Natural hierarchy acknowledges the reality of difference. When the dynamism of evolutionary tension and the reality of natural hierarchy are held in awareness together, a new type of organisation appears. That new organisation is adaptable. It has the merits of any configuration of co-operative people, but it can also quickly adapt and objectively reposition its members to meet new challenges. More intelligent than a rigid hierarchy, the fusion of evolutionary tension and natural hierarchy produces an organisation that is better able to serve evolution.

The Author's Christianity

In this book, I have said that my father was an Anglican priest and, at two key moments, I have referred to the Christian story. These references might lead some readers to wonder about my form of Christianity and how I relate to Jesus and his life.

As a boy, I liked the New Testament stories. I liked their simplicity. I loved Jesus's vigour, his success, and his down-to-earth metaphors. Even then, I thought the creeds (virgin birth, resurrection, etc.) were symbolic, not literal, stories, while, with schoolboy confidence, I decided that Jesus didn't want to be worshipped because that, I figured, would not have fitted with his selflessness.

What I now love about Jesus is his effectiveness. He worked effectively with humanity's most profound aspiration: our desire for self-knowledge. At one level, he engaged with people, correcting their priorities. At another level, his booming victory - over humanity's doubt in God's existence - altered the course of history. For myself, his example gives weight to my highest aspirations.

I hope this book shows that my time with Andrew has enabled me to manage my mind and trust the force of evolution. I see my relationship with Jesus as a parallel source of inspiration and instruction, less sophisticated, but unsurpassable. To me, the invaluable influences of both men are compatible.

Two Questions Answered

1. What was talked about in students' meetings?

In some formal meetings, the subject of discussion was the state of consciousness being shared at the time. But many meetings started with a more material focus. Before listing the range of subjects which students might focus upon, I'd like to offer a metaphor that, I hope, illustrates how their discussions had a specific purpose, and then explain what that purpose was.

Please imagine a group of artists observing an oil painting: a vase of daffodils. One might reasonably expect the artists to be more interested in the painting's colours and depiction of light, than the daffodils' botanical classification or the vase's manufacturer: the artists would have their particular interests. Similarly, when Andrew's students discussed a subject, they had a specific purpose: to understand their experience of that subject in order to *see through it*. Here is an explanation of what *seeing through* a subject means.

In our meetings, we took a feature of human experience – which, of course, was also our experience - and applied ourselves to understanding its original purpose, current function, depth of history, and the strength of the feelings associated with it. We sought to understand that feature so thoroughly –

conceptually and emotionally - that it became completely familiar to us. This is what is meant by seeing through a subject. Once seen through, features of human nature cease to be obstacles, and that is when we - human beings in general - become more open conduits for the passage of Spirit.

Regarding the content of our meetings, any facet of the human condition was a possible subject for discussion. Frequent topics were: human interest in improvement (the impulse to evolve); the pros and cons of progressive social values, gender conditioning, ego, cultural values, and the classifications of developmental models such as Clare Graves' *Spiral Dynamics* and Ken Wilber's *AQAL (All Quadrants All Levels)*. We also had our personal experience and the community's progress to discuss and learn from, and Andrew's teachings to study.

2. How were formal meetings different from 'good', social conversations?

There are tangible, physical differences between the formal meetings held by Andrew's students and good, social conversations. I will come to these. But first, the foundational difference is one of self-importance: students' sense of self-importance was – and should have been - less than the sense of self-importance that generally exists in members of a social group.

There is a reason for this difference: students worked hard at this matter. Dissolving self-importance was the aim of the community's years of ego-engagement. To recap: each student's task in those years was to 'cage' the human species' sense of self-importance – of ruling the earth with unrivalled intelligence – while bringing forward the view that our purpose as human beings is to contribute to a project greater than ourselves: the awakening of the universe. I hope that Chapter 15, *Engaging with Ego*, shows how difficult it is to achieve this displacement. But if it is achieved - if ego is successfully displaced - an individual sees himself or herself as both subordinate to a greater process and, vitally, an integrated part of that process. The experience of being an integrated part of a greater process is thrilling and enriching. Critically, it makes one willing to give up the kind of personal concerns often found in social conversations.

One obvious physical difference between formal meetings and social conversations is the number of participants. Formal meetings might contain between five and sixty people, but the meetings always had one, shared conversation. Further differences are to do with individual behaviour. In formal meetings, students would not consume more attention than they needed. Nor would they let preoccupations affect their responsible participation. They would not fidget, sit with casual posture, or otherwise fragment the discussion's progress by making comments or jokes, for example. They would care for the theme of the meeting by staying focused upon it and, if they had a contribution to make, they would be sensitive about when they entered the dialogue. Students would not withdraw if something they said failed to receive expected recognition, and their attention would not be distracted by concern for others in the meeting: with everyone being fully responsible for themselves, there was no need for that concern. Of course, in the community's early years, the meetings contained many of these fragmenting behaviours but, in the honed meetings of later years, the purpose was clear and students had enough attainment to filter out intrusive habits, at least for the duration of the meeting.

We found that when everyone was engaged – and it did require everyone, because a self-centred person could ruin a meeting – we became more than the sum of our parts. Perhaps, like any team, we relaxed when we knew everyone was intent on giving their best. Then, when relaxed, students were able to give of their best. It was at these times, when we were united in the service of Spirit, that we were able to invoke the Authentic Self.

What is Enlightenment? Magazine
(Later, *EnlightenNext Magazine*)

Subjects, Contributors and Interviewed Luminaries

The issues of the magazine listed below are arranged chronologically, starting with the most recent. Because Andrew Cohen's reputation is currently tarnished, the names of the magazine's editors are omitted, along with those of contributing students and the magazine's graphic designers. Please note, however, that many of the articles in each issue were written by Andrew and the editorial team. In particular, the transcribed dialogues between Andrew and Ken Wilber are a central feature of many editions. Lastly, for information, the magazine's subtitle was, *redefining spirituality for an evolving world.*

The Cosmic Dimensions of Love.
Exploring the hidden depths of the evolutionary process.

Issue 47	2011
Contributors:	Brian Swimme, Gary Lachman, Peter Heehs, Mark Vernon
Interviews:	Ken Wilber, Deepak Chopra, Hardin Tibbs

Quantum Dreams.
Have scientists finally solved the mystery of consciousness?

Issue 46	Spring/Summer 2010
Contributor:	Gary Lachman
Interviews:	Stuart Hameroff, Ken Wilber, Marilyn Schlitz, Michael Grosso, Henry Stapp

The Evolving Faces of God.
New perspectives on the meaning of spirituality for our time.

Issue 45	Sept-Nov 2009
Contributors:	Jun Po Denis Kelly, Dennis Genpo Merzel Roshi
Interviews:	Ken Wilber, Aliya Haeri, Jean M. Twenge, Terry Patten

Envisioning the future.
What today's brightest minds have to say about the road ahead.

Issue 44	June-August 2009
Contributors:	Gary Lachman, Peter Ragnar, Alex Steffen
Interviews:	Thomas PM Barnett, John L. Petersen, Jim Garrison

Sex.
The Good, the Strange, and the Sacred

Issue 43	March-May 2009
Articles on:	David Deida, One Taste community
Contributors:	Steve McIntosh, Peter Ragnar, Gary Lachman
Interview:	Ken Wilber

What does the future look like to You?

Issue 42	Dec 2008–Feb 2009
Article on:	John F Haught
Contributors:	Jushua Dugdale, Peter Ragnar, James N Gardner
Interviews:	Susan Neiman, Arianne Huffington, Ken Wilber

Constructing the New Man
4 Unique Perspectives on Masculinity in the 21st Century

Issue 41	August–October 2008
Articles on:	Harvey Mansfield, Tripp Lanier, Jayson Gaddis, Erwin McManus, Nathaniel Flick
Contributors:	Jean Houston, Ani Difranco, Cheri Huber, Niurka, Audrey Kitagawa, Asra Nomani, Miranda Shaw, Rabbi Einat Ramon, Judith Glaser, Sally Kempton, Mother Clare Watts, Anne Wilson Schaef, Bina Agarwal, Jenny Wade, Lama Palden Drolma, Wendy Shalit, Chris Griscom, Rebecca Walker, JZ Knight
Interview:	Ken Wilber

Welcome to the centre of the Universe
Science zeros in on the significance of consciousness

Issue 40	May–July 2008
Interviews:	Depak Chopra, Ken Wilber, Joel R Primack, Nancy Ellen Abrams, Neil deGrasse Tyson, Paul Davies, Janna Levin, Deno Kazanis, Bernard Haisch

The Cosmos, The Psyche and YOU
An evolutionary vision for spirituality and psychology in the 21ˢᵗ century

Issue 39	Feb–April 2008
Interviews:	Ken Wilber and Frank Zane

Envisioning the future
... of ecology, politics and consciousness

Issue 38	Oct–Dec 2007
Articles on:	Don Beck, Elza Maalouf, Ajja the Avadhut
Interviews:	Steve McIntosh, Ken Wilber, Corrado Rustici, Jim Marion

Searching for Utopia
Exploring humanity's timeless quest for heaven on earth

Issue 36	April–June 2007
Articles on:	Contemporary communities including Damanhur
Contributors:	James N Gardner, Allan Combs
Interview:	Fritzie P Manuel

The Mystery of Evolution
A spiritual and scientific exploration of where we came from and where we're headed

Issue 35	Jan–March 2007
Contributor:	John Stewart
Interviews:	Robert W Godwin, John Haught, Zoltan Torey, Rick Warren

15-year Anniversary Issue

Issue 34	Sept–Dec 2006
Articles on:	Archimandrite Dionysios, Vimla Thakar, Eckhart Tolle, Teilhard de Chardin, Dr Beatrice Bruteau, Sheikh Ragip/ Robert Frager
Contributors:	Brian Swimme, Peter Ragnar

God's Next Move
Exploring the Next Spiritual Revolution

Issue 33	June–Aug 2006
Article on:	Rev. Jim Ball
Contributors:	Jana Espiritu Santu, Rev. Dr Cynthia Bourgeault, Peter Ragnar
Interviews:	Ken Wilber, James Gardner

Death, Rebirth and Everything in Between

Issue 32	Mar–May 2006
Articles on:	Mother Antonia, Rabbi Menachem Mendel Schneerson
Interviews:	Michael Beckworth, Rickie Byars-Beckworth

Spirituality vs Religion
Where do you stand?

Issue 31	Dec 2005–Feb 2006
Contributors:	Jason D Hill, Karen Armstrong, Rabbi Marc Gafni
Interviews:	Dzongsar Khyentse Rinpoche, Dr Dario Salas Sommer, Tom Callos, Dadi Janki

Do You Want to Live Forever?
Grappling with the science and ethics of immortality

Issue 30	Sept–Nov 2005
Article on:	Jakob von Uexkull
Contributors:	Andrei Codrescu, Joe Orso, Cheri Huber, Barbara Marx Hubbard
Interviews:	Ray Kurzweil, Robert J Sawyer, Connie Barlow, Peter Ragnar, Joe Firmage

Who are You?
Science's quest to solve the mystery of consciousness

Issue 29	June–Aug 2005
Article on:	Thomas de Zengotita
Contributor:	Rick Warren
Interviews:	John Petersen, Jonathan Granoff

Will Big Business Save the World?
Meet the unlikely heroes struggling to evolve the corporate machine

Issue 28	March–May 2005
Articles on:	Dadi Janki, John P Milton, Shawn Phillips, Brother Wayne Teasdale
Contributors:	Douglas Harding, Howard Bloom
Interviews:	Tex Gunning, Carlos and Deborah Santana, Don Beck

Searching for Soul in Hollywood

Issue 27	Nov 2004–Feb 2005
Articles on:	Phoolan Devi, Pir Vilayat Inayat Khan
Contributors:	Audrey Kitagawa, Jason D Hill, Duane Elgin, Howard Bloom
Interview:	Donna Zajonc

Is God a Pacifist?
War vs Peace in a post-9/11 world

Issue 26	Aug–Oct 2004
Contributors:	Mario Cuomo, Thomas de Zengotita, Robert F Kennedy Jr
Interviews:	David Rieff, John McCarthy, Ervin Lazlo, Jan Chozen Bays Roshi, Sheikh Tosun Bayrak, Father Basil Pennington, David Frawley, Ann Druyan, Neil deGrasse Tyson, James Gardner, Brian Swimme, Robert Wright

Come Together!
The power of collective intelligence

Issue 25	May–July 2004
Contributors:	Howard Bloom, Michael Murphy, Wayne Teasdale, Duane Elgin, John Petersen, Dr Munawar Anees, Peter Senge, Claus Otto Scharmer, Joseph Jaworski, Betty Sue Flowers
Interview:	Phil Jackson

Morality Bites!
Searching for ethics in a Postmodern Age

Issue 24	Feb–April 2004
Articles on:	Byron Kate, Eckhart Tolle, Robert Wright, Pilot Baba
Contributors:	His Holiness the Dalai Lama, Duane Elgin, John Petersen, Jim Garrison
Interview:	Robbie Wootton

Can God Handle the 21st Century?

Exploring the perils and potentials of the new millennium

Issue 23	Spring/Summer 2003
Article on:	Vissarion Christ
Contributors:	Don Beck, Brian Swimme, Peter Senge, Jeremy Rifkin, Elisabet Sahtouris, Barbara Marx Hubbard, Ray Kurzweil
Interviews:	Douglas Moore, Huston Smith, Douglas Harding, Vernon Kitabu Turner Roshi, Toni Packer, Lama Ole Nydahl, Leslie Temple-Thurston, Arnaud Desjardins, Ram Dass, Michael Barnett, Richard Moss, Lama Surya Das, Swami Niranjanananda, Byron Katie

Are You Ready to Change Now?

Exploring the dynamics of human transformation

Issue 22	Fall/Winter 2002
Articles on:	His Holiness Reverend Sri Swami Satchidananda Maharaj, Sri Chinmoy, Ashrita Furman
Contributors:	Robert Thurman, Don Beck
Interviews:	Yasuhiko Kimura, Dee Hock, Robert Kegan

The Future of God

Evolution & enlightenment for the 21st century

Issue 21	Spring/Summer 2002
Articles on:	Sri Aurobindo, Babaj
Contributors:	Robert Wright, Desmond Tutu, His Holiness the Dalai Lama, Dr Mihaly Csikszentmihalyi, Rigoberta Menchu Tum, Lech Walesa, Jody Williams, Oscar Arias Sanchez
Interview:	Dr Beatrice Bruteau

Celebrating 10 years of Radical Spiritual Inquiry.

Special tenth anniversary edition

Issue 20	Fall/Winter 2001
Contributor:	Ken Wilber
Interviews:	Georg Feuerstein, Rupert Sheldrake, Amit Goswami, Father Thomas Keating, Miranda Shaw, Stephen Batchelor, Ramesh Balsekar, Jack LaLanne, Vernon Kitabu Turner, Jetsunma Ahkön Lhamo, José Cabezón, Ajja, Lee Lozowick, Vimalar Thakar

Can Enlightenment Save the World?

Issue 19   Spring/Summer 2001

Contributors: Vimalar Thakar, Wayne Liquorman, Satyam Nadeen, Tony Parsons.

Interviews: Duane Elgin, Brian Swimme, Rabbi Michael Lerner, Brother Wayne Teasdale, Roshi Bernie Glassman, Ma Jaya Sati Bhagavati, John White, Joe Firmage

What Does it Mean to be in the World but not Of It?

Issue 18   Fall/Winter 2000

Contributors: Ken Wilber, Peter Masefield

Interviews: Elizabeth Lesser, Eckhart Tolle, Joseph Goldstein, Rabbi David Edelman, Sheikh Tosun Bayrak al-Jerrahi, Father William McNamara, His Holiness Penor Rinpoche

What is Ego?
Friend or foe?

Issue 17   Spring/Summer 2000

Contributors: Deepak Chopra, Cheri Huber, Paul Lowe, Saniel Bonder, Leon Hoffman, James Hollis, Henry Stein

Interviews: Ammachi, Yogi Amrit Desai, Venerable Master Sheng-Yen, Archimandrite Dionysios, Sheikh Ragip Frager al-Jerrahi, Robert Frager, Jack Engler, Kaisa Puhakka, Taylor Hackford, Otto Kernberg, Bannanje Govindacharya

Men's Liberation? Women's Liberation? Gay Liberation?
How free do we really want to be?

Issue 16   Fall/Winter 1999

Contributor: Daniel Piatek

Interviews: Mary Daly, Sam Keen, José Cabezón, Jetsunma Ahkon Lhamo, Father Basil Pennington, Tamar Frankiel, Swami Bharati Tirtha, Kate Bornstein, Marion Woodman

The Self Masters
Are They Enlightened?

Issue 15   Spring/Summer 1999

Interviews: Anthony Robbins, Jack LaLanne, Susan Powter, Dan Millman, Michael Murphy, Jean Houston, Beverly Slade, Vernon Kitabu Turner, Evander Holyfield

What IS Enlightenment?
Does anyone know what they're talking about?

Issue 14	Fall/Winter 1998
Interviews:	Ajja, Ramesh Balsekar, Swami Dayananda Saraswati, Dr Vijai Shankar, Helen Tworkov, His Holiness the Dalai Lama, Stephen Batchelor, Peter Masefield, Frances Vaughan

What is the Relationship Between Sex and Spirituality?

Issue 13	Spring/Summer 1998
Interviews:	Father Thomas Keating, Swami Chidananda, Bhante Gunaratana, Margot Anand, Barry Long, Miranda Shaw

The Modern Spiritual Predicament
An Inquiry into the popularization of East-meets-West spirituality

Issue 12	Fall/Winter 1997
Contributor:	Ken Wilbur
Interviews:	George Feuerstein, Deepak Chopra, Andrei Codrescu, Dr Laura Schlessinger, Sam Bercholz

Can Science Enlighten Us?
Science, Spirituality and the Revelation of the Unknown

Issue 11	Spring/Summer 1997
Articles on:	David Bohm and J Krishnamurti, E F Schumacher, Frank Tipler
Contributors:	F David Peat, Fritjof Capra, Michael Toms, Renee Weber
Interviews:	Huston Smith, Amit Goswami, Rupert Sheldrake

Women, Enlightenment and the Divine Mother
Do Women have the Inside Track on Spirituality?

Issue 10	Fall/Winter 1996
Articles on:	Mother Meera, Anandamayi Ma
Contributors:	Georg Feuerstein, Arnaud Desjardins, Daniel Roumanoff
Interviews:	Vimlar Thakar, Z Budapest, Elizabeth Debold

Is the Guru Dead? Questioning the "New Paradigm"
An exploration of purity and authority in spiritual life

Issue 9	Spring/Summer 1996
Articles on:	Da Free John, Joel Kramer, Diana Alstad
Contributor:	Georg Feuerstein
Interviews:	Metropolitan Anthony of Sourozh, Brother David Steindl-Rast, Rabbi Adin Steinsaltz

Impersonal Enlightenment
A Revolutionary Change of Perspective
> 'Issue 8'   Summer 1995
> Article on: Swami Krishnananda
> Contributors: John Wren-Lewis, Barry Long
> Interview: Lee Lozowick

Beyond the Boundaries of Tradition
Conversations on the Nature of Truth
> 'Issue 7'   January 1995
> Articles on: Penor Rimpoche, Chatrul Rinpoche, Tulku Urgyen
> Interviews: Lex Hixon, Rabbi Yitzchak Ginsburgh

Come Together
Who Has the Courage to Stand Alone/Together in the Truth?
> 'Issue 6'   July 1994
> Contributor: Francis H Cook

Cynicism
The Modern Spiritual Predicament
> 'Issue 5'   January 1994
> Interview: Amit Goswami

What is the Relationship Between Love and Truth?
> 'Issue 4'   July 1993

Descent from Heaven: The Last Frontier
> 'Issue 3'   January 1993

Corruption, Purity and Enlightenment
> 'Issue 2'   July 1992

A Passion for Death
> 'Issue 1'   January 1992
> Interview: Irina Tweedie